全国外语翻译证书考试必备

本书配有音频资料，请访问北京大学出版社主页www.pup.cn，进入下载专区获得。

口译句型强化

蒋凤霞　编著

图书在版编目（CIP）数据

口译句型强化／全国外语翻译证书考试必备／蒋凤霞编著 .—北京：北京大学出版社，2010.7
（全国外语翻译证书考试系列）
ISBN 978-7-301-17172-1

Ⅰ. 口… Ⅱ. 蒋… Ⅲ. 英语—口译—资格考核—自学参考资料　Ⅳ. H315.9

中国版本图书馆 CIP 数据核字（2010）第 077490 号

书　　　名：口译句型强化
著作责任者：蒋凤霞　编著
责 任 编 辑：孙　莹
标 准 书 号：ISBN 978-7-301-17172-1/H·2500
出 版 发 行：北京大学出版社
地　　　址：北京市海淀区成府路 205 号　100871
网　　　址：http://www.pup.cn
电　　　话：邮购部 62752015　发行部 62750672　编辑部 62765217　出版部 62754962
电 子 信 箱：zpup@pup.pku.edu.cn
印 　刷 者：北京鑫海金澳胶印有限公司
经 　销 者：新华书店
　　　　　　787 毫米×1092 毫米　16 开本　15.5 印张　299 千字
　　　　　　2010 年 7 月第 1 版　2016 年 8 月第 3 次印刷
定　　　价：32.00 元

未经许可，不得以任何方式复制或抄袭本书之部分或全部内容。
版权所有，侵权必究　举报电话：010-62752024
　　　　　　　　　　电子邮箱：fd@pup.pku.edu.cn

前　言

口译考试是国内含金量最高的素质英语考试之一，试题难度大，题量多，通过率控制严格，其证书也就有了很高的可信度。目前，国内比较被认可的口译考试有教育部的全国翻译考试；人事部的翻译考试；上海口译考试。口译考试包括汉译英和英译汉，内容上跨越了科技、经贸、旅游、城市发展、时事新闻、历史文化等多个领域，考查学生对地道英文的理解和判断能力，同时拓展了他们的逻辑思维和视野。因为一次性通过口译考试意味着巨大挑战，学生在复习口译教材和参加培训的基础上就需要大量的训练。

由于此类图书在市场上极为紧缺，北京外国语大学口译培训始于 2000 年，口译专家，教授在教授口译的同时，花了大量时间进行题型细分、考试趋势分析、资料收集筛选、难度评估讨论等工作。由于口译考试除了教材的知识点以外，没有完整的考试大纲知识汇编，考题内容广泛，包罗万象，因而大量实战学习是必经之路，考生需要大大扩充练习量，以提高应试技能，这也意味着这三本强化训练会发挥巨大的助考作用。考生可以根据自身能力安排进度，磨练口译的节奏、质量和熟练度，在考前做到胸有成竹。

当然，学习口译不仅仅是为了考试。读者除了把这三本强化训练用作应试训练外，还可以把其中的内容作为重要的英语学习资料，积累词汇和重要知识点，分析长难句，增加新闻听说机会，苦练听、说、读、写、译技能，奠定坚实基础，实现职场飞跃。

本丛书较前取材更为广泛，编排更为合理。《汉英口译强化 100 篇》《英汉口译强化 100 篇》和《口译句型强化》采取难度循序渐进原则，可以视译，交传，或用作同传练习，也可由使用者依具体情况和训练要求自行决定。做好翻译除了依赖广博的知识为前提以外，学员要系统地认识和掌握两种语言特别是外语的规律。说到语言知识，人们最容易想到词汇和语法。当然，这也是语言中最基础的元素，是必不可少的。但是，语言的表达不是这些元素的简单堆砌。语言表达最核心的东西是"意义"，语言的功能在于表达思想，在于对主客事物的分门归类和表述。人的语言之所以能够做到这一点，一方面是它的创造性和开放性，另一方面在于它的系统性。离开了这两点，语言表达是无法实现的。正是基于上述这样的考虑，本书在练习材料的组织编写过程中，既没有按照语法结构的顺序也没有采用按内容分类的方法进行安排；而是按口译训练难易，篇幅长短来进行排序。语言材料多取自英语国家的权威刊物、杂志、报章、书籍和国际组织的出版物，内容真实鲜活，语言文字地道流畅，用词简练精确，对学员的语言能力要求也是很高的，这与专业口译的要求相一致。做好翻译，要具备多方面的知识。学员应尽量做到举一反三，以一斑而窥全豹，才能够达到较好的学习效果。

　　我们在讲话时，不会有意识地去想，我这一句是要表达我的行为还是我的思想或者什么其它的方面，但是只要我们使用语言，我们就要依赖语言所固有的这些特征来表达我们的意思，从一定意义上说，语言的功能分类体系为我们提供了一个掌握语言使用规律的"路线图"，它有别于语言的语法分类和知识分类。

　　作为一套口译教程，本丛书中的英语材料基本上采自国外媒体，有些是外国名人或政要的言论。适合学生特点、高效而又实用的训练方法，突出了口译技能和实战演练的重要性。这种跨学科的大合作是一次前所未有的大胆尝试，体现了团队协作、集思广益、取长补短、资源共享和共同发展的合作精神。教程的编写体现了"培养优秀口译人才"和"强调技能训练过程"这两个指导思想。对此，我们首先导入来源语的单句听练，包括听懂、听记（心记与笔记）和听说。随着单句字数的不断增加和结构内容的愈加复杂，重点训练学生的记忆、笔记与双语口头表达能力和拓展学生的知识面。为进入下阶段的互动训练打好扎实的基础。

　　本丛书的又一大特色是总结了国际高级口译通用的100个符号，可以代替3000多个词的笔记，较全面地揭示了口译员记得快，翻得准的中心环节，为口译学习者提供了便利。在此，祝所有心怀口译梦想的人早日成功！

北京外国语大学
蒋凤霞

目 录

口译笔记符号系统
01

汉译英练习
1

答 案
123

口译笔记符号系统

1. / 动词省略符；成分分隔符
2. ≈ about, approximate, roughly
3. = the same as, be equivalent to, which means
4. ≡ persist, continue, endure, last, persevere, prevail, insist on
5. ≠ differ from, not equal to, disparity, inequality
6. ∵ because, due to, thanks to
7. ∴ so, hence, therefore, so that, consequently
8. > more than, superior than, exceed, surpass, prospect, wish, hope
9. < less than, inferior to, worse than, look back on, in retrospect, review
10. + plus, in addition, another, furthermore
11. − minus, deduct, except, subtract, few, little
12. ∧ over, above, top, head, tip, peak, superior, consolidate, uttermost, maximum, climax, supreme, crown, king, queen, leader, director, chancellor, boss, manager, officer, captain, emperor, empress, majesty, dictator, ruler, commander, governor, mayor, administrator, supervisor, monitor, minister
13. ∨ below, beneath, under, lower, basic, fundamental
14. ∈ belong to
15. ○ whole, entire, complete, integrate
16. ⊙ meeting, conference, convention, session, forum, seminar, council, congress, assembly, gathering, committee, commission, association, union, senate, parliament, convocation, symposium
17. ∽ relationship, trade, exchange, communication, dialogue, conversation, each other, mutual
18. √ good, right, correct, positive, affirmative, approval
19. X bad, wrong, mistake, error, negative, notorious

口译句型强化

20. ⌐ ago, past, long before
21. ⌐ in the future, next
22. ° people, person, -ist, -cian, -or, -er
23. □ country, nation, state, republic, kingdom, federal, union
24. △ city, urban, metropolitan, cosmopolitan
25. ▽ village, rural, countryside, farm, suburb, outskirt
26. ☆ important, significant, key, outstanding, extraordinary, eventful, famous, glorious, emphasize, magnificent
27. ✶ feature, nature, characteristics, personality, symbolize, sigh, embody, exemplify, represent, on behalf of, stand for, epitomize
28. ♀ female
29. ♂ male
30. ↑ increase, go up, rise, raise, lift, improve, enhance, grow, advance, elevate, escalate, boost, nourish, climb up, stand up, bring up, expand, enlarge, extend, augment, launch
31. ↓ decrease, decline, reduce, drop, fall, descend, sink, weaken, devalue, degrade, dwindle, lessen, diminish, cut down, go down, fall off, abate, subside, landing
32. ← come from, origin, deprive from
33. → lead to, in the direction of, to
34. ± probably, possibly, maybe, could, might, not necessarily, uncertain
35. : say, think, believe, express, speak, insist, maintain, claim, hold
36. ? problem, issue, question, disagreement, what, which, how, doubt
37. ! danger, warning, alarm, alert, hazardous, perilous, jeopardy, watch out, look out
38. ·· steady, stable, sustain
39. ··· very much, for a long period, for ever, permanent
40. ∥ way, method, measures, means, channel, tunnel, tube, pipe, ditch, duct
41. ⊥ influence, effect, affect, impact, pressure, tress, burden, load
42. $ dollar, money, invest, rich, property, investment, prosperous
43. [ ] among, within, according to, quotation, cite
44. θ thank you, thanks, grateful, appreciated
45. ◎ environment, atmosphere, situation, condition
46. # end, finish, conclude, conclusion, wind up, close, be over, sum up

47. @ locate, location, at, in, on
48. & and
49. ⊕ hospital, medical
50. Σ total, add up to
51. ∞ endless, boundless, limitless
52. ⌒ challenge
53. ⌣ chance, opportunity
54. ∿ unsteady, fluctuate, wave, unsettle, rise and fall, undulate, popple
55. ⌂ development
56. ⌐ to see, observe, watch
57. ⌐ admire, look back, remember
58. ⌐ delete, discard, give up
59. ⊟- import
   ⊟- export
60. ⊗ stop, cease, halt, suspend, call off, setback, dwelling, interruption, quit, rest, throw-out action
61. A 原级
    A^+ 比较级
    Â 最高级
62. î industry
63. ⼈ agriculture
64. ⊘ globe, world, international
65. ☺ happy, exited, satisfied, pleased, delighted, joy
    ☹ unhappy, sad, dissatisfied, displeased
    ◠ worry, concerned, bother, trouble
66. ⊙ surprised, amazed, shocked
67. ⊙⊙ afraid, scare, frighten, threaten
68. ○̇ opinion, idea, view, point, thought
69. ◯ hear, hear about, well known
70. ⁒ bilateral
71. h preside, host, chair
    $h°$ president, chairman, host
72. ( ) what he said, what he does...

73.)(contradict, conflict, fight, war, battle

74. ' omit part. Eg: 1986: '86

75. A̅ 地方上面 north

　　A̲ 地方下面 south, 其他词下面 very, quite

　　|A 地方左边 west

　　A| 地方右边 east

76. a   action, act,

77. b   but

78. c   can, ability, talent, genius

　　¢   century, 100

79. d   day

80. e   economy, economic

81. f   financial

82. g   government

83. n   numerous, many, a lot

84. p   party, policy, political

85. r   reform

86. s   science, social

87. t   think, consider

88. v   victory, win

89. y   year

90. M   month

91. m   minute

92. R   register, recruit, enroll

93. bz   business

94. co   company, cooperation

95. eg   for example, for instance

96. nz   news

97. tx   tax

98. ed   education

99. tho although, though, in spite of, even

100. demo   demonstration

汉译英练习

1. 人们谴责他们放弃了自己的原则。(abandon)
2. "Dr"是"Doctor"的缩写形式。(abbreviation)
3. 健康中心为所有病人提供医疗服务,不管他们是否有支付能力。(ability)
4. 他们对饮酒有种异乎寻常的爱好。(abnormal)
5. 他们把那些土著人全部灭掉了。(aboriginal)
6. 植物吸收二氧化碳。(absorb)
7. 你对计划的所有细节都完全了解了吗?(absorbed)
8. 她全神贯注于自己的思绪中。(abstract)
9. 他被要求为这本小说做一摘要。(abstract)
10. 人类是唯一能够进行抽象思维的动物。(abstract)
11. 你的问题在于不能从讲座中提取要点。(abstract)
12. 他出神遐想,在名字被叫了两遍后才答应。(abstract)
13. 对药物和酒精的滥用导致了皮特的过早死亡。(abuse)
14. 我从未想到他会滥用我对他的信任。(abuse)
15. 孩提时代遭受虐待的人往往会变成虐待儿童者。(abuse)
16. 他不具备任何学术资格。(academic)
17. 她的先生现就职于中国科学院。(academy)
18. 这篇论文谈论了现代社会中高等教育的职能。(academy)
19. 汽车加速超过那辆公共汽车。(accelerate)
20. 他们使用特殊的化学物质来促进农作物的生长。(accelerate)
21. 只有高层管理人员才有权看这些文件。(access)
22. 通过右手的一个小门进入。(access)
23. 这一新技术被称为医学上的一大突破。(acclaim)
24. 曾有很多难民儿童住在这个岛上。(accommodate)

25. 她的眼睛花了一段时间才适应黑暗的环境。(accommodate)
26. 14 岁以下的儿童必须由成人陪同。(accompany)
27. 这种病伴随有打喷嚏和发烧症状。(accompany)
28. 他们怎能这么快就完成这么多工作？(accomplish)
29. 实现这个政策目标花了六个月的时间。(accomplishment)
30. 消减预算是一项不小的成绩。(accomplishment)
31. 我相信你对事情发生的经过做了很好的描述。(account)
32. 我想在你们这儿开个账户。(account)
33. 我们一定会顾及你的感受。(account)
34. 你对车上的凹痕做何解释？(account)
35. 计算机软件占我们产品的 70% 左右。(account)
36. 脂肪容易在臀部和大腿周围囤积。(accumulate)
37. 要得到有关人口数目的准确数字很困难。(accurate)
38. 他被指控犯了抢劫罪。(accuse)
39. 我需要花时间来适应变化。(accustom)
40. 她最终实现了自己的目标，成为一名教授。(achieve)
41. 这些橘子很酸。(acid)
42. 她讲话时的语调很尖刻。(acid)
43. 醋是一种酸。(acid)
44. 两位被告都拒绝承认法庭的权威。(acknowledge)
45. 我们希望对大学的支持表示感谢。(acknowledge)
46. 汤姆瞥了她一眼，算是看到她出席，和她打招呼。(acknowledge)
47. 他有许多商业上的熟人，但真正的朋友却很少。(acquaintance)
48. 他因为认识总统而获得了那个职位。(acquaintance)
49. 这个学院由于其高教学标准获得美名。(acquire)
50. 他花了数年时间学到外科医生的技能。(acquire)
51. 为了公司的进一步发展，他们的团队致力于获得新的场地。(acquisition)
52. 艺术协会正举行一场展览，展出其近期获得的艺术品。(acquisition)
53. 鱼的嗅觉非常敏锐。(acute)
54. 孩子们发现很难适应这所新学校。(adapt)
55. 很多小孩子购买那些已被改编成电视节目的书籍。(adapt)

56. 他嗜巧克力如命。(addict)
57. 他拿出笔来，记下他的姓名和住址。(address)
58. 她对皇家学会做了演讲。(address)
59. 她在信封上写好了地址，贴上了邮票。(address)
60. 你要投诉就得向总部反映。(address)
61. 对于抗菌素治疗的适宜性已做了检验。(adequacy)
62. 她的表现能够胜任工作，但缺乏创意。(adequate)
63. 这家公司还没有就其举动给出足够的解释。(adequate)
64. 这些鱼的鱼卵粘附在植物的叶子上。(adhere)
65. 我们坚持所有人享有平等权利和言论自由的原则。(adhere)
66. 我们俩的房间挨着。(adjacent)
67. 要我父母适应公寓里的生活很困难。(adjust)
68. 该地区一直由南非管理。(administer)
69. 考试举办得公平，公正。(administer)
70. 我们正在寻找一有管理经验的人。(administration)
71. 这个问题被尼克松政府忽略了。(administration)
72. 我一向欣赏她的画。(admire)
73. 我们上山中途停下来欣赏风景。(admire)
74. 只有持请帖者才可进入展览会。(admission)
75. 法庭也许会将你的缄默作为认罪的表示。(admission)
76. 他们要收五元入场费。(admission)
77. 他承认了自己有罪／错误。(admit)
78. 只有持票者才可进入体育场。(admit)
79. 聚会上挤满了长有青春痘的青少年们。(adolescent)
80. 他有时如此幼稚。(adolescent)
81. 在这一问题上，加利福尼亚已经采取了强硬立场。(adopt)
82. 经过两年的争议，国会最终批准了这项法令。(adopt)
83. 这对夫妻不能生育自己的孩子，希望收养。(adopt)
84. 她敬爱她的姐姐。(adore)
85. 人们将会非常喜欢这部影片。(adore)
86. 有些孩子发现和成年人讲话很困难。(adult)

87. 成年以后，他大多数时间都生活在苏格兰。(adult)
88. 鉴于其语言和成年人的主题，这部电影被评定为 R 级。(adult)
89. 他提前半小时到达。(advance)
90. 医学方面最近有了长足的进步。(advance)
91. 我们对宇宙的认识已经前进了很多。(advance)
92. 生活在纽约有很多有利因素，其中一条就是什么时候想出去吃东西都可以。(advantage)
93. 她在埃及有一些令人兴奋的奇遇。(adventure)
94. 他们收到了许多关于变革的不利宣传。(adverse)
95. 我们决定在当地的报纸上为我们的汽车登广告。(advertise)
96. 他总是大肆宣传自己愿意对新闻界讲话。(advertise)
97. 她热情地支持婴儿自然顺产的生育方法。(advocate)
98. 在那宗案件中，他是被告的辩护律师。(advocate)
99. 极端主义者公开主张暴力。(advocate)
100. 从美学角度看，这是个很不错的设计。(aesthetic)
101. 这把椅子也许很美观，但并不是很舒适。(aesthetic)
102. 美学的中心问题之一是美存在于观者眼中，还是事物本身存在着令其美好的东西。(aesthetic)
103. 她过世了，我们深受影响。(affect)
104. 她对他没什么感情，当然谈不上爱他了。(affection)
105. 他送花给她，想赢得她的爱情。(affection)
106. 嫌疑犯声称自己整晚都在家里。(affirm)
107. 就他的问题，她给出肯定的回答。(affirmative)
108. 对于发生的事情，他不是很乐观。(affirmative)
109. 他们两人都来自比较富裕的家庭。(affluent)
110. 政府就改革宪法制定了议事日程。(agenda)
111. 在市中心限制停车的尝试使交通阻塞的问题更加严重。(aggravate)
112. 少数派总共获得 1327 张选票。(aggregate)
113. 希拉所有来源的收入总计达十万美元。(aggregate)
114. 他已被给予法律援助。(aid)
115. 她惊慌地看看四周。(alarm)
116. 警报器响了。(alarm)

117. 尽管有点犹豫，他还是接受了这份工作。(albeit)
118. 我滴酒不沾。(alcohol)
119. 大多数葡萄酒含有 10% 到 15% 的酒精。(alien)
120. 那是个被强加了一个外国政府和一种外国语言的国家。(alien)
121. 你抵达英国之后必须向外侨登记处报到。(alien)
122. 报纸的所有这些改变都使它与它的老读者疏远了。(alienate)
123. 这两个男人声称警察逼迫他们做了假供。(allege)
124. 这笔钱应该能缓和我们的财政问题。(alleviate)
125. 一百万美元被分配来用于救灾。(allocate)
126. 他在大学里的时候，他的父母给他的零用钱太少以至于他不得不到饭店打工赚钱。(allowance)
127. 我出国的时候，几乎从没有用完我的全部免税额度。(allowance)
128. 这么多年来，她的容颜依旧。(alter)
129. 我别无他法，只得将他报告警察。(alternative)
130. 你有其他可供选择的建议吗？(alternative)
131. 我们目前正在海拔 10000 米的高空飞行。(altitude)
132. 那是一次非常业余的演出。(amateur)
133. 约翰突然间结婚，令朋友们大为吃惊。(amaze)
134. 部长在声明中使用的语言非常含糊不清。(ambiguous)
135. 他的雄心是最终开办一家自己的公司。(ambition)
136. 急需外国援助来缓解水灾的影响。(ameliorate)
137. 被告后来修改了自己的证据。(amend)
138. 等演讲完了，你们会有充分的机会提问。(ample)
139. 在学校里，她总是会想出一些游戏来逗乐同学。(amuse)
140. 她将婴儿的出生和创造过程进行了类比。(analogy)
141. 细胞样本在实验室中分析。(analyse)
142. 这些数据需要进一步的分析。(analysis)
143. 房间的墙上挂着他祖先的肖像。(ancestor)
144. 他出生在一个古老的天主教家庭。(ancient)
145. 据宣布，首相将在当天晚上发表电视演说。(announce)
146. 他郑重其事地对妻子说他打算离开。(announce)

147. 你这么说无非是要惹我生气。(annoy)
148. 爵士乐节每年都举行。(annual)
149. 销售情况比预想的还要好。(anticipate)
150. 我为自己的迟到而道歉。(apologize)
151. 那件新设备在实验中使用。(apparatus)
152. 我们遇到了一个大问题,这很快就变得显而易见。(apparent)
153. 牵涉到的组织已向政府发出急切的恳求,要求再拨专款。(appeal)
154. 所有囚犯都有申诉权。(appeal)
155. 这个节目拥有非常广泛的吸引力。(appeal)
156. 她对这个决定不满,计划上诉。(appeal)
157. 农夫们已向政府求助。(appeal)
158. 到国外工作的想法很是吸引我。(appeal)
159. 这两姐妹的外貌非常相像。(appearance)
160. 幸亏警察马上赶到,殴斗才很快被制止了。(appearance)
161. 文件后附加了客户调查的结果。(append)
162. 克里斯蒂不得不去医院切除阑尾。(appendix)
163. 食欲突然减退有时是生病的征兆。(appetite)
164. 保罗不喜欢卖力气。(appetite)
165. 那首歌唱完时孩子们鼓掌叫好。(applaud)
166. 这些变革将受到赞许。(applaud)
167. 我已经申请了另外一份工作。(apply)
168. 他希望能得到一份能使他的外语有用武之地的工作。(apply)
169. 这张图表不再适用了。(apply)
170. 我想预约一下,今天上午来找位医生看病。(appointment)
171. 我被委任为编辑,他向我致贺。(appointment)
172. 对于你的关心我表示感激,但是说实话,我很好。(appreciate)
173. 她的能力没有得到雇主的充分赏识。(appreciate)
174. 人们期望大多数投资都能稳定增值。(appreciate)
175. 我们走近,吓着了鸟儿。(approach)
176. 他决定采用一种不同的方法,通过讲故事的方式教授《圣经》。(approach)
177. 她听到脚步声逼近。(approach)

178. 我觉得现在不是谈钱这个话题的恰当时机。(appropriate)
179. 我不赞成整形手术。(approve)
180. 会议批准了公民投票的建议。(approve)
181. 每个班大约有多少个学生。(approximate)
182. 这个数字接近英国年消费量的四分之一。(approximate)
183. 他有从事新闻工作的才能。(aptitude)
184. 我们今年夏天去意大利而不是西班牙只是一时随意决定的。(arbitrary)
185. 今年非洲的很多地区遭受了严重的干旱。(area)
186. 这门课程囊括了三个主要的课题领域。(area)
187. 我们惊奇地发现有一位新的候选人在选举即将开始之前参与角逐。(arena)
188. 在和老公的争执中,我打破了这个花瓶。(argument)
189. 关于改变系统的原因,我们需要提供一个令人信服的理由。(argument)
190. 新的法律引起了公众很大的关注。(arouse)
191. 这个名单按照字母顺序排列。(arrange)
192. 联络你们当地的分支机构安排一次约见。(arrange)
193. 有一大批颜色可供选择。(array)
194. 一件家具 (article)
195. 旅客们被告知不要将任何贵重物品留在旅馆房间内。(article)
196. 昨天报纸上有一篇关于教育的有趣的文章。(article)
197. 这次入侵违反了联合国宪章第 51 条。(article)
198. 虽是 80 岁高龄,她依然是思维敏捷,口齿清晰。(articulate)
199. 你认为女人比男人更善于表达自己的情感吗? (articulate)
200. 我不喜欢人造纤维的衣服。(artificial)
201. 他们的快乐表情看上去很勉强而做作。(artificial)
202. 潜水员们开始向水面上升。(ascend)
203. 我工作的最重要的方面就是与人打交道。(aspect)
204. 一大群人聚集在美国使馆外。(assemble)
205. 硬说吸烟不会损害人们的健康纯属一派胡言。(assert)
206. 这项生意的价值被估为 125 万英镑。(assess)
207. 这个方法正在课堂上试用,以评价其可能造成的影响。(assess)
208. 他拥有一家 90 亿美元资产的公司。(asset)

209. 我认为瑞秋将是这个部门里难得的人才。(asset)
210. 给每个学生分配一个搭档。(assign)
211. 简被指派到亚洲事务局。(assign)
212. 他在国外执行任务时被杀。(assignment)
213. 他被通知被选派为利物浦副领事。(assignment)
214. 你将受雇去协助进行开发新设备。(assist)
215. 琼是他的一个生意上的合伙人。(associate)
216. 流血和战争是形影相随的。(associate)
217. 彼得过去是位陪审法官。(associate)
218. 莎拉是《时尚》杂志的副主编。(associate)
219. 在那次会议上我遇到兄弟单位的许多朋友。(associate)
220. 我不会将他与运动扯上关系。(associate)
221. 他不赞成民主运动。(associate)
222. 我不喜欢这些和你交往的懒虫。(associate)
223. 一小束各式各样的野花。(assorted)
224. 这一理论假定劳动力和资本都是流动的。(assume)
225. 我没看到你的车,所以想当然地以为你出去了。(assume)
226. 无论他们任命谁当职,都要为所有的财政问题负责。(assume)
227. 很多人主观臆断贫穷仅仅存在于第三世界国家。(assumption)
228. 他傲慢的样子使人们讨厌他。(assumption)
229. 我向你保证,文件是真的。(assure)
230. 良好的评论保证了电影的成功。(assure)
231. 她的从政前景看起来很有保证。(assured)
232. 一般来讲,他是一个很自信的人。(assured)
233. 你可以放心,一切都很好。(assured)
234. 他们闹离婚的事使我很吃惊。(astonish)
235. 在你的地图册里查一查明尼苏达在哪。(atlas)
236. 火星与地球的大气层是很不相同的。(atmosphere)
237. 这房间里的空气太闷了,我简直没法呼吸。(atmosphere)
238. 我们办公室里有一种非常友好的气氛。(atmosphere)
239. 每个二氧化碳分子由一个碳原子和两个氧原子构成。(atom)

240. 在申请表上贴一张近期照片。(attach)
241. 请填好附上的回执单并将其返回。(attach)
242. 爱上和你一起工作的人很容易。(attach)
243. 敌军对该城发动了一次进攻。(attack)
244. 大多数野兽若非被激怒，一般是不会袭击人的。(attack)
245. 由于削减教育经费，政府收到来自各方面的抨击。(attack)
246. 他撰文抨击了那些法官及其在审案中的行径。(attack)
247. 一年后，她达到了自己的理想体重。(attain)
248. 他试着开了一个玩笑，但得到的反应只是沉默。(attempt)
249. 这枚炸弹是今年对总统的第三次行刺企图。(attempt)
250. 很多人出席了丧礼。(attend)
251. 你的孩子上哪所学校？(attend)
252. 彼得对待女人的态度实在让我觉得可怕。(attitude)
253. 他后来成了一位著名的律师。(attorney)
254. 这些花的颜色鲜艳，可以吸引蝴蝶。(attract)
255. 通常人们把心脏病死亡人数的下降归因于饮食结构的改善。(attribute)
256. 不应该认为人的（做事）动机属于动物。(attribute)
257. 一个优秀的经理人应该具备什么样的特质。(attribute)
258. 她新出的那本书将会吸引大批读者。(audience)
259. 这些账目必须由一家外聘审计员的公司来稽查。(audit)
260. 这家公司在每个财政年度末进行一次审计。(audit)
261. 随着他第三个儿子的出生，他感到有必要想办法增加收入。(argument)
262. 本书对那次可怕的战争做了可靠的报道。(authentic)
263. 他著有两本有关中国的书。(author)
264. 李先生是有关中国食品的首席专家。(authority)
265. 美国和哥伦比亚当局试图达成一项协议。(authority)
266. 我可以和管事儿的人说句话吗？(authority)
267. 现今机器自动执行银行的两项基本职能——存款和取款。(automate)
268. 自动武器可以连续射击，直到你的手指离开扳机。(automatic)
269. 出生于该国内的孩子自然获得该国的公民权。(automatic)
270. 如果消化过程不再是自发的活动，生命将不能继续维持下去。(automatic)

271. 停电的时候，他们依赖后备供电设施。(auxiliary)

272. 可以在票房买到票。(available)

273. 巴黎的香榭丽舍大街是世界上最美的大街之一。(avenue)

274. 我们必须在探索过一切途径后再承认失败。(avenue)

275. 1996年教师的平均年龄是38岁。(average)

276. 我们不需要爱因斯坦那样的天才，才智平平的人即可。(average)

277. 物价的平均上涨率比去年高出3%。(average)

278. 在西欧，每天工作7至8小时基本上属于平均水平。(average)

279. 他们是航空初期的驾驶员。(aviation)

280. 孩子们没有意识到吸食毒品的危险。(aware)

281. 他很好地应付了那个颇为尴尬的局面。(awkward)

282. 不雅的姿势。(awkward)

283. 背景是一颗高大的松树。(background)

284. 他俩的婚姻不会成功。他们的家庭背景差得太远了。(background)

285. 饮用水中的细菌传染了疾病。(bacteria)

286. 出席会议时我们必须戴上标有名字的胸章。(badge)

287. 脚夫提着她的行李送她上了出租车。(baggage)

288. 我们都背着沉重的感情包袱。(baggage)

289. 她不得不抓紧栏杆以免失去平衡摔倒。(balance)

290. 我不得不权衡一下孩子的需要和我的需要究竟哪个重要。(balance)

291. 供需可以平衡。(balance)

292. 政党领导人由秘密选举产生。(ballot)

293. 昨天职员们投票决定罢工行动。(ballot)

294. 电影院里应该禁止喧哗和吃东西声音过大。(ban)

295. 这家餐馆内禁止吸烟。(ban)

296. 甲壳虫乐队可能是世界上最有名的乐队。(band)

297. 无线电信号是以不同的波段传播的。(band)

298. 请将下边条形图中的信息描述一番。(bar chart)

299. 酒吧几点关门？(bar)

300. 没有空桌子了，所以只好在吧台前坐下。(bar)

301. 一条形巧克力。(bar)

302. 不要光着脚在屋外到处走。(bare)
303. 他们公寓的木地板没铺地毯。(bare)
304. 管理部门和雇员最终达成了协议。(bargain)
305. 这件外套半价出售，真是件便宜货。(bargain)
306. 工会为争取更好的工资与就业条件与雇主交涉。(bargain)
307. 他们听见外面有狗叫。(bark)
308. 中士咆哮着对新兵发出一系列命令。(bark)
309. 土地仍然贫瘠。(barren)
310. 不能生育的妇女受到部落男子的排斥。(barren)
311. 群山形成两国之间的自然屏障。(barrier)
312. 语言隔阂使得辩论不可能进行。(barrier)
313. 她刚刚买了本书，叫做《烹饪概要》。(basic)
314. 这个农场连最基本的设备都没有。(basic)
315. 他们声明没有事实根据。(basis)
316. 面包是他们每天饮食的主要部分。(basis)
317. 将军在战斗中阵亡了。(battle)
318. 政府对全国矿工联盟进行了两场决定性的斗争。(battle)
319. 我可以看见他手电筒的光束在黑暗中舞动。(beam)
320. 这场灾难是他们中有些人承受不了的。(bear)
321. 让他个人承担相关的巨大开支是不公平的。(bear)
322. 我怀疑那把椅子能否承受得了你的体重。(bear)
323. 他们躺在帐篷里能听见外面野兽在黑暗中走动时发出的响声。(beast)
324. 我知道她那天下午要来，因为她事先打电话跟我说过。(beforehand)
325. 她叫医生替她去和她的父母谈一谈。(behalf)
326. 校长不会容忍课上不规矩的行为。(behaviour)
327. 不管她在台下的行为如何，她的表演为全世界歌手树立了新标准。(benchmark)
328. 他弯下身子，解开了鞋带。(bend)
329. 两臂弯曲然后向上伸展。(bend)
330. 大多数科学成果对人类确实是很有益的。(beneficial)
331. 我希望今天的决定对全国人民都有好处。(benefit)
332. 你或许会得到住房补助金。(benefit)

333. 他们齐心协力地工作，使整个社区受益。(benefit)
334. 我们不出售含酒精的饮料。(beverage)
335. 一个新环境能难住和吓住孩子。(bewilder)
336. 在摒弃偏见和偏爱的基础上，学生得到评估。(bias)
337. 有几个因素很可能影响到了研究的结果，使其产生了偏差。(bias)
338. 请查阅参考书目了解本书参考的所有书籍。(bibliography)
339. 他的两手被绑在柱子后面。(bind)
340. 我姐姐的狗咬了我。(bite)
341. 今天鱼上钩了吗？(bite)
342. 他和他的朋友有过几次稀奇古怪的谈话。(bizarre)
343. 乔治把他缺乏自信心归咎于他母亲。(blame)
344. 她将事故的原因推到他的身上。(blame)
345. 我从来不知道珍妮在想什么——她的表情是如此木然。(blank)
346. 在表格末有一空白处让你签名。(blank)
347. 将奶油与糖搅拌在一起。(blend)
348. 标签上写着此咖啡是各种最好的咖啡豆的混合品。(blend)
349. 幸运的是我们碰上了好天气。(bless)
350. 牧师在教堂里为人们祝福，说"上帝与你同在"。(bless)
351. （别人打喷嚏时说）长命百岁！(bless)
352. 一大块冰。(block)
353. 博物馆离此只有六个街区远。(block)
354. 一棵倒下的树挡住了路。(block)
355. 他们的花园开满了美丽的花朵。(bloom)
356. 这些花整个夏天都会绽放。(bloom)
357. 从医院出来后她一直精力旺盛。(bloom)
358. 签上名字后我吸干了纸。(blot)
359. 风越来越大。(blow)
360. 在沙滩上信被风吹走了，我不得不追赶它。(blow)
361. 哨子声响起，上半场结束。(blow)
362. 他企图盗窃绝密导弹系统设计蓝图时被抓获。(blueprint)
363. 他们经济改革的计划要付诸实际是不大可能的。(blueprint)

364. 我的铅笔不尖了。(blunt)

365. 让我问一个直率的问题。(blunt)

366. 他夸口说这是有史以来耗资最大的一部电影。(boast)

367. 水烧开后让它冷一下。(boil)

368. 她不会煮蛋。(boil)

369. 如今创办企业是个冒险之举。(bond)

370. 本句就是用粗体字排印的。(bond)

371. 部队连续炮击了城市,死伤了数百人。(bombard)

372. 他停止讲话后,学生们连珠炮似的问了许多问题。(bombard)

373. 他交了保释金获释。(bond)

374. 正是这一行动似乎加强了他与我之间的联系。(bond)

375. 我父亲把他所有的钱都投在了股票市场的债券上。(bond)

376. 两个表面不到 10 分钟就粘合一起。(bond)

377. 他付给我工资,又因为我新争取到客户给我发了红包。(bonus)

378. 我们听到远处炸弹爆炸的轰鸣。(boom)

379. 今年图书销售激增。(boom)

380. 大炮在晚上隆隆作响。(boom)

381. 这里的休闲产业正在蓬勃发展。(boom)

382. 新的度假区推动了旅游业的发展。(boost)

383. 她参与了推销新式时装的广告活动。(boost)

384. 展览会上本公司的展室就在我们主要竞争对手的隔壁。(booth)

385. 电话亭。(booth)

386. 火车穿越法国和德国的边界。(border)

387. 我从不费心去熨烫我的衬衫。(bother)

388. 使我烦恼的是,这样做不合法的。(bother)

389. 别拿这种鸡毛蒜皮的事来烦我。(bother)

390. 你必须留在你所在的郡界之内。(boundary)

391. 他向观众深深地鞠了一躬。(bow)

392. 讲话前他们向女王鞠躬。(bow)

393. 他们吹嘘说从没被打败过。(brag)

394. 科比突然想到一个好办法。(brainstorm)

395. 雇员聚集在一起，集体自由讨论，激发想法。(brainstorm)
396. 除了顶端的树枝外，这些树都没有叶子。(branch)
397. 等你一安顿下来就向分行经理报到。(branch)
398. 免疫学是生物科学的一个分支。(branch)
399. 你用什么牌子的洗发水。(brand)
400. 画眉同大多数鸟一样在春天繁殖。(breed)
401. 美国公民自由协会呈递了一份摘要反对这一决定。(brief)
402. 格林在剑桥度过了一段短暂的时光。(brief)
403. 工作人员向总统全面介绍了海地目前局势的基本情况。(brief)
404. 他们将成堆的旅行手册带回了家。(brochure)
405. 他手臂和背部布满了瘀痕。(bruise)
406. 一两只桃子上有碰伤的痕迹，我得将它们切掉。(bruise)
407. 花园里大多数的植物都在发芽。(bud)
408. 树上已长出新叶，花蕾处处可见。(bud)
409. 摄影的预算被削减了。(budget)
410. 这个计划通过固定的月付帮你预算好开销。(budget)
411. 面团的体积会涨至现在体积的两倍。(bulk)
412. 大多数消费者住在城里。(bulk)
413. 办公室大量买进纸张以减少花费。(bulk)
414. 我们可以加入很多图表来扩展这份报告。(bulk)
415. 我的头又撞到了那个架子上！(bump)
416. 我们尽力在车中的位子上坐稳，沿着小路颠簸而行。(bump)
417. 我买了一串香蕉。(bunch)
418. 猫追老鼠进了洞穴。(burrow)
419. 蚯蚓在土里打洞穿行。(burrow)
420. 河流有决口危险。(burst)
421. 我知道他们充满好奇，但我什么也没说。(burst)
422. 孩子们冲进了房间。(burst)
423. 我通常在自助餐厅用餐。(cafeteria)
424. 油价以美元计算。(calculate)
425. 很难估计这些变化会给公司带来什么样的影响。(calculate)

426. 黑人对这些法律的反应是发起一场暴力运动。(campaign)
427. 他们正忙于参加反对在附近建新高速公路的活动。(campaign)
428. 大多数一年级学生住在小院里。(campus)
429. 我打电话给旅馆，取消预订。(cancel)
430. 有三名候选人参加竞选。(candidate)
431. 我们有意接受任何学科的求职者。(candidate)
432. 洪水灾区设立一些救济站。(canteen)
433. 他把水壶举到嘴边。(canteen)
434. 我完全有能力照顾自己，谢谢！(capable)
435. 这个房间大约能做 80 人。(capacity)
436. 这个公司的卡车年生产能力达 1500 辆。(capacity)
437. 澳大利亚的首都都是堪培拉。(capital)
438. 他不动用银行里的本金，靠利息生活。(capital)
439. 两名士兵被杀，其余的被俘。(capture)
440. 花了 24 小时才攻下此城。(capture)
441. 美国的载人登月引起了全世界的关注。(capture)
442. 他意识到自己的演艺事业结束了。(career)
443. 米开朗基罗用一块大理石雕刻出了这个人物形象。(carve)
444. 有人将自己名字的首字母刻在树上。(carve)
445. 我通过邮购目录买了一些衣服。(catalogue)
446. 许多植物还没被归类就已经灭绝了。(catalogue)
447. 他们希望他的选举会促进改革。(catalyst)
448. 有五类工人。(category)
449. 选民分为三个范畴。(category)
450. 我们曾经为很多活动供应饮食，这次是最大的一次活动。(cater)
451. 大多数香水广告迎合男性的幻想。(cater)
452. 在开具抗抑郁药时，医生必须非常谨慎。(caution)
453. 由于超速，她受到警告。(caution)
454. 雨停了，天空放晴。(cease)
455. 他们举行了一个晚会庆祝通过考试。(celebrate)
456. 该国每十年进行一次人口普查。(census)

457. 他参加了奥林匹克运动会的开幕仪式。(ceremony)
458. 价格不久就要上涨了，这是肯定的事。(certainty)
459. 谁也无法肯定自己将来会在哪里。(certainty)
460. 我的考试合格证书今天寄到了。(certificate)
461. 在这儿签名以证实这个声明是正确的。(certify)
462. 她在1990年被授予教师资格证书。(certify)
463. 看，山姆给我买的金链子。(chain)
464. 引发第一次世界大战的一系列事件。(chain)
465. 连锁餐馆 (chain)
466. 我喜欢赛车的速度和挑战。(challenge)
467. 这是对总督权威的直接的质疑。(challenge)
468. 午饭后，凯里提出和我进行一场网球比赛。(challenge)
469. 心脏有四个腔室。(chamber)
470. 世界重量级拳击冠军 (champion)
471. 她游过了圣乔治海峡。(channel)
472. 他们正在建一个灌渠。(channel)
473. 一个高效的灌溉系统输送水去灌溉农作物。(channel)
474. 冰雪造成了道路上秩序混乱。(chaos)
475. 这个国家的经济政策只能用混乱来形容。(chaotic)
476. 这一章探讨了权力以及人们如何使用权利的问题。(chapter)
477. 我们希望他们会和我们一起开始一段崭新的和平合作时期。(chapter)
478. 生活中一连串的灾难事件使他卧床不起。(chapter)
479. 人们受到巴黎特有气氛的感染。(character)
480. 哈代笔下的主要人物是一个命运悲惨的年轻挤奶姑娘。(character)
481. 这个地区出产的奶酪具有奶油味浓郁的特色。(characteristic)
482. 雄心是所有事业有成的商人们的共同特性。(characteristic)
483. 买了西服后可以免费改。(charge)
484. 我不在时由哈里负责部门的事务。(charge)
485. 迪克面临武装抢劫的指控。(charge)
486. 饭店收了我们40美元的酒水钱。(charge)
487. 昨晚他们逮捕的那个人被控犯有谋杀罪。(charge)

488. 音乐会所得收入将全部用作善款。(charity)
489. 好几个慈善机构已向洪灾灾民提供了援助。(charity)
490. 她是个很有魅力的女人,而且她知道如何运用这种魅力。(charm)
491. 他正在看有关去年销售额的图表。(chart)
492. 警车开得这么快,一定是在追赶什么人。(chase)
493. 那个律师正尽全力要争取到这份合同。(chase)
494. 我去看看土豆煮好了没有。(check)
495. 在节食之前先咨询一下医生是明智之举。(check)
496. 这本指南内含有买车时便于查阅的要点一览表。(checklist)
497. 他正在进行土壤的化学分析。(chemical)
498. 尽管我爱护我的孩子们,但我的确允许他们自由。(cherish)
499. 我的祖父怀念他年轻时在军队里度过的时光。(cherish)
500. 把香槟放在冰桶里冰一下。(chill)
501. 过来坐在火炉边,你看上去冻的够呛。(chill)
502. 把洋葱切碎。(chop)
503. 你能劈些木材吗?(chop)
504. 我做完家务以后要去买东西。(chore)
505. 我发现写报告真的很讨厌。(chore)
506. 这儿长期缺乏教师。(chronic)
507. 疼痛很厉害。(chronic)
508. 我们按照时间顺序排列文件。(chronological)
509. 血液在全身循环。(circulate)
510. 把他的名字加到传阅这份报告的人的名单中去。(circulation)
511. 旧钞票正在回收。(circulation)
512. 这份报纸的发行量有 200000 份。(circulation)
513. 我不能想象什么情况下——我会愿意偷东西。(circumstance)
514. 你是否符合贷款的条件取决于你的财政状况。(circumstance)
515. 法官在她的判决中引用了 1956 年最高法院的一次裁决。(cite)
516. 加西亚由于照顾残疾儿童而受到表扬。(cite)
517. 杰克逊花了一天时间和当地的宗教领袖和市民领袖会面。(civic)
518. 当地的艺术馆是老百姓骄傲的根本。(civic)

519. 他们于五月举行了仪式，结为夫妇。(civil)

520. 很多民事案件可以庭外和解。(civil)

521. 有人认为核战争将意味着文明的终结。(civilization/civilisation)

522. 回到舒适的文明世界，感觉怎么样？(civilization/civilisation)

523. 警察说如果没有人来认领这只表，你可以留着它。(claim)

524. 公司声称它对河流污染没有责任。(claim)

525. 她的房子被盗后，她要求领取保险赔偿金。(claim)

526. 你能举出任何证据支持你的说法吗？(claim)

527. 你能给我澄清一两点吗？(clarify)

528. 这篇报告目的在于弄清楚如何得到这些结论。(clarify)

529. 第九十分钟，罗伊射进一个非常漂亮的球。(classic)

530. 他为这个典礼选择了一套传统样式的海军装。(classic)

531. 简·奥斯汀的《傲慢与偏见》是英国文学中的经典作品。(classic)

532. 法律上，啤酒被列为一种食品。(classify)

533. 作为音乐家，凯奇很难被划入某一类别。(classify)

534. 他就是区别不开主句和从句。(clause)

535. 合同附加了一条机密性条款。(clause)

536. 现在他正和一位很重要的主顾面谈。(client)

537. 我不能忍受生活在热带地区。(climate)

538. 小企业发现在当前的经济形势下很难生存。(climate)

539. 当人们在下星期进行最后投票时，竞选活动将达到高潮。(climax)

540. 奥林匹克运动会在壮观的闭幕式中达到高潮。(climax)

541. 抓牢，否则你会掉下去的。(cling)

542. 他仍然保持着旧式的习惯举止。(cling)

543. 如果你不给我一点线索的话，我绝对猜不到答案的。(clue)

544. 他是我见过的最好的网球教练。(coach)

545. 她给学生进行法语辅导，通常是为了考试。(coach)

546. 她脚下的粗砂又烫又扎脚。(coarse)

547. 所有的报告必须加密发出。(code)

548. 美国的每个州都有不同的刑法和民法。(code)

549. 纺织服务协会已草拟了一份实践准则。(code)

550. 他正在学习认知心理学。(cognitive)

551. 他们从来就不是一个协调的团队。(coherent)

552. 这门课程开设三年,这三年被计划为一个连贯的整体。(coherent)

553. 历史上讲,体育运动在国际关系中一直是一种凝聚力。(cohesive)

554. 同一时间,他入了党也结了婚。(coincide)

555. 美国的利益和那些岛民的利益不一致。(coincide)

556. 两个作家合写了这部电影的脚本。(collaborate)

557. 这栋古老的修道院处于倒塌的危险之中。(collapse)

558. 股票市场崩溃了,他失去了所有的钱。(collapse)

559. 很久以前屋顶就塌啦。(collapse)

560. 我想没有我,整个项目就会崩溃。(collapse)

561. 他和几个同事谈了谈这个想法。(colleague)

562. 那你是什么时候开始收藏古代酒杯的?(collect)

563. 这是管理层的集体决定。(collective)

564. 他们成功的秘诀就是大量制造廉价商品。(colossal)

565. 很多因素结合在一起造成了这个困境。(combine)

566. 好的地毯毛需要兼备柔性和韧性。(combine)

567. 莎士比亚的许多戏剧都是喜剧。(comedy)

568. 在工作中遇到困难时,我从家人那里寻求安慰。(comfort)

569. 我的穿着通常讲究舒适而不追求时尚。(comfort)

570. 我试图安慰他,但是无济于事。(comfort)

571. 我们聚集在这座教堂里,怀念那些在大战中死去的人们。(commemorate)

572. 开始上班后六个月要对你进行第一次评估。(comment)

573. 演讲在新闻界得到很多评论。(comment)

574. 有人有什么问题或意见吗?(comment)

575. 人们总是对我妹妹的容貌发表评论。(comment)

576. 战争期间两国间的贸易中止了。(commerce)

577. 这个商人从卖出的商品中抽取百分之二十的佣金。(commission)

578. 政府建立了一个委员会调查对于警察暴力的指控。(commission)

579. 犯了罪,你至少应该觉得羞耻。(commission)

580. 和男性相比,女性犯罪案例更少。(commit)

581. 他已经将自己交付给经济改革事业。(commit)
582. 我没法去开会,因为我另有约定。(commitment)
583. 我不想要孩子,他们需要我承担太多的义务。(commitment)
584. 他是财经委员会的成员。(committee)
585. 商品价格急剧下降。(commodity)
586. 城镇的这个地段偷车现象很平常。(commonplace)
587. 这个新建的艺术中心将为整个社区服务。(community)
588. 他是旧金山同性恋团体的一员。(community)
589. 火车里积满满身大汗不停抱怨的上/下班旅客。(commuter)
590. 宿舍房间虽小却安排紧凑,配有书桌、床和壁橱。(compact)
591. 他的狗成了他晚年最亲密的伙伴。(companion)
592. 你不能将索马里那场战争比作越南战争。(compare)
593. 和他以往的电影相比,李作为一个导演已有所进步。(comparison)
594. 这位作家将两位总统的相似之处进行比较。(comparison)
595. 史蒂芬的政治观点常常和她的不一致。(compatible)
596. 新的软件和IBM电脑兼容。(compatible)
597. 他不想去看她,但他的良心迫使他这么做。(compel)
598. 尽管她缺乏实践经验,但她的聪明很好地弥补了这一弱点。(compensate)
599. 他是唯一一位有足够能力统治这个国家的领导人。(competent)
600. 这两家公司相互竞争。(competition)
601. 这份文件由卫生部编纂。(compile)
602. 吃烧烤时有这种酒,真是美上加美。(complement)
603. 每个新细胞都带有自己全套的染色体。(complement)
604. 约翰和鲍勃两个人互补性很强。(complement)
605. 中国是由众多不同的民族组成的统一体。(complex)
606. 过去我对自己的长相有种夸大的情结。(complex)
607. 两个复杂的人之间关系很复杂。(complex)
608. 我必须填写这张十分复杂的表格。(complicated)
609. 他抱怨说她丈夫再也不赞美她了。(compliment)
610. 我正在赞美他做的美味佳肴。(compliment)
611. 运动是健康生活方式的重要组成部分之一。(component)

612. 音乐是为影片专门创作的。(compose)
613. 过去宫院里有很多神秘的事情。(compound)
614. 他与房东太太关系不好,这使得他的问题更加复杂。(compound)
615. 他对会议的叙述面面俱到。(comprehensive)
616. 这个隐喻使他难以理解。(comprehensive)
617. 这幢房子包括两个卧室,一个厨房和一个客厅。(comprise)
618. 委员会由很有名的登山运动员组成。(comprise)
619. 成员们不愿妥协使党内团结受到威胁。(compromise)
620. 政府声称不会对恐怖分子让步。(compromise)
621. 在我所在的学校里,游泳是必修的。(compulsory)
622. 最终的结果还没有计算出来。(compute)
623. 小路被深深的草丛掩盖了。(conceal)
624. 我找遍了所有我能想到的地方,但还是找不到我的钥匙。(conceivable)
625. 很多人不能设想一顿没有肉或鱼的正餐。(conceive)
626. 她怀孕有困难。(conceive)
627. 人口集中在河流沿岸。(concentrate)
628. 医生们正力争集中更多的精力在预防而不是治疗上。(concentrate)
629. 一旦你掌握了这一概念,事情就变得很简单啦。(concept)
630. 让人们挂虑的事情之一就是治疗的副作用。(concern)
631. 她明显很关心,这让他很感动。(concern)
632. 这家餐馆是家族生意。(concern)
633. 税收变动和大公司有关,与小企业没什么关系。(concern)
634. 类似食品添加剂的问题确实让我担心。(concern)
635. 回答要清楚简明。(concise)
636. 这份报告最终得出结论,马上关闭该校。(conclude)
637. 在今天上午的会议上你有没有做出什么决定?(conclusion)
638. 这项调查没能提供任何结论性的证据。(conclusive)
639. 那是幢令人压抑的灰色混凝土建筑,窗户很小。(concrete)
640. 他们认为她杀了丈夫,可是他们没有具体证据。(concrete)
641. 我们对需要什么有个总的想法,但目前还没有具体化。(concrete)
642. 展览回顾了同期国外的发展情况。(concurrent)

643. 我的观点和你的一致。(concurrent)
644. 我喜欢在图书馆看书。我觉得这样更有益。(conducive)
645. 参议院的品行正在接受道德规范委员会的调查。(conduct)
646. 他经商很成功。(conduct)
647. 无论在场上还是场下,他都是一个为人无懈可击的球员。(conduct)
648. 管弦乐队由约翰·威廉姆斯指挥。(conduct)
649. 大学授予他一个荣誉学位。(confer)
650. 富兰克林斜过身子,和他的律师交换意见。(confer)
651. 要我为这次会议预定会议室吗? (conference)
652. 她缺少自信。我从没见过如此胆怯而不自信的人。(confidence)
653. 她从未经历过她自己那紧密团结的家庭以外的生活。(confine)
654. 你被要求将电话机的使用限制在业务往来上。(confine)
655. 他被监禁在一间狭小黑暗的房间长达两个月。(confine)
656. 总统拒绝证实一个谣言。(confirm)
657. 为了进一步确定我的诊断,我需要做个试验。(confirm)
658. 她的话使我进一步认定她是个很无礼的少女。(confirm)
659. 多年来这个地区都被武装冲突弄得四分五裂。(conflict)
660. 马克思指出社会表面下潜在冲突。(conflict)
661. 新的证据与从前的科学发现相冲突。(conform)
662. 拒绝遵守校规,学生可能被逐出校园。(conform)
663. 所有建筑的大厦都必须与地区发展方案一致。(confront)
664. 军队迎面遇到一群愤怒的暴徒。(confront)
665. 我们试图帮助人们正视他们的问题。(confront)
666. 顾客面临很多选择。(confront)
667. 你把他搞糊涂了!慢慢地告诉他,一次说一件事。(confuse)
668. 你把我当成我姐姐了——在你的沙发上呕吐的是她。(confuse)
669. 她热烈祝贺我考试取得好成绩。(congratulate)
670. 她选举获胜,他寄去了祝贺信。(congratulation)
671. 国际 / 医学代表会议 (congress)
672. 国会否决了总统最近关于枪支的提议。(congress)
673. 警察把这起入室窃案和近期该地区其他失窃案联系起来。(connect)

汉译英练习

674. 电话接通了吗？(connect)
675. 请给我解释一下结缔组织。(connective)
676. 诺曼人于1066年攻占了英格兰。(conquer)
677. 祖鲁人打败了所有临近的部落。(conquer)
678. 我注意到她有点局促不安。(conscious)
679. 当救护车赶到事故现场时，司机仍然神志清醒。(conscious)
680. 这是连续第五个周末加班，我有点厌倦了。(consecutive)
681. 我们能在该问题上达成一致吗？让我们来表决。(consensus)
682. 没有得到车主的同意，他把车取走了。(consent)
683. 他很少同意面谈。(consent)
684. 安全程序被忽视了，这有可能带来悲剧性后果。(consequence)
685. 农民遭受严重的干旱，结果造成市场上食品匮乏。(consequent)
686. 保守党的政策 (conservative)
687. 对教育非常保守的态度 (conservative)
688. 一套非常老式的衣服 (conservative)
689. 这个系列已经引起人们很大的兴趣。(considerable)
690. 自助餐包括几份不同的印度菜肴。(consist)
691. 幸福并不在于你拥有多少财产。(consist)
692. 她工作有时不错，但问题是她坚持不了。(consistent)
693. 科学家们对这个数字很满意，直到1975年这个常量才有人问及。(constant)
694. 这户人家不断有人来访。(constant)
695. 道路意外事故死亡人数在过去五年保持不变。(constant)
696. 他对公司非常忠诚。(constant)
697. 我们必须重新定义一个家庭的组成。(constitute)
698. 这一联盟建立于1949年。(constitute)
699. 政治因素不应妨碍医生给病人提供最好的治疗办法。(constrain)
700. 国外经济不景气很可能限制对美国出口商品的需求。(constrain)
701. 有计划要在河上建造一座新桥。(construct)
702. 罗伊斯已经构思出一个新的管理理念。(construct)
703. 我需要咨询我的律师。(consult)
704. 你查过字典吗？(consult)

705. 小一点的车辆会消耗更少的燃料。(consume)
706. 校园里不许喝酒。(consume)
707. 消费者很快就要付更高价的机票。(consumer)
708. 两个部落之间的联系很少。(contact)
709. 他在媒体里有很多熟人。(contact)
710. 如果你有任何疑问,请不要犹豫,联系我。(contact)
711. 这篇文章中有一些有用的信息。(contain)
712. 要努力控制住你的愤怒。(contain)
713. 奥斯卡在研究院里深受同辈的敬仰。(contemporary)
714. 人们认为墙上装饰有墙帷与地面镶瓷砖基本属同一时代。(contemporary)
715. 她的新书是有关当代英国生活的。(contemporary)
716. 箱子翻了,里面的一些东西散落出来。(content)
717. 如果信的内容被外交大臣知道的话,后果会非常严重。(content)
718. 约翰似乎很满意整晚坐在电视机前。(content)
719. 简单的表扬就已经让他心满意足了。(content)
720. 我强烈反对那种主张。(contention)
721. 这个问题已经解决——不再有争议了。(contention)
722. 他们一连输了三场比赛,从而失去了争夺冠军的资格。(contention)
723. 我们参加了一次钓鱼比赛。(contest)
724. 资方和工会之间一直存在着斗争。(contest)
725. "funny"这个单词的含义取决于上下文。(context)
726. 要领会这些变化的含义,有必要将它们放在一定的背景下看。(context)
727. 我的电脑不停地发出低低的嗡嗡声。(continuous)
728. 仔细阅读这份合同,然后签字。(contract)
729. 随着金属冷却,它的体积缩小。(contract)
730. 医生们与医院签订合同,提供医疗服务。(contract)
731. 那里三分之二的成人感染了艾滋病。(contract)
732. 这篇文章彻底地否定了他们的主张。(contradict)
733. 证人的证词自相矛盾,事实仍然不明。(contradict)
734. 尽管有反对意见,他还继续喝酒。(contrary)
735. 除非有反面的证据,不然我们应该相信他们。(contrary)

736. 与大众了解的情况相反的是，沙漠里有可能很冷。(contrary)
737. 两种对立的观点出现了。(contrary)
738. 这个股票于去年同期相比，每股跌了 60 美分，当时是涨了 21 美分。(contrast)
739. 虽然两种文化之间有相似之处，但仍然有很大的差别。(contrast)
740. 这些结果与在澳大利亚进行的其他医疗实验形成鲜明对比。(contrast)
741. 城里的雇员不能给政治运动捐款。(contribute)
742. 他是这本书的几个撰稿人之一。(contribute)
743. 关于在水果和蔬菜上使用化学制品产生了争议。(controversy)
744. 10月25号宣布全国大会将于11月4号召开。(convene)
745. 政府只考虑到供应商的便利。(convenience)
746. 如果你买得起，折叠式浴缸倒不失为一种方便设备。(convenience)
747. 传统医药治不好的病，有时替代性医药却能治好。(conventional)
748. 我想显得友好、平易近人些，却发觉给人印象恰恰相反。(converse)
749. 能和讲她的语言的人交谈，她很享受这个机会。(converse)
750. 他们最近转而皈依这一事业的。(convert)
751. 他们将空闲的卧室改为办公室。(convert)
752. 欧洲传教士使成千上万的人皈依基督教。(convert)
753. 股票可以轻易地兑换成现金。(convert)
754. 要是你见到詹姆斯，请转达我的歉意。(convey)
755. 官员们急于说服我们核反应堆是安全的。(convince)
756. 美洲豹在猎食时相互协作。(cooperate)
757. 相匹配的包和配饰构成了一个色彩和谐的整体。(coordinate)
758. 这些机构一起工作来协调食品安全政策。(coordinate)
759. 贫困的家庭必须应付许多沉重的压力。(cope)
760. 谁拥有这本书的版权？(copyright)
761. 去核，将苹果烘烤 40 分钟。(core)
762. 债务是这个问题的核心。(core)
763. 听到这个消息时，我的内心感到很震撼。(core)
764. 这家公司将公司总部从纽约迁至休斯顿。(corporate)
765. 她为一家大公司工作。(corporation)
766. 这份文件的前半部分和后半部分不一致。(correspond)

767. 有关这些事件的描述与当时的其他记载很类似。(correspond)
768. 母亲过世后,她便停止和他通信了。(correspond)
769. 在卖这所房子以前,我们将对它的外部稍事装修 (cosmetic)。
770. 你节食是为了健康还是为了漂亮?(cosmetic)
771. 伦敦给我留下了非常深刻地印象——因为它是那样地富于世界性。(cosmopolitan)
772. 许多见多识广的专家认为,牛津是欧洲最令人愉快的大学城之一。(cosmopolitan)
773. 孩子们都是万圣节打扮。(costume)
774. 歌唱家在演出莫扎特的歌剧时经常穿古装。(costume)
775. 或许我们应该见一下婚姻顾问。(counsellor)
776. 我进银行时柜台后没人,我只得等候有人出来服务。(counter)
777. 首相将会见其他欧洲国家的总理或首相讨论反毒品战。(counterpart)
778. 有两个女孩子在等你。(couple)
779. 他们新婚。(couple)
780. 这一点必须和创建一个迷人的环境联系起来。(couple)
781. 这张赠券值五英镑。(coupon)
782. 如果想更多了解我们的新型计算机,请填好这张资料索取单,按以下地址寄给我们。(coupon)
783. 遇见莎莉改变了他整个一生的进程。(course)
784. 我同意,这是唯一明智的举动。(course)
785. 安迪正在上一门为期一年的新闻学课程。(course)
786. 这张票包括门票和四道菜的一餐饭。(course)
787. 眼泪迅速地流下他的脸颊。(course)
788. 尽管她常常和我意见不一致,但她总是谦恭有礼。(Courteous)
789. 伦敦占地 1579 平方公里。(cover)
790. 灯光太亮了,我只好用手遮住眼睛。(cover)
791. 这本小册子的内容比我们刚才讨论的更详细。(cover)
792. 三小时我们赶了 400 公里路。(cover)
793. 剑桥出版的词典语法内容很详实。(coverage)
794. 对英国广播公司的大选报道你怎么看?(coverage)
795. 我只为自己的车投了火灾险。(coverage)
796. 窗户被石块击中破裂了。(crack)

797. 鞭子啪地抽在马头上方。(crack)
798. 保育员轻轻摇着摇篮。(cradle)
799. 化石证据表明非洲是早期人类进化的发源地。(cradle)
800. 我正在把这一手艺传授给我的侄子。(craft)
801. 飞机在起飞后几秒钟内便坠毁了。(crash)
802. 她的母亲死于汽车撞车事故。(crash)
803. 这个软件使得创作色彩斑斓的图标变得容易。(create)
804. 有些人相信宇宙是由一场大爆炸创造的。(create)
805. 几个孩子引起了一场骚乱。(create)
806. 鳄鱼是一种模样古怪的动物。(creature)
807. 我完全相信你有能力做这个工作。(credit)
808. 他很快在外交界中取得声望。(credit)
809. 我的学分不够毕业。(credit)
810. 请相信我还是有点头脑的！(credit)
811. 曼联的很多成功都可归于它的经理人。(credit)
812. 为了不吵醒婴儿，我们蹑手蹑脚地上了楼梯。(creep)
813. 狗趴到汽车下藏着。(creep)
814. 犯罪率继续上升。(crime)
815. 我父亲是个跛子，我母亲则身体不好。(cripple)
816. 职工们要求提高工资的呼声使公司面临一场危机。(crisis)
817. 学生必须达到一定的标准才有资格得到奖学金。(criteria)
818. 我们试图给学生们有建设性的批评。(criticism)
819. 她已经读过一打有关文学评论的文章。(criticism)
820. 这笔救济款对政府的经济政策而言很重要。(crucial)
821. 你就非得这么粗鲁不可吗？（或：你何必这么粗鲁呢？)(crude)
822. 包裹在邮运途中被压得一塌糊涂。(crush)
823. 我收到一副可爱的水晶耳环作为 21 岁生日礼物。(crystal)
824. 那儿的大部分土地太贫瘠而无法耕种。(cultivate)
825. 在这所学校里，我们力图陶冶所有学生的心灵。(cultivate)
826. 如果你要寻找文化的踪迹，这个城市有很多博物馆和艺术馆。(culture)
827. 众所周知，他是一个有高度文化修养的人。(culture)

828. 将你的车靠近路缘停放。(curb)
829. 从下周开始对酒后驾车将有新的限制措施。(curb)
830. 为抑制贩运毒品付出了很大努力。(curb)
831. 一年后她的癌症被治好了。(cure)
832. 这种病还找不到一种有效的疗法。(cure)
833. 消除无聊的最好办法是努力工作。(cure)
834. 婴儿对他们周围的一切都充满了好奇心。(curious)
835. 昨天我碰到件怪事。(curious)
836. 小女孩的脸被金色卷发包着。(curl)
837. 银行可向你提供外币。(currency)
838. 他的思想在上个世纪广为流传。(currency)
839. 在某些学校里,孩子们学习时事作为一门课程。(current)
840. 语言课程是学校全部课程里的主要部分。(curriculum)
841. 他没有接住球便狠狠地咒骂起来。(curse)
842. 她向后靠在垫子上。(cushion)
843. 气垫船靠气垫行驶。(cushion)
844. 我有一些积蓄,希望能帮助我度过找工作的那段日子。(cushion)
845. 根据习俗,由新娘的父亲支付婚礼费用。(custom)
846. 他在海关被拦住接受问话。(custom)
847. 他有个逗人喜爱的小弟弟。(cute)
848. 有时打破家庭暴力的唯一办法就是妻子离开。(cycle)
849. 水在机器里循环,重复利用。(cycle)
850. 我常常骑车穿过公园抵达学校。(cycle)
851. 他正在观察蒸汽机活塞的往复运动。(cyclic)
852. 地震造成大量建筑物的毁坏。(damage)
853. 当心别弄坏计时器的机械装置。(damage)
854. 别坐在草地上——湿的!(damp)
855. 我们沿着月台猛冲,勉强赶上火车。(dash)
856. 海浪撞击着礁岩。(dash)
857. 太空船已经传回有关木星大气的新数据。(data)
858. 我们几乎一直谈到天亮。(dawn)

859. 申请的截止日期是5月27号。(deadline)

860. 疯狂驾车时,汽车就成了一种致命武器。(deadly)

861. 她是新任社会科学院院长。(deadly)

862. 关于妇女是否该多花点时间待在家里这个问题,有很多踊跃的讨论。(dean)

863. 如果在白天举行辩论会就会更好一些。(debate)

864. 哲学家们就克隆人类是否正当展开辩论。(debate)

865. 我考虑着,是否应该告诉谁。(debate)

866. 预期他们将会在未来几十年内继续破坏臭氧层。(decade)

867. 他们声称塑料被埋起来就不会腐烂。(decay)

868. 我被他的制服骗过了,真的以为他是警官。(deceive)

869. 他们无法用比较正确的英语来表达自己。(decent)

870. 你能辨认出这信封上的字迹吗?(decipher)

871. 他们声明支持这项提议。(declare)

872. 家庭规模有所减小。(decline)

873. 人们普遍认为教育标准在逐渐衰退。(decline)

874. 史密斯由于更喜欢现在的工作,便谢绝了主席这个职位。(decline)

875. 汽车销售量已减少百分之二十五。(decline)

876. 几个月来她的健康状况每况愈下。(decline)

877. 他们用彩带和鲜花装饰了喜车。(decorate)

878. 今年我们占据市场的份额急剧减少。(decrease)

879. 我想把这首歌献给我的妻子。(dedicate)

880. 从她儿子的年龄看,我推断她先生至少应该有60岁了。(deduce)

881. 政府严重受挫。(defeat)

882. 经过长时间的战役,威灵顿的军队最终打败了拿破仑。(defeat)

883. 我认为我们的教育制度中存在许多不足之处。(defect)

884. 他们需要更多的部队来保卫边境地区免受可能的攻击。(defend)

885. 工会称他们将采取行动来维护会员们的工作权益。(defend)

886. 谁在为这个案子辩护?(defend)

887. 缺少关于这个主题的真正好书。(deficiency)

888. 新闻界已对教育体制的不足进行了大量的报道。(deficiency)

889. 这一职位的职责很难定义。(define)

890. 现在我将尽力弄清"流行文化"这个说法。(define)

891. 图形的外边界常常限定了它的大小。(define)

892. 关于新厨房的样子,约翰有明确的想法。(definite)

893. 我不可能给你一个肯定的答案。(definite)

894. 将烤箱预热至425度。(degree)

895. 20世纪60年代的英国,其特点是与从前相比,自由程度更高。(degree)

896. 申请人必须有工程学学位。(degree)

897. 他想把会议推迟几天,对你可方便?(delay)

898. 该书的出版延迟了。(delay)

899. 代表们已经投票赞同这项动议了。(delegate)

900. 由四名教师组成的小组被选派到工会会议上作学校代表。(delegate)

901. 经济决定权已交付给一个特别委员会。(delegate)

902. 他的名字被从名单上删掉了。(delete)

903. 我们故意决定分开住一段日子。(deliberate)

904. 他在慎重考虑要不要接受人家提供的新工作。(deliberate)

905. 莫利的体质一直很弱。(delicate)

906. 冬季,娇嫩的植物要养在温室里。(delicate)

907. 这玫瑰有股清香。(delicate)

908. 这种蛋糕好吃极了。(delicious)

909. 每天给我们办公室送两次邮件。(deliver)

910. 政府拒绝对恐怖分子提出的要求做出让步。(demand)

911. 抗议者绝食示威,要求释放所有政治犯。(demand)

912. 这是一首很难演奏的乐曲。它需要高度集中的注意力。

913. 艾米丽要大人花很多力气照看。(demanding)

914. 她妈妈有时很难伺候。(demanding)

915. 如果你缺席会议会被记过。(demerit)

916. 那栋建筑已在数年前拆掉。(demolish)

917. 这项研究证明了贫穷与营养不良之间的关系。(demonstrate)

918. 他们将说明如何操控现代高精度汽车。(demonstrate)

919. 英文单词"family"过去还表示包括仆人在内家里的所有人。(denote)

920. 这张地图上的十字形代表乡村。(denote)

921. 本国北部地区明天将有浓雾。(dense)
922. 我从未否认存在住房问题。(deny)
923. 儿子要什么，她就给什么。(deny)
924. 开往爱丁堡的火车将从第五站台发车。(depart)
925. 那时，罗伯特·肯尼迪是司法部部长。(department)
926. 埃里森现在任教育系的系主任。(department)
927. 这个国家主要依靠旅游业。(depend)
928. 你可以相信简——她一向信守诺言。(depend)
929. 治疗时间的长短取决于疾病的严重程度。(depend)
930. 她的画描绘出上个世纪普通人的生活。(depict)
931. 要是我们继续耗损地球的自然资源，就会给环境造成严重破坏。(deplete)
932. 上周我们付了房子的定金。(deposit)
933. 你得预付一个月的租金，外加500美元的押金。(deposit)
934. 我想办理一下存款。(deposit)
935. 这种雌性动物把卵直接产在水中。(deposit)
936. 河流流速变慢时，一层泥沙便沉积下来。(deposit)
937. 建议您把贵重物品存到旅馆的保险箱里。(deposit)
938. 看起来没人关心，这让我很沮丧。(depress)
939. 几个因素综合起来，导致美国经济不景气。(depress)
940. 他声称自己已经被剥夺了自由。(deprive)
941. 他跟他副手合作得很好。(deputy)
942. 从医学角度看，我们将从这一技术中获得巨大利益。(derive)
943. 这个单词来源于拉丁语。(derive)
944. 飞机开始下降。(descend)
945. 我妈妈声称自己是亚伯拉罕·林肯的后代。(descend)
946. 这人描述了他所看到的情形。(describe)
947. 沙漠里通常都非常炎热。(desert)
948. 凭你的一番勤奋工作，你理应得到一次休假。(deserve)
949. 你的建议值得认真考虑。(deserve)
950. 新飞机处于最终的设计阶段。(design)
951. 他对公司有些宏伟的规划。(design)

952. 她为公司设计了一个新的标志。(design)
953. 我最渴望没有别人来打扰我。(desire)
954. 他对财富没有渴求。(desire)
955. 连输六局之后,球队似乎产生了绝望的感觉。(despair)
956. 他令他的父母绝望,因为他对找工作毫无兴趣。(despair)
957. 他们生活在极度贫困中。(desperate)
958. 对付不断加剧的毒品问题需要采取极端的措施。(desperate)
959. 别干冒险的事!(desperate)
960. 尽管医生让她休息,她还是去了西班牙。(despite)
961. 老城区多半在战争期间被炸弹摧毁了。(destroy)
962. 这种长柄煮锅的把手可以拆下。(detach)
963. 他详细描述了这个过程。(detail)
964. 这份报告详细说明了过去一年我们所取得的进步。(detail)
965. 如果发现得早,很多种癌症都能治愈。(detect)
966. 不是所有的变节者都能被查出来。(detect)
967. 国家经济已经经历了一段时间的衰退。(deteriorate)
968. 专家查明,签名是伪造的。(determine)
969. 这些检查将帮助医生们决定使用何种治疗方法。(determine)
970. 这些化学物质对环境有不利影响。(detrimental)
971. 地震摧毁了整个地区。(devastate)
972. 这笔资金将应用于市场推广和产品开发。(development)
973. 全城到处都是新建的住宅区。(development)
974. 飞机不得不偏离正常的航道。(deviate)
975. 这家公司制造检测一氧化碳的设备装置。(device)
976. 他们的建议只不过是迷惑反对派的手段。(device)
977. 他擅长设计能和学生在课堂上玩的语言游戏。(devise)
978. 他们把所有的时间用来帮助生病的人。(devote)
979. 会议主要探讨健康和安全问题。(devote)
980. 医师把它诊断为风湿病。(diagnose)
981. 老师画了张示意图,显示血液如何流过心脏。(diagram)
982. 全国仍然存在各种各样的方言。(dialect)

983. 池塘直径六英尺。(diameter)
984. 口述这封信花了他很长时间。(dictate)
985. 房东们出租房子时可以定出他们的条件。(dictate)
986. 声音和优良的措辞备受关注。(diction)
987. 均衡、健康的日常饮食很重要。(diet)
988. 下周我要节食，希望圣诞节前减掉五磅。(diet)
989. 人与其他哺乳动物的不同之处在于人能说话。(differ)
990. 将事实与观点区分开来很重要。(differentiate)
991. 电视是传播知识的强有力手段。(diffuse)
992. 公司变得又大又分散。(diffuse)
993. 大多数婴儿能容易地消化多种食物。(digest)
994. 这篇报告内容太多，读一遍无法了解吸收。(digest)
995. 即使在战俘营里我们也尽力保留一些做人的尊严。(dignity)
996. 总统在如何应对危机上明显处于两难境地。(dilemma)
997. 我深信孜孜不倦的研究会有结果。(diligent)
998. 灯发出昏暗的光。(dim)
999. 一幢大型建筑物朦胧的轮廓在雾霭中隐现出来。(dim)
1000. 早日解决争端的希望非常渺茫。(dim)
1001. 我们需要知道这个房间确切的长宽高。(dimension)
1002. 我们将接受一场大规模灾难的洗礼。(dimension)
1003. 没有宗教信仰，你的生活也可以有精神层面。(dimension)
1004. 这些药减少大脑的血流量。(diminish)
1005. 不要让他贬低你的成就。(diminish)
1006. 他把手指伸进糖浆瓶蘸了一蘸。(dip)
1007. 我希望今年拿到教师证。(diploma)
1008. 我们在寻求一个外交上的和平解决方法。(diplomatic)
1009. 这位秘书在通电话时沉着镇定，说话很得体。(diplomatic)
1010. 这种病每年使数千人残疾。(disable)
1011. 这个项目主要的缺点是费用太高。(disadvantage)
1012. 有120人在这次空难中死亡。(disaster)
1013. 由于天气原因，游行彻底泡汤了。(disaster)

1014. 在街上乱扔垃圾的人应受重罚。(discard)

1015. 看不出这些图形有什么格式。(discern)

1016. 武术教人要互相尊重、严于律己、相互合作。(discipline)

1017. 在纪律准则方面，这本书给家长提供了建议。(discipline)

1018. 不同的文化环境有不同的方法训导儿童。(discipline)

1019. 安全部不可能透露任何消息。(disclose)

1020. 利物浦队不足惧——他们有三名伤员。(discount)

1021. 要是我们不得不对我们的价格打折扣，就无利可图了。(discount)

1022. 我以六折买下这些鞋子。(discount)

1023. 你应该在所有的窗户上都安上锁，以防窃贼入室。(discourage)

1024. 你批评学生次数太多，他们很快就会泄气的。(discourage)

1025. 两份账目之间有出入。(discrepancy)

1026. 变化分一系列互不关联的几个步骤产生。(discrete)

1027. 新生儿能辨别男人和女人的声音。(discriminate)

1028. 联邦法规定，区别对待少数民族群体和妇女是违法行为。(discriminate)

1029. 两个宇航局可能合作一个项目，目前该项目正在讨论中。(discussion)

1030. 阿曼达沮丧地看着自己的考试成绩。(dismay)

1031. 他只是笑笑，就以不切实际为由拒绝了我的建议。(dismiss)

1032. 布莱恩特被免职了。(dismiss)

1033. 由于下雪，今天老师或许会提早下课。(dismiss)

1034. 一切都凌乱不堪，但好像并没有丢什么东西。(disorder)

1035. 这个家庭有精神错乱史。(disorder)

1036. 贫富生活的水平相差如此悬殊。(disparity)

1037. 管理人会派一队人去修好损坏之处。(dispatch)

1038. 煤作为主要能源已经被天然气所取代。(displace)

1039. 战争已经使五万人流离失所。(displace)

1040. 昨晚他们去观看了焰火表演。(display)

1041. 今天布莱顿展出了一辆世界上最古老的汽车。(display)

1042. 伊恩确实喜欢公开表露自己的情感。(display)

1043. 画廊四周陈列着中国花瓶。(dispose)

1044. 身体释放出一种化学物质，这种物质使你产生倦意。(dispose)

1045. 两国之间一直有边界争端。(dispute)

1046. 旅行能够开阔视野，几乎没有人会对此提出异议。(dispute)

1047. 他们在和地方政府就所建议的新铁路展开争论。(dispute)

1048. 守军寸土必争。(dispute)

1049. 法官命令陪审团不要理会证人的最后陈述。(disregard)

1050. 该组织的一个目标是散发有关疾病蔓延的消息。(disseminate)

1051. 把糖放在水里溶解。(dissolve)

1052. 国会已被解散。(dissolve)

1053. 两组人的学习需求有很大区别。(distinct)

1054. 轮船的轮廓变得越来越清晰。(distinct)

1055. 我得到的很显著的印象是，他试图激怒我。(distinct)

1056. 他是色盲，不能轻易地分辨红绿。(distinguish)

1057. 他很小年纪就在体育方面崭露头角。(distinguish)

1058. 他的脸由于愤怒而变了形。(distort)

1059. 他的描述受到新闻界的曲解。(distort)

1060. 王室丑闻转移了媒体对经济危机的注意力。(distract)

1061. 有些人搬家时会显得忧虑。(distress)

1062. 我们怎么能防止这种贫穷、艰难和困苦呢？(distress)

1063. 如果因为我问了你所有这些而使你感到苦恼，我很抱歉。(distress)

1064. 衣物和毛毯已分发给了难民。(distribute)

1065. 要保证重量得到均匀分布。(distribute)

1066. 纽约的哪个区最富？(district)

1067. 对不起打扰你，可以借用一下你的电话吗？(disturb)

1068. 塞尔玛还没拿到自己的考试成绩，她很焦虑。(disturb)

1069. 设计一个要满足所有使用者不同需求的程序很难。(diverse)

1070. 加入这一组织的人来自不同的社会、经济和教育背景，可谓形形色色。(diverse)

1071. 我们需要使经济多样化。(diversify)

1072. 大多数金融家建议投资者增加资产种类。(diversify)

1073. 这门课程将考虑到（该国）人口的种族多样性。(diversity)

1074. 在英国，三分之一的婚姻以离婚告终。(divorce)

1075. 他们的婚姻仅维持了六个月。(divorce)

1076. 长时间的睡眠缺乏使我头晕目眩。(dizzy)
1077. 2004 年她拿到了历史学博士学位。(doctorate)
1078. 几份秘密文件在他的办公室丢失了。(document)
1079. 这份文件不可以被用作一项独立调查。(document)
1080. 在美国，主要还是由男性从事体力劳动。(domain)
1081. 这一问题超出了医学的范围。(domain)
1082. 不幸的是，他的家庭生活并不幸福。(domestic)
1083. 国内航班从 1 号候机室出发。(domestic)
1084. 这一产业由五家跨国公司垄断。(dominate)
1085. 大教堂俯视全城。(dominate)
1086. 在选举活动中，教育问题占首要地位。(dominate)
1087. 要求人们献血的呼吁非常成功。(donate)
1088. 整个国家感到某种大灾难的降临。(doom)
1089. 不断增加的债务注定了工厂的倒闭。(doom)
1090. 长期休眠的火山最近显现了活动的迹象。(dormant)
1091. 开始的四个段落由点阵打印机打印出来，信纸的供应不能间断。(dot matrix)
1092. 你不可以在双黄线上停车。(double)
1093. 我要一杯双份威士忌。(double)
1094. 我想订一个双人房间，住两晚。(double)
1095. 美国的制造商们一直在缩小他们工厂的规模。(downsize)
1096. 帕姆午饭后经常坐在椅子上打盹。(doze)
1097. 我父亲 18 岁的时候应征入伍。(draft)
1098. 伊娃正忙于起草会议上的发言稿。(draft)
1099. 在喜剧《睡眠者》中他扮演一个俄罗斯间谍。(drama)
1100. 玛姬的生活充满了戏剧性。(drama)
1101. 我希望能看到显著的改进。(dramatic)
1102. 登上月球是本世纪最为扣人心弦的科学探险之一。(dramatic)
1103. 我有一次看了戏剧版的《白衣女人》。(dramatic)
1104. 政府最近采取严厉的措施控制公用支出。(drastic)
1105. 这是个很棒的城市，唯一的缺点是天气不好。(drawback)
1106. 进口货日后出口时退还其进口关税。(drawback)

1107. 橡皮筏子漂向大海。(drift)

1108. 詹妮一年来一直在欧洲各地漂泊。(drift)

1109. 电钻 (drill)

1110. 发音练习 (drill)

1111. 沙特政府已经宣布在沙漠钻井探水的计划。(drill)

1112. 她在教这个班练习过去时。(drill)

1113. 小心——你的漆刷在往下滴漆。(drip)

1114. 有个男子掉到桥下淹死了。(drown)

1115. 萨姆把煎饼泡在糖浆里。(drown)

1116. 大卫有英美双重国籍。(dual)

1117. 月底得付租金。(due)

1118. 插座里的坏电线引起了火灾。(due)

1119. 我认为这本书既沉闷又无新意。(dull)

1120. 大海呈一片暗灰色。(dull)

1121. 这些因素对聪明和愚笨的儿童都会有影响。(dull)

1122. 她生下来就又聋又哑。(dumb)

1123. 他痛苦地呆望着被撞得不像样的汽车，说不出话来。(dumb)

1124. 谁把这些书乱堆在我的书桌上？(dump)

1125. 让我们把汽车扔在这儿，剩下的路走着去。(dump)

1126. 小偷有复制的保险箱钥匙。(duplicate)

1127. 我丢失了原件，所以他们给我送来了副本。(duplicate)

1128. 你能不能替我复印这份文件？(duplicate)

1129. 塑料窗框比木质窗框耐用。(durable)

1130. 这个课程要持续三年。(duration)

1131. 街灯在黄昏时亮起来。(dusk)

1132. 伊恩对他的父母有一种责任感。(duty)

1133. 葡萄酒税已经上调。(duty)

1134. 白雪公主和七个小矮人 (dwarf)

1135. 她在亚洲一个偏僻的地方住了许多年。(dwell)

1136. 报告细述了过多的暴力。(dwell)

1137. 上电影院看电影的人数似乎在持续下降。(dwindle)

1138. 市场时时都在变化，公司必须学会适应市场的变化。(dynamic)
1139. 很明显，这个年轻女子充满活力，雄心勃勃。(dynamic)
1140. 也许我在那个阶段确实显得有点怪癖。(eccentric)
1141. 在当前的经济氛围里，我们必须降低成本。(economic)
1142. 通货膨胀是很多南美国家经济中的一个重要问题。(economy)
1143. 公司宣布削减五百人，作为精简行动的一部分。(economy)
1144. 这种植物只有叶子可以食用。(edible)
1145. 报纸先将来信进行编辑，然后印出。(edit)
1146. 他在剪辑室里看胶片，将片段链接起来。(edit)
1147. 那酒对我很起作用——我觉得有点头晕。(effect)
1148. 培训往往没有预期的那么有效。(effective)
1149. 降低的利率从星期一开始生效。(effective)
1150. 这家餐厅提供高效且友好的服务。(efficient)
1151. 他们在为婚礼做极为周详的准备工作。(elaborate)
1152. 部长说他将辞职，但拒绝细说。(elaborate)
1153. 48岁的福布斯是个百万富翁，用自己的钱资助自己参选总统，他从来没有组织过选举办公室。(elective)
1154. 给一年级学生开一门有关社会正义的选修课。(elective)
1155. 举止优雅的人／优美的身材／优雅的侧影 (elegant)
1156. 简要明确的观点／计划／解决方法 (elegant)
1157. 诚实是她取得成功的重要因素。(element)
1158. 她连礼貌的基本要素都一无所知。(element)
1159. 他们想提高教师地位。(elevate)
1160. 她敲了门，却没有得到回应，于是她便开了门，探头进去看。(elicit)
1161. 非全日制课程的学生不具备申请贷款的资格。(eligible)
1162. 斯蒂芬被看作合适的单身汉。(eligible)
1163. 有了信用卡就不需要现金或支票了。(eliminate)
1164. 在第一轮比赛中我们队被淘汰出局。(eliminate)
1165. 我们在利物浦上船赴纽约。(embark)
1166. 20世纪50年代中国开始实施工业化的重大计划。(embark)
1167. 我把茶打翻在老师身上的时候真是窘极了。(embarrass)

1168. 乔治在运动场上总是体现出良好的运动员风范。(embody)

1169. 她温柔地拥抱儿子。(embrace)

1170. 不抓住那么好的机会你真是个傻瓜。(embrace)

1171. 这门课程涉及心理学的几个不同方面。(embrace)

1172. 太阳从阴云后浮现。(emerge)

1173. 后来，事情暴露出来，法官雇用了一个非法移民。(emerge)

1174. 多年来，他在社会学领域一直地位卓著。(eminent)

1175. 烟囱里冒出一团团的烟雾。(emit)

1176. 这门课很强调实际工作。(emphasis)

1177. 我只是想强调人们学习外语是多么重要。(emphasize)

1178. 他的理论与实践证据不一致。(empirical)

1179. 这家公司在全世界雇用了 2000 名员工。(employ)

1180. 为得到这些结果使用了精密的数据分析。(employ)

1181. 杨原本希望能赶超道格拉斯的成就。(emulate)

1182. 贷款使简能买下这幢房子。(enable)

1183. 正在计划加长跑道，以便大型喷气式客机的降落。(enable)

1184. 国会拒绝通过该法案。(enact)

1185. 请随求职信寄上简历。(enclose)

1186. 那座纪念碑所在的公园最近被扩建了。(enclose)

1187. 房子占地约 100 平方米。(encompass)

1188. 美国建议建立一个包括整个西半球在内的自由贸易区。(encompass)

1189. 他似乎不记得去年夏天我们曾经邂逅的事情，人家介绍我的时候，他只点了点头。(encounter)

1190. 她见证了两个相互对抗的足球队的支持者之间的敌对冲突。(encounter)

1191. 你初次遇到这个问题是什么时候？(encounter)

1192. 警察对付罪犯必须不危及行人生命。(endanger)

1193. 工程师们试图找到问题的根源。(endeavour)

1194. 这次探险是人类奋勇进取的显著例证。(endeavour)

1195. 竟然有人能忍受如此的痛苦，看起来不可能。(endure)

1196. 他们再也无法容忍的那一天终于来了。(endure)

1197. 她是一个那么充满活力的小女孩！(energetic)

1198. 她全身心地投入到婚礼计划中。(energy)
1199. 假期之后,她干劲十足。(energy)
1200. 如果你总是觉得疲劳的话,有些维生素可以给你提供更多的能量。(energy)
1201. 政府制定法律,警察执行法律。(enforce)
1202. 唱片公司不太可能会强迫一位有声望的艺术家接受自己的意见。(enforce)
1203. 如果一本书的开头几页不能引起我的兴趣,我通常就不继续看下去了。(engage)
1204. 你为什么不雇个木匠给你做一套厨房组合件?(engage)
1205. 在业余时间,他参加志愿工作。(engage)
1206. 推广活动对于提高他的知名度没起什么作用。(enhance)
1207. 儿童电视的作用是娱乐还是教育?(enlighten)
1208. 这个团队做出了巨大努力。(enormous)
1209. 委员会在开始建新住宅区之前将需要进行公众调查。(enquiry)
1210. 教育可以使生活充实。(enrich)
1211. 殖民地的目的就是要增加殖民者与西班牙王国的财富。(enrich)
1212. 1996 年他被一所社区大学录取。(enrol)
1213. 在他 18 岁的时候,父母送他入伍,加入一所军校。(enrol)
1214. 必要的措施都采取了,以保证他们的安全。(ensure)
1215. 医院尽力保证病人很快就医。(ensure)
1216. 对许多父母来说,有了孩子就得做出一定的牺牲。(entail)
1217. 那些年是私营企业兴盛的年头,许多小企业就是那时开办的。(enterprise)
1218. 我们在晚会上雇了一个魔术师给孩子们娱乐。(entertain)
1219. 事情发生之后,他失去了对这项运动的兴趣。(enthusiasm)
1220. 他们得到一整套银餐具作为结婚礼物。(entire)
1221. 失业使你有权享受免费医疗。(entitle)
1222. 她最近的一部小说名为《被遗忘的过去》,本周出版。(entitle)
1223. 这些博物馆紧密合作,但在法律上是分别的实体。(entity)
1224. 小孩子常常在家庭环境中感到更加开心。(environment)
1225. 有些化学物质对自然环境非常有害。(environment)
1226. 这个计划比最初设想的要花更多的钱。(envisage)
1227. 大多数人将财富等同于成功。(equate)
1228. 这些房间配有摄影机。(equip)

1229. 我们使学生掌握那些他们离开学校时会用得上的技能。(equip)
1230. 这个单词在英语中没有对等的说法。(equivalent)
1231. 美国国会相当于英国的议会。(equivalent)
1232. 我没有美元，便给了他同等数量的英镑。(equivalent)
1233. 柏林墙的倒塌象征着一个时代的结束。(era)
1234. 政府声称正在全力以赴地杜绝腐败。(eradicate)
1235. 虽然他现在是个富有的人，但他却无法抹去童年的回忆。(erase)
1236. 他已78岁，但仍个头高挺，腰杆笔直。(erect)
1237. 公园中央的战争纪念碑建于1950年。(erect)
1238. 悬崖常年受到巨浪的腐蚀。(erode)
1239. 一而再，再而三的考试失利逐步削弱了他的自信。(erode)
1240. 我们的计算肯定有错误。(error)
1241. 医生承认自己错了。(error)
1242. 扩展公司的决定是判断失误。(error)
1243. 由于军事管制的实施，激烈的反政府情绪突然爆发了。(eruption)
1244. 采取加强联合国干预的决定是希望尽快结束敌对状态。(escalate)
1245. 关于家庭作业我想让你们写一篇关于濒临灭绝物种的论说文。(essay)
1246. 竞争是所有比赛的本质。(essence)
1247. 她装了一些必需品。(essential)
1248. 提前预订很有必要。(essential)
1249. 山姆和我的本质区别是我认真对待人生。(essential)
1250. 我们的目标是在北部建立一个新的研究中心。(establish)
1251. 大多数钱会被用于创建当地的各个产业以及集中劳动力。(establish)
1252. 在继续工作之前，警方必须让大家认可这一案件的事实。(establish)
1253. 这个国家对职业教育的尊重程度较低。(esteem)
1254. 这处房产是死者产业的一部分。(estate)
1255. 她的工作深受全体同事的敬重。(esteem)
1256. 据政府估计，难民人数至少达1800万。(estimate)
1257. 我们预言石油价格会上涨百分之十，而且那是个保守的评估。(estimate)
1258. 据估计，这棵树至少700岁了。(estimate)
1259. 在一些宗教观点中，生命被看做是善与恶两种力量间永恒的冲突。(eternal)

1260. 电视新闻以道德规范为基准。(ethic)
1261. 这家学校教授来自各个种族群体的学生 (ethnic)
1262. 爱德华不能永远躲着不服兵役。(evade)
1263. 你应该有能力估计自己的工作。(evaluate)
1264. 我们需要评价这次战役的成功之处。(evaluate)
1265. 我们需要对这个新系统做出恰当评估。(evaluation)
1266. 今年的奥林匹克运动会将是最大的体育盛事。(event)
1267. 双方对会谈的最终结果都很满意。(eventual)
1268. 这一研究发现一条有趣的证据。(evidence)
1269. 她拒绝在审判中提供证词。(evidence)
1270. 目前，我们还没有发现在其他行星上存在生命的迹象。(evidence)
1271. 我看得很明白，他在说谎。(evident)
1272. 这所学校已逐步形成自己的教学风格。(evolve)
1273. 鱼类从史前的海洋生物进化而来。(evolve)
1274. 准确距离是 1838 米。(exact)
1275. 敲诈者向受害人共勒索了 10 万美元。(exact)
1276. 这座教堂是哥特式建筑的一个很好的典范。(example)
1277. 她的勇气是我们学习的榜样。(example)
1278. 他由于超速被罚款。(exceed)
1279. 他的表现超出我们的期望。(exceed)
1280. 他擅长体育运动。(excel)
1281. 你必须每个星期二到这里报到，无一例外。(exception)
1282. 饮酒可以但不要过量。(excess)
1283. 看上去我们所带的东西多了些，但情况紧急时，它们会派上用场。(excess)
1284. 有些数据被专门从报告中剔除。(exclude)
1285. 新闻界被刻意地排除在这次活动之外。(exclude)
1286. 在这一阶段，我们不能完全排除裁员的可能。(exclude)
1287. 一两个月之后他们处决了国王。(execute)
1288. 董事们做出决定，但要由经理们来执行。(execute)
1289. 洛杉矶是美国文化多元性的典范。(exemplify)
1290. 他因身体差而被豁免服兵役。(exempt)

1291. 根据目前的医疗制度，孕妇免付牙医费。(exempt)
1292. 如果你们运用自己的影响，他们可能会改变决定。(exert)
1293. 我觉得上一整天课让我精疲力竭。(exhaust)
1294. 他们很快就将周围地区的食物资源消耗一空。(exhaust)
1295. 最古老的展品可追溯到17世纪。(exhibit)
1296. 少儿博物馆举行了几次可亲手触摸的展览会。(exhibit)
1297. 在潜在危险面前表露出极端忧虑情绪的人不可能成为好的军事领袖。(exhibit)
1298. 她的画作已在全世界展出。(exhibit)
1299. 过去的十年里，计算机业得到巨大的发展。(expand)
1300. 温度降低，水的体积增大。(expand)
1301. 法律专家说，宣判此人有罪不合法。(expert)
1302. 我没有烹饪专长。(expertise)
1303. 我的护照再过三个月就到期了。(expire)
1304. 这届政府的任期到2004年已满。(expire)
1305. 绑匪已给出明确的指示，不许报警。(explicit)
1306. 和家人谈钱的问题时，坦率点。(explicit)
1307. 在紧邻的一条街上有一枚炸弹爆炸了。(explode)
1308. 人口在激增。(explode)
1309. 该国的自然资源还没得到充分开发。(exploit)
1310. 新的电视公司正充分开发卫星传送的潜能。(exploit)
1311. 家庭佣工很容易受到雇主的剥削。(exploit)
1312. 对新能源的勘探对于我们地球的未来是至关重要的。(exploration)
1313. 这个岛的每一部分都已做了勘察。(explore)
1314. 会议探讨了进一步密切贸易联系的可能性。(explore)
1315. 她是自学成才的著名典型。(exponent)
1316. 这一艺术手段最著名的倡导者要数查尔斯．麦金托什。(exponent)
1317. 小麦是该国主要的出口产品之一。(export)
1318. 这家公司出口金枪鱼给美国。(export)
1319. 意大利食品已被传播到世界的各个角落。(export)
1320. 报告披露，工人一直暴露在高度的辐射下。(expose)
1321. 有些小孩子从没受过古典音乐的熏陶。(expose)

1322. 他掀起自己的T恤衫，露出胸口的伤疤。(expose)

1323. 森林向四面延伸，一望无际。(extend)

1324. 银行说他们不能继续追加对这个企业的承诺。(extend)

1325. 我们把厨房扩大了六英尺。(extend)

1326. 我应对你的好意表示感谢。(extend)

1327. 从帝国大厦的顶层，你可以看到整个曼哈顿。(extent)

1328. 主建筑外面，有一个小小的建筑可用作办公室或工作室。(exterior)

1329. 房子外面需要粉刷。(exterior)

1330. 必须在该物种灭绝之前停止捕捞。(exterminate)

1331. （婴儿）出生体重过低可能由外界因素造成，例如怀孕期间吸烟。(external)

1332. 中国不会姑息任何外国势力干预其内政。(external)

1333. 许多部落在接触到西方疾病后就灭绝了。(extinct)

1334. 一位空中小姐让他熄掉雪茄烟。(extinguish)

1335. 我们必须抹去对失败的记忆。(extinguish)

1336. 最近他每一天多工作两小时。(extra)

1337. 加一茶匙的香草精。(extract)

1338. 我只看过这部电影简短的选段。(extract)

1339. 你得把那颗牙拔掉。(extract)

1340. 从植物中提取油。(extract)

1341. 他们旨在从奥运会中获取最大的政治利益。(extract)

1342. 大多数家庭都缺少用来资助孩子参加课外活动的钱。(extracurricular)

1343. 他讲述了他不寻常的逃跑经历。(extraordinary)

1344. 她认为他用电很浪费。(extravagant)

1345. 这种产品没有达到广告商们所吹嘘的水平。(extravagant)

1346. 人们能够在极端恶劣的环境下生存下来。(extreme)

1347. 社会不能容忍人类的极端行为。(extreme)

1348. 这些料子是特地从意大利和法国进口的。(fabric)

1349. 这些磁盘的生产成本很高。(fabricate)

1350. 杰克逊被指控伪造钞票。(fabricate)

1351. 你看上去真美啊！(fabulous)

1352. 那幅画卖了一个天价。(fabulous)

1353. 独角兽是神话中的怪兽。(fabulous)
1354. 宝石的表面是些琢刻的小平面。(facet)
1355. 机敏只是他作为船长所具备的各种才能中的一种而已。(facet)
1356. 两个中心之间的电子联络使交流变得更加便利。(facilitate)
1357. 计算机可用于促进语言学习。(facilitate)
1358. 煤气炉使用起来比老式煤炉更方便。(facility)
1359. 这家旅馆有自己的游泳池和休闲设施。(facility)
1360. 犯罪增加主要是由于社会和经济因素。(factor)
1361. 3 是 15 的一个因子。(factor)
1362. 她很有获取信息的天赋。(faculty)
1363. 最后，他被法律系录取。(faculty)
1364. 系里的老师、工作人员和学生都反对这些措施。(faculty)
1365. 和平解决的希望正开始逐渐消失。(fade)
1366. 太阳把窗帘晒得褪了色。(fade)
1367. 还有一线希望，他们可能还活着。(faint)
1368. 几个球迷（歌迷、影迷）在炙热的天气下晕过去了。(faint)
1369. 公众对政府已完全失去信心。(faith)
1370. 我们以为这是真的古董，可实际上只是一件赝品。(fake)
1371. 回到熟悉的环境里真让人释然。(familiar)
1372. 这种情况在约翰看来很普通。(familiar)
1373. 我觉得他和我太太有点亲近。(familiar)
1374. 你们的这些计划太荒唐了，永远不会实现。(fantastic)
1375. 你穿着那套服装看上去棒极了！(fantastic)
1376. 穿越时间之旅的主意把我吸引住了。(fascinate)
1377. 观看如何制造玻璃十分有趣。(fascinating)
1378. 今年夏天流行长长的卷发。(fashion)
1379. 她用报纸为他们做帽子。(fashion)
1380. 系好你的安全带。(fasten)
1381. 格拉芙在比赛中途犯了个致命的错误。(fatal)
1382. 你最喜欢看什么电视节目？(favourite)
1383. 你真聪明，买了巧克力饼干，这是我最喜爱的食品。(favourite)

1384. 你以前一直是爸爸的宠儿。(favourite)

1385. 电动汽车从技术上讲是可行的。(feasible)

1386. 这座大桥的建成是工程技术上的一项业绩。(feat)

1387. 她的眼睛长得最好。(feature)

1388. 梵高的绘画的重要特点是明亮的色彩。(feature)

1389. 在主要故事片之前播出了两个卡通片。(feature)

1390. 这次展览以当代画家的作品为特色。(feature)

1391. 看来暴力在他所有的作品中占有突出的地位。(feature)

1392. 由于宗教原因歧视某人违反联邦法。(federal)

1393. 瑞士是联邦共和国。(federal)

1394. 公园的门票已经涨到了 15 美元。(fee)

1395. 试用过这种新肥皂的客户反馈回来的信息是令人乐观的。(feedback)

1396. 她在第二年比赛中被评选为最佳女歌唱家。(female)

1397. 尼罗河的定期泛滥使其周围地区土地变得肥沃。(fertile)

1398. 大多数男子直到老年还有生育能力。(fertile)

1399. 导演这样一部独特的影片需要丰富的想象力。(fertile)

1400. 尽管她命运多舛，还是狂热地笃信上帝。(fervent)

1401. 这里的大多数人都是自主的热情支持者。(fervent)

1402. 美满幸福的婚姻也许更常见于小说而不是现实生活。(fiction)

1403. 我们必须维持还是正常夫妻的假象。(fiction)

1404. 他是政治界圈外知名度最高的美国人。(field)

1405. 上个周末这两个人在一场激战中被击毙。(fierce)

1406. 分别用文字和数字写出这个数量。(figure)

1407. 他是宪法改革运动中的一位中心人物。(figure)

1408. 她从书架里抽出一个蓝色的文件夹。(file)

1409. 一队士兵齐步行进。(file)

1410. 合同按照字母顺序归档。(file)

1411. 格林先生对部门提起正式申诉。(file)

1412. 有人知道最后的比分吗？(final)

1413. 她不和我们一起走，这是最终决定！(final)

1414. 我们要筹集继续研究的资金。(finance)

1415. 她拒绝回答有关个人财务状况的问题。(finance)

1416. 音乐会得到艺术理事会的资助。(finance)

1417. 这个电影很棒，但是没有取得商业成功。(financial)

1418. 地球的资源有限，我们必须保护这些有限的资源。(finite)

1419. 开始爬梯子之前，检查一下梯子是否结实。(firm)

1420. 他刚开始在剑桥的一家会计事务所工作。(firm)

1421. 突然出现了一道闪光和"之"字形的叉状闪电。(flash)

1422. 羽毛鲜艳的鸟在空中飞掠而过。(flash)

1423. 过去人们都相信地球是平的。(flat)

1424. 经过那次激动人心的聚会，现在的生活好像很没劲。(flat)

1425. 承蒙您过奖，我可没有那么重要。(flatter)

1426. 这酒有种淡淡的水果味。(flavour)

1427. 这一简介应当让你对这本书的特点有所了解。(flavour)

1428. 这块布上有一疵点，不过很小。(flaw)

1429. 你可发现了他论点中的谬误之处？(flaw)

1430. 他跟着成千上万的人逃离了这个国家。(flee)

1431. 新的电脑软件极富弹性。(flexible)

1432. 你开始（工作）的日期可变通。(flexible)

1433. 这种木头能浮起来吗？(float)

1434. 我们让小筏子漂到河中央。(float)

1435. 有一大群海鸥尾随在我们后面。(flock)

1436. 好几百人涌去看足球赛。(flock)

1437. 一些国际机构搞得很红火的同时，另外一些国际机构实际上已经崩溃了。(flourish)

1438. 在这些水域里，细菌繁殖得很快。(flourish)

1439. 昆虫数量每年都有很大的波动。(fluctuate)

1440. 价格在20美元和40美元之间动摇不定。(fluctuate)

1441. 体内失水过多可能会引起死亡。(fluid)

1442. 一个半月以后，它的中心部分仍然完全呈流质状态。(fluid)

1443. 最近的研究重点是环境问题。(focus)

1444. 她转过照相机，将镜头对准马丁的脸。(focus)

1445. 沿虚线将纸折起来。(fold)

1446. 双臂交叉，挺胸坐直。(fold)

1447. 他们已经弄到了一份禁止该项销售的法院指令。(forbid)

1448. 要预测年幼的小孩的未来发展几乎是不可能的。(forecast)

1449. 今后几天的天气预报怎样？(forecast)

1450. 你预见到新制度有什么问题吗？(foresee)

1451. 他一直不原谅这家报纸刊载这篇报道的做法。(forgive)

1452. 文章的版式请看附上的杂志。(format)

1453. 面谈以一问一答的方式写下来。(format)

1454. 我们现在对行星形成的早期阶段了解了很多。(formation)

1455. 他是前总统里根的顾问。(former)

1456. 他们农场的规模已经缩减为从前的一半。(former)

1457. 我们的产品按照传统配方手工制成。(formula)

1458. 我们仍在寻求一个和平方案。(formula)

1459. 查尔斯.达尔文系统地阐述了自然选择理论。(formulate)

1460. 我们在研究这一形式，但还没想出做什么回应。(formulate)

1461. 注意看布告栏，了解以后的活动安排。(forthcoming)

1462. 没有得到答复，她便再次致信。(forthcoming)

1463. IBM 对其产品的市场总是毫不讳言。(forthcoming)

1464. 他是在两星期之前借去的。(fortnight)

1465. 该杂志成了定期交流信息和思想的论坛。(forum)

1466. 科学博物馆里可以看到恐龙化石。(fossil)

1467. 动物的化石骨骼使我们了解过去的生命。(fossil)

1468. 这个城堡建立在一块坚固的岩石上。(found)

1469. 伊顿公学由亨利六世于 1440 年创办。(found)

1470. 建筑工人花了三个星期的时间才打好地基。(foundation)

1471. 所有的理论都应该建立在实际知识的基础上。(foundation)

1472. 这所学校从 1835 年建校以来一直为社区服务。(foundation)

1473. 我稍稍迟疑了一下。(fraction)

1474. 1/4 和 1.25 是同一分数的不同表达。(fraction)

1475. 这只是和约翰长谈的一小部分内容。(fragment)

1476. 这篇论文为以后的研究提供了一个框架。(framework)

1477. 我们的行为必须在现行的法律体系范围内。(framework)
1478. 水在摄氏零度结冰。(freeze)
1479. 像番茄之类的食品如果冷冻起来会丧失原汁原味。(freeze)
1480. 政府冻结了养老金,直到明年年末。(freeze)
1481. "不许动!否则我开枪了!"持枪者尖声叫道。(freeze)
1482. 这艘船既载货又载客。(freight)
1483. 发生严重灾祸的次数似乎在不断增加。(frequency)
1484. 因为摩擦力较小,机器的总效率较高。(friction)
1485. 家庭成员之间的争吵会影响孩子的学业。(friction)
1486. 我想和一些外行一起工作让他很是气恼。(frustrate)
1487. 他们想跟他说话,但被警卫拦住了。(frustrate)
1488. 现在的状况使我们很沮丧。(frustrating)
1489. 他们没有能兑现使经济复苏的诺言。(fulfil)
1490. 既然孩子们不在家,我可以出去尽情地乐一乐了。(fulfil)
1491. 神经系统规范我们的身体功能。(function)
1492. 教堂承担颇有价值的社会职责。(function)
1493. 这个房间可租来举办婚礼和其他重大聚会。(function)
1494. 她的腿已经不会动了。(function)
1495. 图书馆暂时充当医院,用来照顾伤员。(function)
1496. 举行销售活动为学校筹资。(fund)
1497. 他记得大量有关童年的故事。(fund)
1498. 阅读以下有关设计和印刷生产的基本原则的简介。(fundamental)
1499. 我们必须抓住问难的基本原因。(fundamental)
1500. 水对生存而言至关重要。(fundamental)
1501. 我这辈子从来没有这样大发雷霆过。(furious)
1502. 他想搬到一个能自己布置房间的小型疗养所去住。(furnish)
1503. 此外唯一的一件家具是个老式衣橱。(furniture)
1504. 他又老又没人缘,而且他的政治生涯最多只有两年。(furthermore)
1505. 继续谈判是无济于事的。(futile)
1506. 遥远的星辰和星系。(galaxy)
1507. 我从未见过这么一群男女名演员。(galaxy)

1508. 篱笆在大风中被吹倒了。(gale)

1509. 我们被禁止饮酒或赌博。(gamble)

1510. 我们不能降低我们的安全标准——否则我们就是拿人们的命来冒险。(gamble)

1511. 好几个犯罪团伙在这个地区活动。(gang)

1512. 娄的门牙间有很大的缝。(gap)

1513. 贫富之间的差距不断扩大。(gap)

1514. 你走的时候能把垃圾带出去吗？(garbage)

1515. 她穿着一件猩红色亚麻布料子的长外套。(garment)

1516. 我把我的几张地图收起来装进了文件夹。(gather)

1517. 他们采集浆果、坚果和水果作为食物。(gather)

1518. 争取同性恋者的权利的示威活动 (gay)

1519. 她感到兴奋和极度的快乐。(gay)

1520. 我大部分时间都凝视着窗外。(gaze)

1521. 约翰检查了车上的齿轮。(gear)

1522. 我打好行李，走了出去。(gear)

1523. 她继承了价值20000英镑的黄金和宝石。(gem)

1524. 对待有偿工作的态度，不同性别的人会有所不同。(gender)

1525. 我们能对这一原则进行概括吗？(generalize)

1526. 研究结果可以推广到更广阔的人群。(generalize)

1527. 风力涡轮机为当地社区发电。(generate)

1528. 这个计划会提供很多新的就业机会。(generate)

1529. 像我们这一代里的很多人一样，我从来不知道战争是什么东西。(generation)

1530. 音乐天赋 (genius)

1531. 爱因斯坦是个天才 (genius)

1532. 专家们判定这幅画是康斯特布尔的真迹。(genuine)

1533. 她看着我，真的是很惊讶。(genuine)

1534. 这些病菌很容易从一个传到另一个人。(germ)

1535. 这只是初步想法，但我认为我们有可能把它发展成有用的东西。(germ)

1536. 她以一种绝望的姿势蒙住脸，突然大哭起来。(gesture)

1537. 政府捐赠了500,000英镑作为善意的表示。(gesture)

1538. 你读过关于残暴的巨人和邪恶的巫婆的故事吗？(giant)

1539. 他是本世纪知识界的伟人之一。(giant)

1540. 大熊猫 (giant)

1541. 这对耳环是我姑姑送给我的礼物。(gift)

1542. 迪有一种能让大家放松的天赋。(gift)

1543. 他具有非凡的记忆力。(gift)

1544. 整项业务的开支十分庞大。(gigantic)

1545. 我没有听这堂课，你能给我说说它的主要内容吗？(gist)

1546. 她环视房间，想看看谁在。(glance)

1547. 她生气地瞪着每个人。(glare)

1548. 车灯发出刺眼的前光，照向街的尽头。(glare)

1549. 那条蛇轻快地向它的猎物爬去。(glide)

1550. 部长将失业人数的增加归咎于全球的经济萧条。(global)

1551. 我们需要全面看待这一情况。(global)

1552. 我们的商品出口到世界各地。(globe)

1553. 这是该队的又一次光荣胜利。(glorious)

1554. 你的玫瑰真是美极了！(glorious)

1555. 他若有所思地凝视着壁炉中燃烧的火焰。(glow)

1556. 这顶帽子似乎是用胶水粘上去的。(glue)

1557. 已粘上了一块新的并重新上了漆。(glue)

1558. 他的最终目标是建立自己的公司。(goal)

1559. 我射入了第一个球。(goal)

1560. 许多文职人员确信他们能比那些政客治理得更好。(govern)

1561. 她抓住了我的手臂。(grab)

1562. 他们对这个世界的实权之争注定要失败。(grab)

1563. 她的动作十分优雅。(graceful)

1564. 她最后道了歉，但却不够风度。(graceful)

1565. 我弟弟念六年级。(grade)

1566. 他数学得 A。(grade)

1567. 铅笔按照（笔芯的）柔软度分类。(grade)

1568. 牛肉根据脂肪含量分级。(grade)

1569. 计算机化导致了许多手工工作逐渐消失。(gradual)

1570. 他获得了哲学学位。(graduate)

1571. 他父亲毕业于哈佛大学。(graduate)

1572. 凯特去年从医学院毕业。(graduate)

1573. 作为演员,她已经从饰演小角色发展成担当更加重要的角色。(graduate)

1574. 晨曦中的群山是多么宏伟壮观!(grand)

1575. 你做首次单独飞行的重大时刻终于来到了。(grand)

1576. 这家俱乐部获得了卖酒的许可证。(grant)

1577. 他的病情被生动详细地描述。(graphic)

1578. Photoshop 是大多数绘图艺术家使用的程序。(graphic)

1579. 一定用双手抓紧绳索。(grasp)

1580. 他们没有领会他的话的全部意义。(grasp)

1581. 他庆幸自己还活着。(grateful)

1582. 我对弗朗西斯的感激之情难以言尽。(gratitude)

1583. 由于地心引力,任何东西被松开后都会落向地面。(gravity)

1584. 卡尔似乎不理解这种情况的严重性。(gravity)

1585. 领事语速减慢,而且十分严肃。(gravity)

1586. 别贪吃——给我们留点蛋糕。(greedy)

1587. 这家公司过分追求利润。(greedy)

1588. 泰勒先生从桌后站起来迎接我。(greet)

1589. 她因海伦的去世而感到悲痛难当。(grief)

1590. 他们将谷粒放在两块大石头之间碾成面粉。(grind)

1591. 《猫》在美国一个国家的总共收益就超过了四亿六千万美元。(gross)

1592. 他们家一个星期的总收入只有 75 英镑。(gross)

1593. 聚会的时候布莱德吐在了地上,真恶心。(gross)

1594. 他们为销售的电器提供两年产品保证。(guarantee)

1595. 银行持有航空公司的资产作为抵押。(guarantee)

1596. 只有我父母为贷款担保,银行才会借钱给我。(guarantee)

1597. 法律确保男人和女人享有平等的权利。(guarantee)

1598. 在电影界,天赋绝不意味着成功。(guarantee)

1599. 他成为他侄女的合法监护人。(guardian)

1600. 美国把自己描绘成民主政治的捍卫者。(guardian)

1601. 这一章的内容给你一些指导方针,以帮助你的工作。(guideline)

1602. 你离开戴维难道没有任何内疚感吗? (guilt)

1603. 控方有责任证明被告有罪。(guilt)

1604. 老师说山姆根本无法管教,责任在于他父母。(guilt)

1605. 他被判决犯有向国外泄露机密文件罪。(guilty)

1606. 他们为很少去看她而感到内疚。(guilty)

1607. 一阵狂风吹来,把门关上了。(gust)

1608. 一阵怒火涌上他的心头。(gust)

1609. 他总是在健身房里。(gym)

1610. 我们做了一小时体操。(gym)

1611. 它很可能是古罗马人从它的地中海原产地引种到此地的。(habitat)

1612. 詹姆斯照常绕着花园作清晨散步去了。(habitual)

1613. 雹子打在窗户上。(hail)

1614. 乔猛踩刹车,汽车向前滑动后停住了。(halt)

1615. 妇女在工作场所的发展仍受到男性态度的羁绊。(hamper)

1616. 我准备给新的浴室小橱用螺丝拧上几个拉手。(handle)

1617. 顾客被要求不要触摸商店里的商品。(handle)

1618. 这是一种很困难的局势,但他应付得很好。(handle)

1619. 我们说过,我们不愿意把自己的未来寄托在任何人的施舍上。(handout)

1620. 传单解释那件事的意义。(handout)

1621. 从我们所在的宾馆房间可以俯视一个美丽的小鱼港。(harbour)

1622. 他们唱得和谐。(harmony)

1623. 产业界和大学界人士合作得很融洽。(harmony)

1624. 获取这种动力并为我们所用的计划着手进行。(harness)

1625. 他这一家人不会活过这个严寒难熬的冬天。(harsh)

1626. 蛋十天以后孵化。(hatch)

1627. 如果你拉网太猛鱼会游走的。(haul)

1628. 这个房间据说闹鬼。(haunt)

1629. 战争时常浮现在我们的脑海中。(haunt)

1630. 这个村庄是游客常爱去的地方。(haunt)

1631. 抽烟既是健康的敌人又是火灾隐患。(hazard)

1632. 伤口很快就会愈合。(heal)
1633. 石膏绷带有利于治好断骨。(heal)
1634. 我们把所有的报纸堆成一堆。(heap)
1635. 他年纪大了,听力也不好了。(hearing)
1636. 他们每公顷产量,每公顷雇佣的人手都比小农场更少。(hectare)
1637. 我们对纽约做了三天紧张繁忙的访问。(hectic)
1638. 惊慌感不断增加,人们开始跑向出口。(heighten)
1639. 地球被赤道划分为北半球和南半球,被一些经线划分为东半球和西半球。(hemisphere)
1640. 大脑的主要部分分为左、右大脑半球。(hemisphere)
1641. 交通成本是工业的主要支出。因此,工厂的地点要重点考虑。(hence)
1642. 一群牛 (herd)
1643. 他相信科学和艺术或建筑一样是我们文化遗产的一部分。(heritage)
1644. 她把手放在电话上,迟疑了一会,然后拿起听筒。(hesitate)
1645. 经过一番犹豫,他同意由我写这篇文章。(hesitation)
1646. 他从基层做起,在公司的等级制度中一路升职成为总裁。(hierarchy)
1647. 在威尼斯度过的周末的确是我们的旅程中的亮点。(highlight)
1648. 你的简历应重点强调你的技能和已经取得的成就。(highlight)
1649. 明天我们要徒步旅行四英里到湖边去。(hike)
1650. 我已绕苏格兰徒步旅行一个月。(hike)
1651. 高利率将会阻碍经济增长。(hinder)
1652. 她对自己的生日做了几次暗示,以确保别人不会忘记此事。(hint)
1653. 我想在白色中加入少许蓝色来粉刷卧室。(hint)
1654. 在这本书中你可以找到一些对去中国旅行者的有益指点。(hint)
1655. 妈妈暗示如果我通过了所有的考试,她可能会为我的墨西哥之行出资。(hint)
1656. 租一辆车用两个星期要多少钱? (hire)
1657. 我们应该雇佣一名公共关系顾问来改善我们的形象。(hire)
1658. 需要更多的资金保护古建筑和纪念碑。(historic)
1659. 使用空心砖是因为他们更轻。(hollow)
1660. 他真是个诚实的人,把钱还给了他们。(honest)
1661. 我们很欣赏她坦白的回答。(honesty)
1662. 把你的外套挂到钩上。(hook)

1663. 一只兔子笔直跳进门口。(hop)
1664. 月亮缓缓地升上了地平线。(horizon)
1665. 这次远东之行确实开拓了我们的眼界。(horizon)
1666. 恐怖的谋杀案 (horrible)
1667. 样样费用都贵，这个旅馆糟透了。(horrible)
1668. 感谢你们过去几星期的热情款待。(hospitality)
1669. 我在伦敦学习时，住在青年招待所。(hostel)
1670. 总统受到一群愤怒的农民很不友好的接待。(hostile)
1671. 老鹰在空中盘旋，伺机俯冲抓地上的兔子。(hover)
1672. 我注意到几名记者在法庭外走来走去。(hover)
1673. 他正处于生死之间。(hover)
1674. 简张开双臂紧紧地拥抱他。(hug)
1675. 他抱着一大堆书。(hug)
1676. 保罗热情的拥抱了我一下，脸上带着微笑。(hug)
1677. 反人类罪 (humanity)
1678. 但愿他这一次能表现出一点仁慈。(humanity)
1679. 雅科卡出身卑微，后来成了福特公司的总裁。(humble)
1680. 他带着卑微的微笑再次向我们表示感谢。(humble)
1681. 我不介意这么炎热的天气，但是我讨厌这么高的湿度。(humidity)
1682. 他们的卫生标准和我们的不一样。(hygiene)
1683. 我们希望进一步的研究能证实我们的假设。(hypothesis)
1684. 在理想的世界中不需要警察。(ideal)
1685. 社会正义和平等，如许多理想一样，是难以实现的。(ideal)
1686. 和同类竞争产品相比，成分是一样的。(identical)
1687. 这对姐妹外表和性格都不相同。(identical)
1688. 警察采集指纹鉴定尸体。(identify)
1689. 她一直被认为是"左派"激进分子。(identify)
1690. 杀手的身份还是未知数。(identity)
1691. 小孩子需要连续性安全感和认同感。(identity)
1692. 他们确实没能保持自己的思想意识，至少这是可能的。(ideology)
1693. 一个健康的孩子不可能闲着不动，他从早到晚总得干点什么。(idle)

1694. 这个医生讨厌把时间浪费在闲聊上。(idle)
1695. 请恕我无知,但是它到底是怎么运行的呢。(ignorance)
1696. 如果肖恩没提起此事,我还被蒙在鼓里呢。(ignorance)
1697. 恐怕我对电脑相当无知。(ignorant)
1698. 在增加利润驱使下,公司经理们有意忽视安全规则。(ignore)
1699. 把烟草卖给16岁以下的儿童是违法行为。(illegal)
1700. 我们对自由抱有幻想。(illusion)
1701. 让我举例说明这个观点。(illustrate)
1702. 这本书配有一百多个图表,表格和图片。(illustrate)
1703. 她凝视自己在镜子中的映像。(image)
1704. 他画了一幅很生动的画,描绘了工人阶级的社区。(image)
1705. 他想不起她的模样,只对她的名字有印象。(image)
1706. 其他社会已经开始效仿西方的挥霍浪费。(imitate)
1707. 对住在附近的人来说,这里是个日趋繁华的购物中心。(immediate)
1708. 他许诺立即采取措施帮助失业的人。(immediate)
1709. 这一发展非常非常重要。(immense)
1710. 把你的脚泡在冰冷的水中可以消肿。(immerse)
1711. 他两岁那年,父母移民了。(immigrate)
1712. 我认为战争已迫在眉睫。(imminent)
1713. 冲击的力量让她喘不过气来。(impact)
1714. 领导层的更迭会对政府政策产生很大影响。(impact)
1715. 新法律将如何影响健康保健,还搞不清楚。(impact)
1716. 由于最近生病,他的消化功能变差了。(impair)
1717. 那音乐赋予该电影一种紧张的感觉。(impart)
1718. 他对他们说,他有一则极坏的消息要透露。(impart)
1719. 恶劣的天气严重阻碍了他们的前进。(impede)
1720. 目前的冲突会增强和平谈判的动力。(impetus)
1721. 最好用锄头之类的工具将杂草从根部割掉。(implement)
1722. 这些衣服不是聪明人穿的。(implement)
1723. 我们已经决定完全执行委员会的建议。(implement)
1724. 三位警官参与到这次卧底行动中。(implicate)

1725. 新的证据暗示斯蒂芬先生和夫人参与了这桩勒索案。(implicate)
1726. 她的话中隐含着威胁。(implicit)
1727. 任何团队会议上都应该包含计划和回顾两部分。(implicit)
1728. 自由贸易意味着分享价值。(imply)
1729. 民主必然包含尊重个人自由。(imply)
1730. 政府禁止买卖象牙。(impose)
1731. 有些父母把自己的道德价值观念强加于他们的孩子们。(impose)
1732. 我希望以我的勤奋给新老板留下好印象。(impress)
1733. 那一天晚些时候天气转好了。(improve)
1734. 我忘记带笔记,因此只能即兴发言。(improvise)
1735. 安妮临时造了一个沙坑让孩子们进去玩。(improvise)
1736. 资本主义的首要推动力是赚钱。(impulse)
1737. 格里抵制不了放下工作去海边的冲动。(impulse)
1738. 这栋大厦的电气系统安全不达标。(inadequate)
1739. 奖品激励年轻人提高自己的技能。(incentive)
1740. 孩子喋喋不休,使他烦躁起来。(incessant)
1741. 为什么吸食海洛因的发生案例持续攀升? (incidence)
1742. 吸烟者最易感冒。(incidence)
1743. 一次严重的边境事件增加了我们对战争的恐惧。(incident)
1744. 他们声称我们在煽动人民反对政府。(incite)
1745. 如果我是你的话,我个人的意向是会另找一份工作。(inclination)
1746. 这个区域地势倾斜,这条小径也逐渐向上倾斜。(incline)
1747. 望远镜倾斜43度角 (incline)
1748. 这次意外使他们重新考虑自己的事业。(incline)
1749. 这个价格包括一切费用。(inclusive)
1750. 房租每星期50英镑,包括暖气和照明。(inclusive)
1751. 收入高的人应该缴更多的税。(income)
1752. 我们在这座建筑的设计中加进了许多环保特点。(incorporate)
1753. 我们最初的一些提议没有并入新的立法中。(incorporate)
1754. 火器的使用已经显著增加。(increase)
1755. 这一世纪的上半期人口数量有巨大增长。(increase)

1756. 她只有12岁么，我觉得那完全难以置信。(incredible)
1757. 最新的导弹有惊人的射击精度。(incredible)
1758. 每年九月你会得到加薪。(increment)
1759. 最后的报偿将足以补偿你可能蒙受的任何损失。(incur)
1760. 不知有多少人已经死于这场战争。(indefinite)
1761. 这个项目因缺少资金而被无限期延迟了。(indefinite)
1762. 幼儿的头部大小的变化被认为是大脑增长的标志。(index)
1763. 图标标示出了销售目标。(indicate)
1764. 这一研究表明贫穷和犯罪之间有很深的渊源。(indicate)
1765. 所有的主要经济指标都表明贸易在增长。(indicator)
1766. 该地区固有的医学传统广泛利用植物。(indigenous)
1767. 在我的工作中，电话是必不可少的。(indispensable)
1768. 每个人都从父母身上分别继承一个基因。(individual)
1769. 树上的每片叶子都是与众不同的。(individual)
1770. 小班授课中，孩子们得到更多关注。(individual)
1771. 没有什么能诱使我再次投票给他。(induce)
1772. 饮食紊乱的病人可能需要用药让自己呕吐。(induce)
1773. 罗沙是个勤奋聪颖的学生。(industrious)
1774. 他总是不善于运动。(inept)
1775. 金与某些可溶解其他金属的酸发生作用。(inert)
1776. 生活条件差必然会生病。(inevitable)
1777. 护士抱着一个刚出世的婴儿走进房间。(infant)
1778. 约翰已经进幼儿学校了。(infant)
1779. 这项计划是为了保护这个国家的新兴产业而设计的。(infant)
1780. 携带这种病毒的人可能毫无症状，却仍可传染给他人。(infect)
1781. 鲁西的热情很快就感染了班里的其他人。(infect)
1782. 从这些统计数字中可以推断出很多东西。(infer)
1783. 证据表明，受害人认识杀死她的人。(infer)
1784. 这是个价廉质次的产品。(inferior)
1785. 他们感到低人一等，直到球队在国际上取得了成功才带给他们一些骄傲。(inferior)
1786. 年度通货膨胀率下降了。(inflation)

1787. 这一理事会对很多政府决策都有影响。(influence)
1788. 数百年内,这个国家都没有受到外界势力的影响。(influence)
1789. 影响这一决定的因素可能有几个。(influence)
1790. 每个星期涌入这个城市的移民约达 1000 人。(influx)
1791. 请尽快将地址的变更通知我们。(inform)
1792. 她就抚养孩子的不同方面做了一次内容丰富的讲话。(informative)
1793. 有些国家缺乏适合的经济基础结构。(infrastructure)
1794. 这些植物演化出绝妙的方法从空气中提取养分。(ingenious)
1795. 把所有的这些原料放在大的平底锅里拌和。(ingredient)
1796. 去国外旅行是你的经商生涯中必不可少的重要部分。(ingredient)
1797. 这些遥远的岛屿上只有鸟类和动物栖息。(inhabit)
1798. 村庄的居民反对铺设这条新公路。(inhabitant)
1799. 每种生意都有其固有的冒险成分。(inherent)
1800. 她所有的子女将平均继承遗产。(inherit)
1801. 乔治继承了他父亲的坏脾气 (inherit)
1802. 家庭生活不幸福很可能妨碍孩子的学习。(inhibit)
1803. 他的名字首字母缩写为 DPH,代表大卫 佩里 毫尔沃斯。(initial)
1804. 最初的反应让人很受鼓舞。(initial)
1805. 知识分子发起一场针对恐怖主义的辩论。(initiate)
1806. 老年人在冬天必须打流感预防针。(inject)
1807. 一次道路交通事故中两人受重伤。(injure)
1808. 卡车司机只是四肢受了点轻伤。(injury)
1809. 有几套公寓俯瞰内院。(inner)
1810. 她渴望求得内心平静。(inner)
1811. 他坚信她是无罪的。(innocent)
1812. 那时我很年轻,而且非常单纯幼稚。(innocent)
1813. 他是个理财天才,可是在政治上却一窍不通。(innocent)
1814. 这家公司成功推出了新的产品和服务。(innovate)
1815. 他们的创新能力使他们得以在世界市场上竞争。(innovate)
1816. 如果公司要保持竞争力,我们必须鼓励创新。(innovation)
1817. 信息技术方面的新奇事物已经彻底改变了学生的学习方式。(innovation)

1818. 他们收到了大量对该计划的投诉信。(innumerable)
1819. 增加施肥量会提高庄稼的产量。(input)
1820. 这是我通过询问了解到的情况。(inquiry)
1821. 他用探索的目光环视四周,看看是否每个人都听懂了。(inquiry)
1822. 但是,经进一步调查,我发现那天晚上家里没有人。(inquiry)
1823. 大多数青蛙以昆虫为主食。(insect)
1824. 他的手微微颤抖着,将钥匙插入锁中。(insert)
1825. 经理给他的合同添加了一条新的条款。(insert)
1826. 这篇文章洞悉了导致当前经济危机的诸多原因。(insight)
1827. 尼克坚持认为他是正确的。(insist)
1828. 我从车里出来检查损伤。(inspect)
1829. 艾兰彼将军来检阅军队。(inspect)
1830. 希望这次成功能激励你更加努力。(inspire)
1831. 他们终于安装了新网络。(install)
1832. 我分四个月付清100美元,每月交付25美元。(installment)
1833. 他们碰到很多歧视的例子。(instance)
1834. 希望你们在这件事情中能满足我们的要求。(instance)
1835. 他的直觉告诉他呆在车旁,等待援助。(instinct)
1836. 她的工作经验很丰富,曾经担任过一个环境研究机构的负责人。(institute)
1837. 我的同事是麻省理工学院的科学家。(institute)
1838. 几乎每个州都建立了一个学生测试项目。(institute)
1839. 我们别无选择,只能对航空公司提起诉讼。(institute)
1840. 这些大学招收学生的标准低于较有名望的高等学府。(institution)
1841. 需要更多的努力教孩子们注意道路安全。(instruct)
1842. 他吩咐秘书取消他的所有安排。(instruct)
1843. 闪电损坏了飞机上的仪表,仪表上没有任何指示。(instrument)
1844. 你玩哪一种乐器?(instrument)
1845. 龙卷风过后,只有壁炉完好无损。(intact)
1846. 尽量减少脂肪摄入量。(intake)
1847. 音乐应该是儿童教育基本组成部分。(integral)
1848. 交通计划应该与能源政策结合起来。(integrate)

1849. 公交和地铁服务已经完美地结合在一起了。(integrate)
1850. 他是个极为耿直的好人。(integrity)
1851. 他们已发誓保护国家的领土完整。(integrity)
1852. 他很伶俐，但不是你所说的那样智力很高。(intellectual)
1853. 他出生在一个知识家庭。(intellectual)
1854. 很小的时候，约翰就表现出很高的智商。(intelligence)
1855. 我们的情报来源表明下一步进攻正在酝酿之中。(intelligence)
1856. 除非你已经了解了遗传学方面的许多知识，否则这篇文章没法读懂。(intelligible)
1857. 如果一切都顺利，我们计划明年去澳大利亚。(intend)
1858. 剧烈的疼痛让我无法睡眠。(intense)
1859. 她对我有点儿太热情了。(intense)
1860. 短暂的强化培训之后，我被允许进行第一次跳伞。(intensive)
1861. 她不想在有生之年一直作饭店女招待。(intention)
1862. 露西和班里的其他孩子处得很好。(interact)
1863. 我从不会干涉夫妻之间的事。(interfere)
1864. 它的内部容积为104立方英尺。(interior)
1865. 这本书的读者群是中级以上水平的学生。(intermediate)
1866. 对整个事件会进行内部调查。(internal)
1867. 医生说，他们发现一些体内器官出血的痕迹。(internal)
1868. 我们无意干涉别国内政。(internal)
1869. 他拒绝工作到很晚，这被别人理解为缺少对公司的奉献精神。(interpret)
1870. 他们的西班牙语很好，并许诺为我做翻译。(interpret)
1871. 对不起打断一下，我有紧急口信带给你。(interrupt)
1872. 该城市位于三条汽车道的交叉口。(intersection)
1873. 他离开了房间，短暂的间隔之后，带回一条信息。(interval)
1874. 他的事业刚刚开始，战争爆发了。(intervene)
1875. 为了避免进一步斗争，陆军将不得不干预。(intervene)
1876. 他在应聘面试之前很紧张。(interview)
1877. 在昨晚的电视采访中，他否认了有辞职的打算。(interview)
1878. 他的最后一次采访是在他去世前一天录下的。(interview)
1879. 我们今天下午要对六位候选人进行面试。(interview)

1880. 你在电视上采访过的人中谁最出名？(interview)
1881. 她和政府中的要人有很亲密的关系。(intimate)
1882. 她被问到生活中的私密细节。(intimate)
1883. 手表的机械结构非常复杂精细，很难修理。(intricate)
1884. 灵活性是有创意的管理的内在特质。(intrinsic)
1885. 非常抱歉，还没有介绍你们两人互相认识吧？(introduce)
1886. 我们刚引进这套系统时没有人认为它会有用。(introduce)
1887. 你的建议对我们非常宝贵。(invaluable)
1888. 亚历山大·贝尔于1876年发明了电话。(invent)
1889. 但我没有胡编，我告诉你的都是真的。(invent)
1890. 奥利弗投资古董家具，赚了很多钱。(invest)
1891. 这个家我们已投入了很多东西，要离开它很难。(invest)
1892. 州警察正在调查这件事。(investigate)
1893. 我们应请谁来参加聚会？(invite)
1894. 采访记者请参议员评论近来的事件。(invite)
1895. 这些货物的发货清单一张也找不到。(invoice)
1896. 他们有没有给我们开文具发票？(invoice)
1897. 瘟疫袭来时，人们总是向圣吉纳维芙祈求保佑。(invoke)
1898. 我恳求市长大人运用他所有的权力为你组织一场搜查。(invoke)
1899. 蕾莉忙于公司的每项业务。(involve)
1900. 自己做生意常常要工作到很晚。(involve)
1901. 我们对不相干的细节关注过多。(irrelevant)
1902. 这个水坝的主要用途是提供灌溉及水力发电。(irrigation)
1903. 洪水将这个城镇孤立起来。(isolate)
1904. 流鼻血就是血从鼻子里流出来。(issue)
1905. 关键问题是工人是不是要归为"雇员"。(issue)
1906. 他的嗓子发出低低的呼噜声。(issue)
1907. 所有的工人都得到防护服。(issue)
1908. 美国国务院每年颁发数百万个护照。(issue)
1909. 我们继续进行到议事日程的下一个条目。(item)
1910. 我也看到了《星期日时报》上的那则新闻。(item)

1911. 愿意制订自己旅行计划的旅行者可以避开成群的旅客。(itinerary)

1912. 草莓酱 (jam)

1913. 对不起，我们来晚了，路上堵车。(jam)

1914. 我无法拧开这个罐子的盖子。(jar)

1915. 你为什么如此嫉妒他的成功？(jealous)

1916. 你的工作做得愉快么？(job)

1917. 我的职责是确保工作按时完成。(job)

1918. 她每天早饭前慢跑20分钟。(jog)

1919. "这顿饭是谁做的？""事实上是我们大家一起做的。"(joint)

1920. 膝关节 (joint)

1921. 雨水渗透过水泥板的接合处。(joint)

1922. 我有权查阅他私下写的文章和日记。(journal)

1923. 她的书吸收了信件、日记、期刊和历史文献里的内容。(journal)

1924. 你旅途愉快吗？(journey)

1925. 她仔细翻看旧相册，踏上了回到童年的怀旧之旅。(journey)

1926. 按照最近的法庭判决，公司被罚六百万英镑。(judgement)

1927. 据我判断，我们应该接受他提出的条件。(judgement)

1928. 我已经认识他很多年，相信他的判断力。(judgement)

1929. 你在开车接近交叉路口时一定要减速。(junction)

1930. 河的两岸是茂密而难以穿越的丛林。(jungle)

1931. 初级医生们已对不得不长时间工作提出意见。(junior)

1932. 我弟弟比我小三岁。(junior)

1933. 期末三年级学生在演戏。(junior)

1934. 这些废旧杂物我必须全部处理掉。(junk)

1935. 我有时真怀疑世上还有没有正义。(justice)

1936. 不把杀害她的凶手缉拿归案，我们决不罢休。(justice)

1937. 没人怀疑我们事业的正义性。(justice)

1938. 我们花了这么多钱购买武器。怎样能证明这样做正确呢？(justify)

1939. 没什么能为谋杀开罪。(justify)

1940. 最近几年青少年犯罪大幅度增长。(juvenile)

1941. 许多人对选举结果有浓厚的兴趣。(keen)

1942. 这份工作的竞争十分激烈。(keen)

1943. 我在火车站月台的售货亭里买了一份杂志和一些香烟。(kiosk)

1944. 战斗机的机组人员都有一套救生设备在被击落时用。(kit)

1945. 她跪下，想从门下面张望。(kneel)

1946. 我奶奶为我织了几副手套。(knit)

1947. 她想开门，可圆把手脱落在她手里。(knob)

1948. 在绳子上打个结，以免松开。(knot)

1949. 这条船的最高航速约为 20 节。(knot)

1950. 做这份工作需要专业知识。(knowledge)

1951. 他们的风流韵事大家都知道。(knowledgeable)

1952. 她是个知识渊博的女人。(knowledge)

1953. 标签上说明要干洗。(label)

1954. 皮肤敏感的小孩，他们衣服上的商标应该去除。(label)

1955. 这份文件标明为"绝密"文件。(label)

1956. 报纸很不公平地将他称为麻烦制造者。(label)

1957. 研究室在实验室测试中使用动物来检测一些药品的功能。(laboratory)

1958. 很多妇女从事重体力劳动。(labour)

1959. 戴安两点钟时分娩了。(labour)

1960. 太多的老师没有得到足够的尊敬。(lack)

1961. 艾力克斯的真正问题是不够自信。(lack)

1962. 你腿瘸，这样走路你学不来。(lame)

1963. 我勉强推脱，说我还有好多好多别的事要做。(lame)

1964. 黑暗中我找不到任何标志，完全迷路了。(landmark)

1965. 硅片的发明是电脑历史上的里程碑。(landmark)

1966. 景色中点缀着露营者和徒步旅行者的帐篷。(landscape)

1967. 我们要花几个月的时间美化花园。(landscape)

1968. 在狭窄的乡村路上开快车是很危险的。(lane)

1969. 我觉得在快车道开车压力很大，所以我宁可留在中速或慢车道。(lane)

1970. 冠军在第五跑道上跑。(lane)

1971. 这个镇所处的纬度低。(latitude)

1972. 在选择职业时，我们给他们发表自己意见的自由。(latitude)

1973. 后面的案子中，买方支付百分之十五的佣金。(latter)
1974. 计划十一月下旬搞庆祝活动。(latter)
1975. 发射导弹前，发射员使它锁定目标。(launch)
1976. 政府开展一场大规模的扫盲运动。(launch)
1977. 家具上落了厚厚的一层尘土。(layer)
1978. 他们在超市外面散发广告传单。(leaflet)
1979. 地板上有水——一定有地方漏了。(leak)
1980. 水正从管子里漏出来。(leak)
1981. 减薪的消息迅速传了出去。(leak)
1982. 1961年她租下了这栋房子。(lease)
1983. 他已说服当地市政委会出租一栋房子给他。(lease)
1984. 他定期做有关现代法国文学的讲座。(lecture)
1985. 我爸爸逮住我，并对喝酒的种种危险对我进行训斥。(lecture)
1986. 他在曼彻斯特大学讲授欧洲艺术课程。(lecture)
1987. 他开始训斥我们，说我们太吵了。(lecture)
1988. 她威胁要对医院采取法律行动。(legal)
1989. 这家公司的行为完全合法。(legal)
1990. 她正在写一篇有关爱尔兰民间传说和神话的论文。(legend)
1991. 路易斯阿姆斯特朗是爵士乐的传奇人物。(legend)
1992. 图表上的说明显示发动机是怎样工作的。(legend)
1993. 传说中巨人的家就在这个洞穴里。(legend)
1994. 他的字迹写的太小了，几乎看不清楚。(legible)
1995. 控制毒品，我们必须立法。(legislate)
1996. 将病人和健康人分开，可减少传染的危险。(lessen)
1997. 他们起初要价五百万美元，最后接受了一个比较少的数目。(lesser)
1998. 要支付不多于四万五千英镑薪水的雇主免于缴税。(levy)
1999. 政府要求征兵，组织军队来应对危机。(levy)
2000. 如果政府意欲增加税收去资助穷人，应该对电影收税。(levy)
2001. 国家征召所有体格健壮的男性参战。(levy)
2002. 多吃一些维生素会减少你患感冒的可能性。(liability)
2003. 照顾孩子是父母必须承担的责任。(liability)

2004. 如果你所负的债超过你的资产，你就可能要破产。(liability)
2005. 我的旧汽车真是个累赘，我不但不能用它，还要为它付停车费。(liability)
2006. 镇上靠近河的地方容易被水淹。(liable)
2007. 你不经常锻炼，更容易受伤。(liable)
2008. 法律规定如果孩子没有的上学的话父母将负有责任。(liable)
2009. 如果他们对待现金能够那么慷慨就好了。(liberal)
2010. 我的父母极为开明。(liberal)
2011. 这家代理处得到绝对的许可在任何友好的国家进行运作。(licence)
2012. 他由于无证驾驶被捕。(licence)
2013. 已有几家被批准生产这些产品。(licence)
2014. 在高速行驶中，船头会抬离水面。(lift)
2015. 再抬一下我们就可以把它放到楼梯顶了。(lift)
2016. 他们乘电梯去下面的酒吧间。(lift)
2017. 这些蛤的味道鲜美。同样，茄子的味道也很好。(likewise)
2018. 只有最好的语言专家才能成为联合国的翻译。(linguist)
2019. 这两个理论有些关联。(link)
2020. 强大的家庭的联系使他们现在还保持联络。(link)
2021. 航天飞机使用的燃料是由液氢和液氧混合而成的。(liquid)
2022. 水是液体。(liquid)
2023. 发明了印刷机之后，人们才有可能读书识字。(literacy)
2024. 这个奶酪的名字是Doleclatte，字面意思是"甜美的牛奶"。(literally)
2025. 毫不夸张地讲，爸爸非常生气。(literally)
2026. 文学作品包括小说，短篇小说，故事戏剧和诗歌。(literature)
2027. 保持接触你这一领域中最新的文献是很重要的。(literature)
2028. 街上有一堆垃圾。(litter)
2029. 凯特坐在地板上，四周乱放着杂志。(litter)
2030. 街道上到处都是乱扔的旧罐头瓶和其他垃圾。(litter)
2031. 我们以三年期限偿还贷款。(loan)
2032. 你能把网球拍借给我用一下吗？(loan)
2033. 我们将在门口的大堂见面。(lobby)
2034. 这群人正在对政府官员进行游说，要求减少国防开支。(lobby)

2035. 附近有哪些休闲设施？(locality)

2036. 店铺坐落于市中心。(locate)

2037. 如果你找不到某本书，请叫一位图书管理员帮忙。(locate)

2038. 他的公寓所处的位置很好。(location)

2039. 保罗刚开始工作时寄宿在布里斯托尔的一户人家里。(lodge)

2040. 我们在学期中把房子租给大学生。(lodge)

2041. 他们到苏格兰的一个狩猎小屋去度周末。(lodge)

2042. 你的论据有什么逻辑？(logic)

2043. 警探必须通过逻辑推理找出杀人凶手。(logical)

2044. 这个镇位于东经21度。(longitude)

2045. 我犹豫了一下，然后才做出如此重要的长期承诺。(long-term)

2046. 你再走近一些，它们便如冰山似的赫然耸现在你面前。(loom)

2047. 他松开座位上的安全带。(loosen)

2048. 她在一次州举办的抽奖中赢了一大笔钱。(lottery)

2049. 杰克已经是这家公司近50年的忠实员工了。(loyal)

2050. 这根链条可能要加润滑油了。(lubricate)

2051. 几杯威士忌就会打开他的话匣子。(lubricate)

2052. 他们的行李不多。(luggage)

2053. 浴室很奢华，配有金质的水龙头和厚厚的地毯。(luxurious)

2054. 这枚针被磁铁吸出。(magnet)

2055. 我要把这张照片放大。(magnify)

2056. 这个报告有夸大所涉风险的倾向。(magnify)

2057. 他们认识不到问题的严重性。(magnitude)

2058. 她是一个温柔而警觉的少女。(maiden)

2059. 英国想保住它世界强国的地位。(maintain)

2060. 报告称，安全设施没有得到恰当的维护。(maintain)

2061. 评论员坚持认为这些改革将导致教育水平的下降。(maintain)

2062. 首相前来拜谒您，陛下。(majesty)

2063. 我把专业改为政治学。(major)

2064. 美国有两大政党。(major)

2065. 大多数学生发现自己很难用手上的那点钱过日子。(majority)

2066. 成年后，他成为家族公司的一位合伙人。(majority)
2067. 对进口肉类的检查是强制性的。(mandatory)
2068. 他们犯了一个明显的判断错误。(manifest)
2069. 到目前为止，他们对我们所关注的事物一直摆出一副漠不关心的态度。(manifest)
2070. 工人熟练地旋动了几个旋钮和操作杆。(manipulate)
2071. 你一直有种自己被人操纵了的感觉。(manipulate)
2072. 如果你有问题的话，查阅一下电脑使用指南。(manual)
2073. 手动搜索所有的数据会花费很多时间。(manual)
2074. 从事体力劳动的人寿命较短。(manual)
2075. 这家公司制造汽车。(manufacture)
2076. 他捏造证据。(manufacture)
2077. 成本将决定制造方法。(manufacture)
2078. 我读过他小说的手稿。(manuscript)
2079. 她正坐在游泳池边。(margin)
2080. 左手边的空白处有人写了一条笔记。(margin)
2081. 每月的预算中你最好富裕出 30 英镑。(margin)
2082. 美国海军陆战队的一个旅 (marine)
2083. 路中央的那些标记是什么意思？(marine)
2084. 搬家具时别碰坏了油漆。(mark)
2085. 你能在期末前批改完我的试卷吗？(mark)
2086. 花费两百万美元进行市场推广运动之后，公司销量狂飙。(marketing)
2087. "我的天啊，"福斯特惊叹道，"我从未见过这么多的钱！"(marvel)
2088. 一座巨大的冰山正漂离阿根廷的海岸。(massive)
2089. 如果没有大量追加投资，公司就会倒闭。(massive)
2090. 我想要六米那种窗帘布料。(material)
2091. 在一些社会，财富是按照母系代代相传的。(maternal)
2092. 一般长成的苹果树有 20 英尺高。(mature)
2093. 我们都足够成熟，明白事理，在这一问题上持不同意见，但是仍然相互尊重对方。(mature)
2094. 她已经成长为一个很棒的作家。(mature)
2095. 公司主要的功能就是使利益最大化。(maximize)
2096. 职业中心将帮助你充分利用你的机会。(maximize)

2097. 他最多在狱中服刑七年。(maximum)
2098. 我们或许会有第三个孩子,但是最多三个。(maximum)
2099. 这个地区的最高温度是 33 摄氏度。(maximum)
2100. 这台机器测量你的心率。(measure)
2101. 厘米是长度计量单位。(measure)
2102. 需要采取更强有力的措施来与犯罪作斗争。(measure)
2103. 这些自动相机有一个特殊的对焦装置。(mechanism)
2104. 陆军建立了一些机构帮助失业的转业军人找到工作。(mechanism)
2105. 一个人生病的时候,身体的自然防御机制就开始运转了。(media)
2106. 这一丑闻在全国的媒体中广为报道。(media)
2107. 前总统同意为和谈进行斡旋。(mediate)
2108. 伤口需要及时的医疗处理。(medical)
2109. 他穿几号的衬衫——小号,中号还是大号? (medium)
2110. 将洋葱在中火上加热至金黄色。(medium)
2111. 糖在水中溶解。(melt)
2112. 你需要养成一种积极的思想态度。(mental)
2113. 要理解这些想法要花很多脑细胞。(mental)
2114. 这个中心为精神病患者提供帮助。(mental)
2115. 我想检查一下货物。(merchandise)
2116. 我不会对他们心慈手软的。(mercy)
2117. 毫无疑问,第一个译本具有清晰明了的优点。(merit)
2118. 他留下口信说他可能会晚一会儿。(message)
2119. 某些人的代谢作用要比另外一些人更有效。(metabolism)
2120. 我认为我们应该使用不同的方法再试一次。(method)
2121. 用显微镜察看,从池塘取出的一滴水里充满了细小的微生物。(microscope)
2122. 今晚我可能去听音乐会。(might)
2123. 鸟类为何知道什么时候迁移,又如何找到回家的路呢? (migrate)
2124. 去年我们度过了一个异常暖和的冬天。(mild)
2125. 他沿途经过的每一块里程标,都逐一指明了开往巨石阵的距离。(milestone)
2126. 他感到搬出他父母的家是他生命中的转折点。(milestone)
2127. 如果叛军不从这一地区撤军的话,政府威胁采取军事行动。(military)

2128. 旅程计划得极为准确。(military)
2129. 几千年来的风雨将它们摧毁了。(millennium)
2130. 他在模仿我们办公室里各式各样的人。(mimic)
2131. 这是一块矿产异常丰富的大陆。(mineral)
2132. 矿泉水 (mineral)
2133. 暴风雨只造成了最低限度的损失。(minimal)
2134. 为了将平民死伤人数降到最低人们已经尽力了。(minimize)
2135. 我们决不能轻视种族歧视的问题。(minimize)
2136. 她已经将脂肪和糖类的消费量减少到最低水平。(minimum)
2137. 她的父亲过去任职于农业部。(ministry)
2138. 1855 年，他还是个十几岁的小孩子的时候就成了神职人员。(ministry)
2139. 这部电影含有不适合未成年人观看的内容。(minor)
2140. 我选择了历史作为辅修科目。(minor)
2141. 他只受了点轻伤，逃跑了。(minor)
2142. 我们给这个计划做了些小小的调整。(minor)
2143. 生活在大城市里有利也有弊。(minus)
2144. 他们遭受到四十亿英镑的贸易赤字。(minus)
2145. 夜间温度有时降到零下三十度。(minus)
2146. 支付的额款减去一点服务费，余额原数退还给您。(minus)
2147. 我过五分钟就回来。(minute)
2148. 开车之前检查一下后视镜和侧视镜。(mirror)
2149. 通货膨胀的加剧是由于食品与各种各样的日用品价格越来越高。(miscellaneous)
2150. 你看上去愁眉苦脸的，怎么啦？(miserable)
2151. 他的任务是鼓舞员工的士气及提高产量。(mission)
2152. 在这个会议上，你会听到多种不同的语言的混杂使用达到惊人的程度。(mixture)
2153. 他们侮辱我们，还嘲笑我们的宗教。(mock)
2154. 参加考试之前你应该进行一次模拟面试。(mock)
2155. 他们的生活方式很轻松，这很适合他们。(mode)
2156. 不用相机的"自动式"，就将旋转钮转向"M"。(mode)
2157. 他们给我们展示了大楼的模型。(model)
2158. 她是诚实和得体的典范。(model)

2159. 他们利用计算机来塑造全球变暖的可能后果。(model)

2160. 吉姆总是效仿他的伟大英雄马丁•路德•金。(model)

2161. 我们正在找一所带中等大小花园的住房。(moderate)

2162. 对于这种式样的车,这是个中等价。(moderate)

2163. 他对自己在遗传学研究方面的成功很是谦逊。(modest)

2164. 就他们的财富而言,他们的住所不大。(modest)

2165. 这些规则只能由一个特别委员会修改。(modify)

2166. 播种之前要确保土壤湿润。(moist)

2167. 树木的巨大根茎能深入地下深处汲取水分。(moisture)

2168. 他怀疑自己的电话被监听了。(monitor)

2169. 温度受到认真监测。(monitor)

2170. 政府密切注视这一局势。(monitor)

2171. 一个旅馆房间收那么多钱真是太没道理了。(monstrous)

2172. 宏伟的国家纪念碑是为纪念开国者而建立的。(monument)

2173. 我不得不向逼迫穷人付医药费的道德观提出质疑。(morality)

2174. 小船晃来晃去,使西尔维娅感到恶心。(motion)

2175. 好教师必须能激发学生积极学习。(motivate)

2176. 你认为凶手的动机是什么?(motive)

2177. 他家族的座右铭是"天助自助者。"(motto)

2178. 事故发生后的数日内,死亡人数持续上升。(mount)

2179. 他骑上自行车走了。(mount)

2180. 这房子装有双层玻璃窗来减轻飞机的噪音。(muffle)

2181. 3 乘以 4 等于 12。(multiply)

2182. 过去五年中军事装备的开支大大增加。(multiply)

2183. 他在角落里轻声地自言自语。(murmur)

2184. 第二天我胳膊上的肌肉有些酸痛。(muscle)

2185. 他希望自己更强壮些,而不要有这样扁平的胸膛。(muscular)

2186. 不幸的是有些毒蘑菇看上去像可食用的一样。(mushroom)

2187. 他默默地一鞠躬,向他们表示感激之情。(mute)

2188. "debt"这个单词中有一个不发音的字母。(mute)

2189. 互相尊重对于任何合作关系都很必要。(mutual)

2190. 他的突然失踪完全是个谜。(mystery)
2191. 大多数社会都有它们自己的创世神话。(myth)
2192. 我们幼稚地相信民主和自由会带来繁荣。(naïve)
2193. 孩子光着身子在湖里游泳。(naked)
2194. 瑞士被四个大国包围，即法国、德国、奥地利和意大利。(namely)
2195. 该电影叙述了这个故事的部分情节。(narrate)
2196. 在国家的层次上，宗教是个大问题。(national)
2197. 我们拒绝签署任何违反我们民族利益的条约。(national)
2198. 你真是个淘气鬼！瞧你干了些什么！(naughty)
2199. 这段河道太浅，不能通航。(navigable)
2200. 船员有专门的仪器帮助他们导航。(navigate)
2201. 罗盘是航行的仪器。(navigation)
2202. 过去，航行在很大程度上依靠星星的位置。(navigation)
2203. 电话是做这项工作绝对必需的。(necessity)
2204. 证人的证词否定了被告的证词。(negate)
2205. 这一决定将使去年最高法院的判决无效。(negate)
2206. 大多数人在被问到他们是否具有独创精神的时候都会给出否定答案。(negative)
2207. 这个问题的消极面要多于积极面。(negative)
2208. 没有任何解释，他给出了否定答案。(negative)
2209. 酗酒开始对我的工作产生负面影响。(negative)
2210. 妊娠检查呈阴性。(negative)
2211. 这些想法中有许多都被现代历史学家们忽略了。(neglect)
2212. 政府拒绝与恐怖分子进行谈判。(negotiate)
2213. 年长者小心地通过旅馆的台阶。(negotiate)
2214. 我在公众面前讲话从不紧张。(nerve)
2215. 牙医在钻我的牙齿时碰到了神经，真是疼死了！(nerve)
2216. 建立起专业人士之间的联系网络很重要。(network)
2217. 您正在收看的是CNN，即有线新闻网。(network)
2218. 他们开始争吵时，我总是试图保持中立。(neutral)
2219. 二战时，瑞典是中立国。(neutral)
2220. 你所说的都对，只不过有点不友善。(nevertheless)

2221. 事故发生很多年之后，我依然做噩梦。(nightmare)
2222. 虽然第一天糟糕透了，但还不是彻底失败。(nightmare)
2223. 早期工商界的新贵着力模仿贵族阶层。(nobility)
2224. 他信念坚定，刚直不阿。(nobility)
2225. 仓鼠是夜间活动的动物。(nocturnal)
2226. 这个地区美极了。不过，杰勒德不能想象自己的余生都生活在那里。(nonetheless)
2227. 乔伊斯的写作风格与文学规范背道而驰。(norm)
2228. 团队中队友评估已成为准则。(norm)
2229. 考试前觉得紧张是正常的。(normal)
2230. 我想要的只是过一种规范的生活。(normal)
2231. 明年她就要从师范大学毕业了。(normal)
2232. 该书以引人注目的插图著称。(notable)
2233. 酒精对人体有显著的作用。(noticeable)
2234. 值得注意的是，参加聚会的人平均大于40岁。(noticeable)
2235. 系统的任何变化都会通知你。(notify)
2236. 八月我们被告知，文章已被拒绝。(notify)
2237. 对于自己想做什么，她只有一个模糊的概念。(notion)
2238. 传统的婚姻观念可以追溯到几千年前。(notion)
2239. 这个地区因谋杀案件多而出名。(notorious)
2240. 尽管名利双收，堂娜没有忘记家乡。(notwithstanding)
2241. 最初几个星期的新奇感消失之后，你是否依然感到愉快？(novelty)
2242. 就电影表演而言仍然是个新手。(novice)
2243. 这是核反应的第一阶段，它可以导致爆炸。(nuclear)
2244. 你住得那么远，真麻烦。(nuisance)
2245. 为掩盖事实进行了许多尝试。(numerous)
2246. 你认为是先天条件还是后天因素对孩子的发展影响最大？(nurture)
2247. 她想待在家里抚养孩子而不出去工作。(nurture)
2248. 营养和运动是保持健康所必不可少的。(nutrition)
2249. 她是个听话的小女孩。(obedient)
2250. 谁来听我的课我都不反对。(objection)
2251. 他发誓要在总统任期内实现一定的目标。(objective)

2252. 世界上存在客观事实。(objective)
2253. 对自己的孩子持客观看法很难。(objective)
2254. 依照法律，雇主们必须付最低工资。(oblige)
2255. 还有什么我可以做的，我随时乐意帮忙。(oblige)
2256. 我非常感激你。(oblige)
2257. 那是太平洋里的一座不为人知的岛。(obscure)
2258. 官方的政策变了，原因尚不清楚。(obscure)
2259. 浓云遮住了星星。(obscure)
2260. 这次事故不能掩盖这样一个事实：火车旅行是非常安全的。(obscure)
2261. 他已被送入医院观察。(observation)
2262. 我想就你到目前为止的工作说几点一般性看法。(observation)
2263. 很难看出他的表情有什么变化。(observe)
2264. 科学家的任务是观察和描绘世界而不是试图控制它。(observe)
2265. 我不喜欢那个聚会，但我还是遵从了社会习俗。(observe)
2266. 我只想说他完全胜任这一职位。(observe)
2267. 害怕变革是进步的最大障碍。(obstacle)
2268. 一架小飞机现在堵塞了跑道。(obstruct)
2269. 一小部分人阻挠了将对大多数人有益的若干政策。(obstruct)
2270. 清除掉运河中的这些障碍物，可能需要花去数周时间。(obstruction)
2271. 你需要得到校长的许可。(obtain)
2272. 减少污染的明显办法是少用汽车。(obvious)
2273. 工作会占据你的心灵，帮你忘记他。(occupy)
2274. 三分之一的意外死亡发生在家里。(occur)
2275. 他从没想到，他可能和她坠入爱河。(occur)
2276. 这桥下发大水是常事。(occurrence)
2277. 这项研究比较在不同国家心脏病的发病情况。(occurrence)
2278. 他有些古怪。(odd)
2279. 他穿的两只袜子不成对。(odd)
2280. 空气中漂浮着一股宜人的树木幽香。(odour)
2281. 她所说的一切都带有伪善的意味。(odour)
2282. 总统前往墨西哥进行四天的正式访问。(official)

2283. 你必须首先得到官方许可。(official)
2284. 他是一个好管闲事的小男人，在公司里人们普遍都不喜欢他。(officious)
2285. 牛奶、黄油和奶酪价格降低会从直接付给农场主的款项中得以抵消。(offset)
2286. 他金色的头发衬托出日晒后深深的肤色。(offset)
2287. 父母的基因是如何传给子女的？(offspring)
2288. 请忽略任何细节，不管看似多么琐碎。(omit)
2289. 讨论仍在进行。(ongoing)
2290. 一组三个人操控这个水坝。(operate)
2291. 修女们在经营一家急诊医院。(operate)
2292. 这两个女人对毒品持截然不同的观点。(opinion)
2293. 他们对保拉的作品评价很高。(opinion)
2294. 连他的对手都很佩服他。(opponent)
2295. 两个候选人反对他。(oppose)
2296. 杂货店在街对面。(opposite)
2297. 我以为这药会使他入睡，但效果完全相反。(opposite)
2298. 我们在面对着政府办公室的大楼里。(opposite)
2299. 住在街对面的人总是发出许多喧闹声。(opposite)
2300. 多年来，土著部落一直受着政府和警方的压迫。(oppress)
2301. 怪梦和噩梦使他感到烦恼不安。(oppress)
2302. 他很乐观地认为我们成功的机会很大，我不同意。(optimism)
2303. 外国银行家们对该国的经济前景持谨慎的乐观态度。(optimism)
2304. 这不是他的唯一选择。(option)
2305. 康拉德现在拥有三十万零两千股票和期权。(option)
2306. 航天飞机已进入轨道飞行。(orbit)
2307. 那颗人造卫星每48小时绕地球轨道运行一周。(orbit)
2308. 按喜欢的程度把你的选择列出来。(order)
2309. 在我走开之前我要整理一下我的书桌。(order)
2310. 早上八点，我们接到了进攻的命令。(order)
2311. 这家商店打电话来说你订的货到了。(order)
2312. 给我一点时间让我整理一下思路，然后我会把这个体系解释给你听。(order)
2313. 经理部命令减少开销。(order)

2314. 我叫了意大利面条和一份什锦沙拉。(order)
2315. 繁殖是生物的最重要的特征之一。(organism)
2316. 工厂和城市是比自给自足的村庄更复杂的机体。(organism)
2317. 这一课程由一培训公司组织开课。(organize)
2318. 他的生活不需要你来料理。(organize)
2319. 东方被用来指世界的东部。(orient)
2320. 新生要花一段时间来适应大学生活。(orient)
2321. 她看了看街名，试图辨别方向。(orient)
2322. 我宁愿读原版。(original)
2323. 徒弟归还给其原先的主人。(original)
2324. 那不是个新颖的建议。(original)
2325. 这主意是怎么来的？(originate)
2326. 谁最先创建了现在这套投诉程序？(originate)
2327. 这家商店供应各种各样的花园装饰物，如雕像、喷泉。(ornament)
2328. 这幢大楼能给人留下深刻的印象全靠巧妙的设计而不是装饰。(ornament)
2329. 星期二我不能和你见面了——我要忙别的事。(otherwise)
2330. 把牛奶放回冰箱去，否则他会变质的。(otherwise)
2331. 糟糕的音质毁了一部在其他方面都很优秀的影片。(otherwise)
2332. 他可能告诉过你他是个合格的工程师，但是事实完全不是这样的。(otherwise)
2333. 有人在审判时听到了这一证据，他们对审判结果感到很吃惊。(outcome)
2334. 这个排水管道是下雨时的出水口。(outlet)
2335. 我用打壁球来排解压力。(outlet)
2336. 人行道上用粉笔勾画出来的受害人尸体的轮廓还依稀可见。(outline)
2337. 不要忘记给评论性文章写个大纲。(outline)
2338. 新总统概述了对付犯罪问题、吸毒问题和教育问题的诸个计划。(outline)
2339. 今年的产量与去年比增长了百分之三十。(output)
2340. 少儿读物已有巨大的增长。(output)
2341. 从一开始就很清楚，会有问题出现的。(outset)
2342. 这一地区具有出众的自然美景。(outstanding)
2343. 该计划的利远大于弊。(outweigh)
2344. 展览的整体费用达四十万英镑。(overall)

2345. 他们已经晚了半个小时。真希望他们能来。(overdue)
2346. 所有这些领域的改革早该实行了。(overdue)
2347. 屋顶上的瓦片一块压着一块。(overlap)
2348. 我和你一块儿度假。(overlap)
2349. 这所大学有很多海外留学生。(overseas)
2350. 道格拉斯当兵时总被派到海外。(overseas)
2351. 一位组长被任命来监管该工程。(oversee)
2352. 绝大多数的人反对这项计划。(overwhelming)
2353. 上周我干额外的工作老板还没付我钱呢。(owe)
2354. 我非常感激父母。(owe)
2355. 他的这条命全亏了这家医院的全体医护人员。(owe)
2356. 平静的河流 (pacific)
2357. 反叛者的和平姿态未得到军队的什么反应。(pacific)
2358. 你能递送一大包书吗？(package)
2359. 这家银行正给学生提供一整套特殊的金融服务。(package)
2360. 那些巧克力包装得很吸引人。(package)
2361. 我刻苦研究了好几个月才写出这本书。(painstaking)
2362. 我随手拿起一本免费的小册子，上面介绍该地区可以参观的一些地方。(pamphlet)
2363. 门上的一块镶板坏了，只能换掉。(panel)
2364. 评判小组里至少有三位高级博士。(panel)
2365. 两枚炸弹在伦敦市中心爆炸之后，购物者惊慌失措地逃离了那条街。(panic)
2366. 越战已经成为强有力的反战范例。(paradigm)
2367. "欲速则不达"这个说法似非而是。(paradox)
2368. 在如此富有的国家却有这么多贫困现象，真是自相矛盾。(paradox)
2369. 这本书一个段落就把各种观点都囊括进来了。(paragraph)
2370. 济慈和浪漫主义诗人有很多相似之处。(parallel)
2371. 直线 AB 和直线 CD 平行。(parallel)
2372. 英国的社会变革是与其他国家的类似趋势相对应的。(parallel)
2373. 铁轨与小溪在几英里内都是并行的。(parallel)
2374. 他的事业可与父亲相媲美。(parallel)
2375. 调查必须在国会指定的界限内进行。(parameter)

2376. 好吧，他的话可以这么解释，电视已成了大众的鸦片。(paraphrase)
2377. 车祸后他的身体部分恢复，但再也不能正常走路了。(partial)
2378. 报纸上的报道完全不公正，而且根本不打算客观。(partial)
2379. 班里的每个人都要积极地参加这些讨论。(participate)
2380. 灰尘一定钻进发动机里面去了，这就是它出故障的原因。(particle)
2381. 我们希望扩大自己的业务，尤其是在欧洲。(particularly)
2382. 尼日利亚是我们在非洲的主要贸易伙伴。(partner)
2383. 她是一家律师事务所的合伙人。(partner)
2384. 克莱尔是我打网球的搭档。(partner)
2385. 有人保证他安全离境。(passage)
2386. 国会通过该法案前将其几度修改。(passage)
2387. 我父母没有钱支付前往美国的旅费。(passage)
2388. 他们目前非常喜欢生物学。(passion)
2389. 凯西在这种(恋爱)关系中处于很被动的地位。(passive)
2390. 阅读是她最喜爱的消遣。(pastime)
2391. 这项专利什么时候到期？ (patent)
2392. 本世纪内，从海浪中提取能量的专利设备已有100种以上。(patent)
2393. 很多艺术家都由一些富有的赞助人支持。(patron)
2394. 他们为身有残疾的主顾提供了一些设备。(patron)
2395. 这本书为40多部历史浪漫传奇建立了典范。(pattern)
2396. 这个孩子的发展很正常。(pattern)
2397. 爱丽丝换磁带的时候有一段暂停。(pause)
2398. 乔停下来考虑自己如何作答。(pause)
2399. 她犹豫了一下。(pause)
2400. 麦金利山是阿拉斯加最高的山峰。(peak)
2401. 这个月的销售额达到了顶点。(peak)
2402. 销售额在八月达到顶点，之后迅速下降。(peak)
2403. 这肉味道很古怪。(peculiar)
2404. 种族歧视问题并不只有这个国家才有。(peculiar)
2405. 将大学生和没上大学的同龄人相比，他们更容易产生感情上的问题。(peer)
2406. 现在对酒醉后开车者有更严厉的处罚。(penalty)

2407. 我做出了错误的决定，只得自食苦果。(penalty)
2408. 当 X 射线穿透人体的时候，一部分被吸收，另一部分穿出体外。(penetrate)
2409. 今年，该公司成功地进入了国外市场。(penetrate)
2410. 了解她的思维很难。(penetrate)
2411. 他们发现靠政府抚恤金生活很困难。(pension)
2412. 这个公园每年吸引四百万的游客。(per)
2413. 根据您的指示开展工作。(per)
2414. 猫不能感知颜色。(perceive)
2415. 虽然很年轻，她也被看作未来的总裁。(perceive)
2416. 我百分之百地同意你的看法。(percent)
2417. 有很大比例的已婚妇女做一些兼职工作。(percentage)
2418. 全部收入的一部分用来缴税。(percentage)
2419. 我们面对资金不足这一长期的问题。(perennial)
2420. 玫瑰和天竺葵是多年生植物，年复一年地开花。(perennial)
2421. 履行他的总统职责 (performance)
2422. 很多人对本届政府的政绩极为失望。(performance)
2423. 演出以后，我顺便到她的化妆室去看她。(performance)
2424. 军备竞赛是当今世界面临的最大危险。(peril)
2425. 在很短的时间内，他的球技迅速长进。(period)
2426. 我的初潮是在 12 岁那年。(period)
2427. 这本期刊每月出版。(periodical)
2428. 轮船沉没，数百人遇难。(perish)
2429. 这种旧宗教正在消亡。(perish)
2430. 暴露于阳光下导致橡胶腐烂。(perish)
2431. 这种疾病导致的失明是永久性的。(permanent)
2432. 为了当一名自由职业者，他放弃了一份固定的工作。(permanent)
2433. 我把车停在这里可以吗？(permissible)
2434. 只允许在公共休息室里抽烟。(permit)
2435. 如果时间许可的话，我开完会去见你。(permit)
2436. 除非你有许可证，否则不许在这儿停车。(permit)
2437. 这是我们坚持记日记的一个原因。(persevere)

2438. 如果还继续疼痛的话就必须看医生。(persist)
2439. 童年经历对个性的形成有很大的影响。(personality)
2440. 这个城镇具有特色的部分原因在于它的建筑。(personality)
2441. 电视名人 (personality)
2442. 我们已登出广告招聘额外的保安人员。(personnel)
2443. 她是一家大公司的人事部门主管。(personnel)
2444. 父亲的过世给了他一个全新的生活观。(perspective)
2445. 最后我终于设法说服她出来和我喝一杯。(persuade)
2446. 你的话与今天的讨论不相干。(pertinent)
2447. 战争过后,全国普遍存在着一种绝望的情绪。(pervade)
2448. 会议的基调很悲观。(pessimistic)
2449. 他们希望我在一份反对动物试验的请愿书上签名。(petition)
2450. 她威胁要正式提出离婚。(petition)
2451. 村民向地方政府正式要求提供更好的公车服务。(petition)
2452. 到街角处的那家药店试试看。(pharmacy)
2453. 现代药学已解决了失眠问题。(pharmacy)
2454. 翻新的第一阶段应该在一月前完工。(phase)
2455. 最近我在想着这个问题的三个方面。(phase)
2456. 无家可归不是什么新的现象。(phenomenon)
2457. 语言是社会和文化方面的独特事件。(phenomenon)
2458. 艾玛在大学研究哲学。(philosophy)
2459. 公司解释了他们的管理哲学。(philosophy)
2460. 他们所处的物质条件糟糕得可怕。(physical)
2461. 她总处于肉体的疼痛中。(physical)
2462. 古老城市里如画的窄街道 (picturesque)
2463. 饼状图能帮助零售商或商人一眼就准确看出钱花到哪里去了。(pie chart)
2464. 隧道尽头的一点点亮光 (pinpoint)
2465. 你能给我在地图上准确地指出它的位置吗? (pinpoint)
2466. 他是心脏移植手术的创始人。(pioneer)
2467. 在该国开创外循环心脏手术的第一家综合性医院 (pioneer)
2468. 他给我提供了如何避免法律程序中的陷阱的建议。(pitfall)

2469. 车中按钮和旋钮的布置考虑得很周到。(placement)

2470. 记录表明，狱卒三次试着去寻找其他的安置地方，后来这事明显被抛在了脑后。(placement)

2471. 这座小镇位于北部大山中的高原上。(plateau)

2472. 她在4号站台上等候开往伦敦的火车。(platform)

2473. 他恳求帮助。(plea)

2474. 人人都为饥民的困境感到震惊。(plight)

2475. 他写的书情节基本上都一样。(plot)

2476. 这项阴谋在实施前就被发现了。(plot)

2477. 房价近几个月来骤跌。(plummet)

2478. 汽车突然停了下来，他被猛地向前抛出了挡风玻璃。(plunge)

2479. 石油价格已跌至新低。(plunge)

2480. 误差幅度不超过三个百分点。(plus)

2481. 大多数小孩子过了五岁就开始上学。(plus)

2482. 这车开起来一点都不刺激，但是它的好处是绝对可靠。(plus)

2483. 三加上六等于九。(plus)

2484. 有很多俱乐部，外加一家赌场。(plus)

2485. 公司已经采取了严格禁止吸烟的政策。(policy)

2486. 我的办法是从不传播流言蜚语。(policy)

2487. 我的职责是每星期六把银器擦亮。(polish)

2488. 他打算花一个夏天的时间改进他的飞行技术。(polish)

2489. 鞋油 (polish)

2490. 这张桌子需要好好擦一擦。(polish)

2491. 这是一部不错的电影，但还需要完善。(polish)

2492. 最近的一次民意测验表明，百分之八十的加利福尼亚人都支持州长。(poll)

2493. 投票结果要到午夜的时候才知晓。(poll)

2494. 总统的受欢迎程度已大大降低。(popularity)

2495. 电脑每年都变得更轻，更小，更容易携带。(portable)

2496. 另一个司机必须承担一部分针对这一事故的指责。(portion)

2497. 你们有提供给儿童的一份食物吗？(portion)

2498. 作家描写了在世纪交替时一个工人社区的生活。(portray)

2499. 安摆出了个姿势，微笑着准备拍照。(pose)
2500. 他卸下了精明律师的伪装，终于变成了真正的自己。(pose)
2501. 我们为拍照摆姿势。(pose)
2502. 布莱斯冒充律师，被撞个正着。(pose)
2503. 官员声称这一化学物品没有造成任何实际的威胁。(pose)
2504. 你绝对有把握自己锁了门吗？(positive)
2505. 我们从公众处得到的反应都是表示赞成的。(positive)
2506. 她的生活态度真的很积极。(positive)
2507. 我把我剩下的财物装进箱子里。(possession)
2508. 这所房子自16世纪以来一直归这个家族所有。(possession)
2509. 有三位研究生帮助他进行研究。(postgraduate)
2510. 部门里的大多数人都持有硕士学位。(postgraduate)
2511. 比赛不得不推迟到下星期举行。(postpone)
2512. 这部电影充满了震撼人心的战争场面。(potent)
2513. 公司绝对有发展的潜能。(potential)
2514. 她第一次意识到自己处境的潜在危险。(potential)
2515. 金往一只玻璃杯里倒了一些水。(pour)
2516. 现在有超过20%的美国家庭生活在贫困线以下。(poverty)
2517. 候选人应该在基础电子学方面具有培训和实践经验。(practical)
2518. 这听起来可不像个切合实际的解决方案。(practical)
2519. 波克郡的普通医师声称1922年中，每1000人他们有31.5次的夜访。(practitioners)
2520. 1967年，菲尔是早期就从事这一危险专业的一员。(practitioners)
2521. 防火措施被忽略了。(precaution)
2522. 午餐前，主席要先进行简短发言。(precede)
2523. 换言之，音乐的地位优于创意。(precede)
2524. 对巴拿马的入侵开了一个危险的先例。(precedent)
2525. 要得到精确的信息很难。(precise)
2526. 尽管有严格的工程计划，我仍然一量再量这个地方。(precise)
2527. 很难预言这一事故的长期影响。(predict)
2528. 移民问题是现在占社会主导地位的问题。(predominant)
2529. 在这幅画中，黑色是主色调。(predominant)

2530. 我们可以吃中餐、意大利或印度餐——你有什么偏爱的吗？(preference)
2531. 发放食品的时候，有小孩的家庭优先考虑。(preference)
2532. 这些单词包含前缀和词干。(prefix)
2533. 佛尔顿的三位数字前都将加上580。(prefix)
2534. 在美国很多地方仍普遍存在着对黑人的偏见。(Prejudice)
2535. 这些讨论只是准备政策文件的初期工作。(preliminary)
2536. 掌握适当程度的英语是学习这门课程的先决条件。(prerequisite)
2537. 这些药片只有凭处方才能配到。(prescription)
2538. 敬请出席定于星期五举行的俱乐部会议。(presence)
2539. 奖品和证书的授予仪式将在大厅举行。(presentation)
2540. 食物的外观和味道一样重要。(presentation)
2541. 每晚有两场卡巴莱歌舞表演。(presentation)
2542. 我认为应该保存这些传统习俗。(preserve)
2543. 8月份记者们不顾一切的捕捉新闻。(press)
2544. 从新闻报道来看，这次音乐会取得了巨大的成功。(press)
2545. 克拉伦登出版社 (press)
2546. 他们正在对投票人施加压力，让他们投赞成票。(pressure)
2547. 工作的困扰能使你病倒。(pressure)
2548. 这家不为人知的英国公司现在获得很大的声望。(prestige)
2549. 国王希望通过战争提高自己的影响力。(prestige)
2550. 从他讲话的方式来看，我推测他是你的老板。(presume)
2551. 这个国家的一些农村地区至今仍然相信魔法。(prevail)
2552. 正义最终赢得了胜利。(prevail)
2553. 前段婚姻中她生了两个孩子。(previous)
2554. 大多数人工作的主要原因都是为了金钱的回报。(primary)
2555. （专业性的）忠告或建议是治疗抑郁的初级疗法。(primary)
2556. 我们担心的主要问题是为难民提供食物和医疗。(primary)
2557. 吸烟是肺病的主要诱因。(prime)
2558. 这家旅馆的位置极好，俯瞰山谷。(prime)
2559. 直到今天村民们仍过着原始的单一作物经济的生活。(primitive)
2560. 后来她成为了王室芭蕾舞团的主要演员。(principle)

2561. 另一个使我感动的老师是姓周的校长助理，还教历史课。(principle)
2562. 教课是她的主要收入来源。(principle)
2563. 接受客户的礼物违背我的原则。(principle)
2564. 他为自己高标准的道德准则深感骄傲。(principle)
2565. 有什么打印错误都用圆圈勾画出来。(printout)
2566. 之前你不需要对这一课题有任何了解。(prior)
2567. 他的亲生子女对继承这份生意有优先权。(prior)
2568. 和其他道路使用者相比，公共汽车应该具有优先权。(priority)
2569. 我要单独呆着好好读这封信并好好理解它。(privacy)
2570. 新法律旨在保护人们的隐私权。(privacy)
2571. 参加本俱乐部的特权之一是可以使用本部的网球场。(privilege)
2572. 在学校时，我得过几次化学奖和物理奖。(prize)
2573. 他给你看过他收藏的最珍爱的古董钟吗？(prize)
2574. 申请签证的程序是怎样的？(procedure)
2575. 这是除掉有毒物质的传统做法。(procedure)
2576. 政府决心继续进行选举。(proceed)
2577. 合同谈判进展得很顺利。(proceed)
2578. 煤炭是经过缓慢的化学变化形成的。(process)
2579. 重复有助于学习过程。(process)
2580. 雇佣了两百万员工为电子公司加工产品。(process)
2581. 所有的大学申请都通过了这一系统进行处理。(process)
2582. 加拿大出产优质小麦。(produce)
2583. 糖作物成了加勒比海岛的主要产品。(produce)
2584. 管理层总是在寻求提高工人生产效率的方法。(productivity)
2585. 你唱歌真像专业歌手。(professional)
2586. 斯洛甫先生是保险业的真正内行人物。(professional)
2587. 得到良好的专业意见很重要。(professional)
2588. 这一商务计划看起来专业。(professional)
2589. 你需要精通簿记才能承担这项工作。(proficiency)
2590. 我只看到了她的侧脸。(profile)
2591. 每周这本杂志都简单介绍一位体育名人。(profile)

2592. 你不要指望在开办公司的头几年里赚取许多利润。(profit)

2593. 许多公司将从利率下跌中获利。(profit)

2594. 母亲的行为对成长中的孩子有深远的影响。(profound)

2595. 由于天气糟糕,我们的活动计划不得不稍微改动。(programme)

2596. 你最喜欢的电视节目是什么?(programme)

2597. 今天下午有什么安排?(programme)

2598. 人权问题上取得的进展很小。(progress)

2599. 尽管下雪,我们还是行进了很远。(progress)

2600. 我问护士我儿子的恢复情况如何。(progress)

2601. 船上的工作进展得很快。(progress)

2602. 工厂内绝对禁止吸烟。(prohibit)

2603. 自从国家独立以来蒂拜一直担任总统,后来宪法不允许他继续连任。(prohibit)

2604. 这一计划旨在提供一份儿童情感的分析。(project)

2605. 我们正在从事一个研究污染的科研项目。(project)

2606. 学校领导正计划下学期扩大招生。(project)

2607. 他将幻灯投射在墙上。(project)

2608. 人们一直在试图延长寿命。(prolong)

2609. 政府应该在提高人权方面起更重要的作用。(promising)

2610. 他是个大有前途的年轻演员。(promising)

2611. 海伦被提升为高级经理。(promote)

2612. 肥料促进叶子的生长。(promote)

2613. 她在伦敦推广自己的新书。(promote)

2614. 她的境况促使我要设法找一份新的工作。(prompt)

2615. 他总是迅速回复来信。(prompt)

2616. 当你疲劳、身体衰弱时更易于生病。(prone)

2617. 这条鱼急速有力地摆着尾巴在水中悄然游动。(propel)

2618. 他们的职责是保护私有财产。(property)

2619. 他已拥有自己的房产。(property)

2620. 铜的一个特性就是导热导电能力强。(property)

2621. 一个《旧约》中的先知 (prophet)

2622. 他是死刑的主要支持者。(proponent)

2623. 近年来女性毕业生的比例有所增加。(proportion)
2624. 减少绘画的成分，这样所有的要素都会比较均衡。(proportion)
2625. 委员会建议缩短时间期限。(proposal)
2626. 下个月希腊人将面对新一轮的大选。(prospect)
2627. 硕士毕业生的工作前景不是很看好。(prospect)
2628. 那时许多生产芯片的公司相当繁荣。(prosper)
2629. 他父亲是一个富裕的农场主和煤商。(prosperous)
2630. 按照礼仪，他将在会议开始前五分钟准时抵达。(protocol)
2631. 这些公司说，他们将分享技术，开始一套标准的交流协议。(protocol)
2632. 俗话说，吃得越多，胃口越好。(proverb)
2633. 可以允许孩子们进来看这些影片，条件是他们只能坐在大厅的后面。(provided)
2634. 协议包括一方有权检查另一方的武器。(provision)
2635. 我们的补给品足够两个星期。(provision)
2636. 我们选择这所房子是由于它离学校近。(proximity)
2637. 为了让人戒烟，你得运用心理学。(psychology)
2638. 他在假期里为出版物撰写评论。(publication)
2639. 他在英格兰忙于新书的出版。(publication)
2640. 他的研究结果的公布，已经掀起了一股新的研究浪潮。(publication)
2641. 音乐会事先没有做很多宣传，所以许多票没有卖出去。(publicity)
2642. 第一版于1765年发行。(publish)
2643. 我们很喜欢读你的信，并且尽可能多地发表它们。(publish)
2644. 他是一个非常守时的人。(punctual)
2645. 这个产品就应在购买当日取用。(purchase)
2646. 你可以在网上购买保险。(purchase)
2647. 她的歌声纯净、清晰、有力。(purity)
2648. 布莱恩穿过空地，一个警官在后边追着他。(pursue)
2649. 她打算在政界寻求发展。(pursue)
2650. 这个公司为追求利润毫不留情。(pursuit)
2651. 强盗逃离了犯罪现场，警察紧追不舍。(pursuit)
2652. 伊娃有不错的学历，但没有工作经验。(qualification)
2653. 这份证书使你有资格担任牙医助理。(qualify)

2654. 这项研究包括对学生的表现进行定性分析。(qualitative)

2655. 他表现出明显的领导特质。(quality)

2656. 这片土地土质很差。(quality)

2657. 如果你对合同有什么疑问，给我们打个电话。(query)

2658. 很多人都在问考试试题是否准确。(query)

2659. 两位球员都对裁判的决定表示质疑。(query)

2660. 所有职员都被要求填写一份有关他们工作的调查表。(questionnaire)

2661. 我们排了半个小时的队。(queue)

2662. 有些排队买票的人天一亮就在那里了。(queue)

2663. 杰克想戒烟。(quit)

2664. 他主持一档很受欢迎的电视问答比赛节目。(quiz)

2665. 我经常一上课就做一次复习词汇内容的小测试。(quiz)

2666. 她从一篇报纸上的文章中引用了一句话。(quote)

2667. 这家公司对整个工作给出的最初报价是 6000 英镑。(quote)

2668. 她在比赛中名列第二。(race)

2669. 法律禁止基于肤色或种族原因而产生的歧视。(race)

2670. 她和本国一些最佳赛跑选手比赛过。(race)

2671. 我们必须快速穿过伦敦赶乘火车。(race)

2672. 燃烧的原木发出温暖舒适的光。(radiate)

2673. 两个机构之间有些根本的区别。(radical)

2674. 投掷圈的半径应为 1.5 米。(radius)

2675. 她大发雷霆。(rage)

2676. 一个乞丐正坐在一堆破毯子上打瞌睡。(ragged)

2677. 飞机正对敌舰进行空袭。(raid)

2678. 公司引进了一个机制，对员工进行随意药检。(random)

2679. 这种药对于治疗一系列细菌引起的疾病都很有效。(range)

2680. 他的家乡位于湖区最长的山脉中。(range)

2681. 他的音域真的是太宽了。(range)

2682. 餐厅的墙壁上挂了一排团队的照片。(range)

2683. 她现在世界排名第五。(ranking)

2684. 不要对你的未来做任何草率的决定！(rash)

2685. 离婚率高的令人难以置信。(rate)
2686. 护士与医生的比例是二比一。(ratio)
2687. 所有的情况应全部通知(孩子的)父母,以便他们做出一个明智的决定。(rational)
2688. 胡萝卜可以煮熟了吃或生吃。(raw)
2689. 我们已经收集了大量原始资料。(raw)
2690. 石油是一种重要的原材料,可以加工成包括塑料在内的许多不同产品。(raw)
2691. 中东地区的危机消息使得石油价格巨变。(react)
2692. 你要现实地对待一天能做的量。(realistic)
2693. 电视是人们逃离现实的一种工具。(reality)
2694. 我们用手工收割。(reap)
2695. 不要让别人坐享你的研究成果。(reap)
2696. 他朝房子后面走去。(rear)
2697. 我过去一直养鸡。(rear)
2698. 我们的母亲一向是非常通情达理的。(reasonable)
2699. 30英镑的票价非常公道。(reasonable)
2700. 他们表示歉意,并向我们保证,问题会立即得到处理。(reassure)
2701. 事后,奥莉维亚回想不起他们谈了些什么。(recall)
2702. 大使被从华盛顿召回。(recall)
2703. 脚步声渐渐远去。(recede)
2704. 痛苦的记忆在他的脑海中渐渐模糊。(recede)
2705. 我们买的每件东西都有收据。(receipt)
2706. 我们有一个专为接待来宾用的房间。(reception)
2707. 我们将出席院长举行的招待会。(reception)
2708. 你在接待处预约一下好吗? (reception)
2709. 收音机的接收情况越来越差。(reception)
2710. 在经济极度萧条时期,公司为了生存常被迫裁员。(recession)
2711. 你知道做全麦面包的好办法吗? (recipe)
2712. 她被邀请去作钢琴独奏表演。(recital)
2713. 弗雷德开始大谈特谈他的奇遇。(recital)
2714. 你估计那要花多少钱? (reckon)
2715. 她认为有风险。(reckon)

2716. 起初她并没有认出我来。(recognize)

2717. 英国的行医资格在加拿大是被承认的。(recognize)

2718. 他也记不起那些名字了。(recollect)

2719. 医生们建议所有儿童都应该接种麻疹疫苗。(recommend)

2720. 你能不能介绍一位好律师？(recommend)

2721. 我的大学导师给我写了封推荐信附在我的求职申请后。(recommendation)

2722. 对公司是否应提起法律诉讼她会在几天内提起建议。(recommendation)

2723. 四幅在美术馆丢失的油画失而复得。(recover)

2724. 他因心脏病突发住进医院，现在正在恢复中。(recover)

2725. 爱玛唯一的娱乐形式似乎是购物。(recreation)

2726. 在书印刷前，人们做了一切努力来改正错误。(rectify)

2727. 矿物燃料不能循环利用，一旦用完会永远消失。(recycle)

2728. 州长宣布了一个降低犯罪率的新计划。(reduce)

2729. 最终，夏洛特沦落在街上乞讨。(reduce)

2730. 你还有胶卷吗？(reel)

2731. 附上了词汇索引以供参考。(reference)

2732. 这本小说中没有直接提到她的童年。(reference)

2733. 汽车制造商不断改进他们的设计。(refine)

2734. 这是四个星期的课程，其宗旨是为加深我们对于管理角色的理解。(refine)

2735. 她可以看到汽车的挡风玻璃里反射出自己的脸庞。(reflect)

2736. 消费者消费的降低反映了他们对经济的担忧。(reflect)

2737. 他有时间反思自己的成功与失败。(reflect)

2738. 现在正是法律进行自身改革的时机。(reform)

2739. 从闷热的教室出来后，和风使人感到凉爽。(refreshing)

2740. 换个人谈话会让人有新鲜感。(refreshing)

2741. 你可以申请退还旅行费。(refund)

2742. 我把收音机送回去，他们给我退款。(refund)

2743. 我拒绝参与任何违法的事情。(refuse)

2744. 他们的开价好得让人无法抗拒。(refuse)

2745. 几位科学家已经尝试过反驳摩尔的理论了。(refute)

2746. 她否定了所有玩忽职守的指控。(refute)

2747. 在这个社会里，教师得不到什么尊重。(regard)
2748. 我老公表达他的问候。(regard)
2749. 就这个方面，这家公司的问题绝不是唯一的。(regard)
2750. 她往后站了站，冷酷地看着他。(regard)
2751. 公司的雇佣政策正受到怀疑。(regarding)
2752. 尽管当地人反对，新建铁路的计划仍在进行中。(regardless)
2753. 这一政权铲除了多数反对者。(regime)
2754. 他带回一份仔细筹划出的饮食起居安排。(regard)
2755. 他们几年都住在肯尼亚的一个偏远地区。(region)
2756. 彼得在旅馆住客登记簿上签了名。(register)
2757. 商务信函应该用正式的语言来书写。(register)
2758. 有多少学生登记参加英语课？(register)
2759. 她的脸表露出震惊和愤怒。(register)
2760. 公司的全部收入如果超过一定数额，就必须呈报增值税。(registration)
2761. 公司定期与员工会面。(regular)
2762. 每隔一段距离就安置一节管道。(regular)
2763. 这已远远迟于他平时上床的时间。(regular)
2764. 肉类和家禽受农业部管理。(regulate)
2765. 人靠出汗来调整体温。(regulate)
2766. 这些日子看起来有太多的规章制度啦。(regulation)
2767. 我该向谁报销旅行费用？(reimbursement)
2768. 煤气公司对他的房屋损坏进行了赔偿。(reimbursement)
2769. 将你的大多数时间投入到培养良好的行为举止上，包括微笑、拥抱和赞许。(reinforce)
2770. 大坝由两万个沙包加固。(reinforce)
2771. 这个电影进一步强化了这一观点，即女人应该既漂亮又无知。(reinforce)
2772. 她的哥哥提出帮忙，但莎拉拒绝了。(reject)
2773. 他的申请为什么被退回，原因太明显了。(related)
2774. 警察现在相信这三个案件之间有联系。(related)
2775. 我很可能和他有亲戚关系。(related)
2776. 表示不同意的人数相对来说还是比较少的。(relatively)
2777. 轻柔的运动可以使僵硬的肩部肌肉得到放松。(relax)

2778. 洗个热水澡应该有助于你放松。(relax)

2779. 西蒙从监狱里获得了提前释放。(release)

2780. 威尔逊先生在一则新闻中说了这番话。(release)

2781. 弹奏乐器可以让感情得到解脱。(release)

2782. 熊最后被放归到野外。(release)

2783. 他昨天出院了。(release)

2784. 她的新专辑月底发行。(release)

2785. 相关文件被呈上法庭。(relevant)

2786. 米勒是个安静的、靠得住的男人。(reliable)

2787. 别担心,我的车很安全可靠。(reliable)

2788. 孩子们都安全到家,这使我们大大松了一口气。(relief)

2789. 镇静剂只能暂时缓解抑郁情绪。(relief)

2790. 她不能接受父母的宗教信仰。(religious)

2791. 我们的父母非常虔诚并且非常爱国。(religious)

2792. 维尔斯最后同意了,但是很不情愿。(reluctance)

2793. 很多职业女性依靠亲人来帮忙照顾她们的孩子。(rely)

2794. 很多人现在指望从因特网上获取信息。(rely)

2795. 他在办公室里度过余下的警察生涯。(remainder)

2796. 十五除以四得到余数三。(remainder)

2797. 他做饭的速度和效率非同寻常。(remarkable)

2798. 现行法律纠正不了这种不公正现象。(remedy)

2799. 他宁愿服用自制的药,也不用即便是最现代的药品。(remedy)

2800. 这景色使她想起了苏格兰。(remind)

2801. 这可能在遥远的将来某时发生。(remote)

2802. 参考书不要从图书馆搬走。(remove)

2803. 他摘下帽子和手套。(remove)

2804. 学院删掉了阻止女性报考的条例。(remove)

2805. 新技术使我的旧电脑过时了。(render)

2806. 我们衷心感谢所有为地震受害者提供帮助的人。(render)

2807. 他在把这本书从法语翻译成英语。(render)

2808. 厂方用机器人替换了大多数工人。(replace)

2809. 他痛恨这所学校以及它代表的一切。(represent)
2810. 这一疗法集中体现了癌症研究领域里的巨大进步。(represent)
2811. 她责备我缺乏先见之明。(reproach)
2812. 她看到他脸上的责备神色大吃一惊。(reproach)
2813. 如果你要安装一部防盗铃的话,确保请一家声誉良好的公司来做。(reputable)
2814. 她是一位出名的好医生。(reputation)
2815. 这一研究在主席的要求下进行。(request)
2816. 雷写了一份正式的申请书要求与道格拉斯见面。(request)
2817. 如果你想拍照的话,必须请求得到允许。(request)
2818. 这一系统需要进行彻底重组。(require)
2819. 法律规定你要系安全带。(require)
2820. 我想尽办法营救他,结果都没用。(rescue)
2821. 我还在为论文进行调研。(research)
2822. 买房子之前做些调查,这个主意不错。(research)
2823. 你可以看出苏珊和她的妹妹很像。(resemblance)
2824. 他长大后简直就是他父亲的翻版。(resemble)
2825. 该国拥有外汇储备八百三十亿美元。(reserve)
2826. 她克服了自己天生拘谨的个性。(reserve)
2827. 管理层保留拒绝接受的权力。(reserve)
2828. 你需要提前订票吗?(reserve)
2829. 江河和水库涨满了水。(reservoir)
2830. 历史是人类经验的宝库。(reservoir)
2831. 他大部分时间都呆在底特律,他的家人都住在那儿。(reside)
2832. 行政权属于总统。(reside)
2833. 辞职还是被辞退由你自己选择。(resignation)
2834. 必要时将以武力抵抗任何攻击。(resist)
2835. 这种特殊涂层是用于防锈的。(resist)
2836. 该决议以三分之二的多数通过。(resolution)
2837. 律师的忠告使这个问题得以解决。(resolution)
2838. 卡罗尔下决心今年要用功学习。(resolution)
2839. 最近发生的事件坚定了她发掘真相的决心。(resolve)

2840. 玛丽决意戒烟。(resolve)
2841. 参议院决定采纳总统的提议。(resolve)
2842. 我认为我们可以不用通过法律解决这个问题。(resort)
2843. 在最近几年,这个小城镇成了一个时髦的旅游胜地。(resort)
2844. 他没有采用暴力,合法地得到了这笔钱。(resort)
2845. 你一定要帮助我——你是唯一可以帮助我的人。(resort)
2846. 警察只能动用有限的财力。(resource)
2847. 他证实自己拥有巨大的潜在策略。(resource)
2848. 新老师必须要赢得其学生的尊重。(respect)
2849. 我非常敬佩戴维所取得的成就。(respond)
2850. 达维没有回复她的任何一封电子邮件。(respondent)
2851. 她的治疗效果很好。(respond)
2852. 只有百分之六十二的民意测验被调查对象说他们很满意。(respondent)
2853. 迫于公众的压力,法律被通过了。(response)
2854. 展览得到参观者的积极响应。(response)
2855. 警察逮捕了那些盗窃犯。(responsible)
2856. 每位委员负责一个部门。(responsible)
2857. 政府许诺将经济恢复到活力十足的状态。(restore)
2858. 战后教堂得到认真地整修。(restore)
2859. 人们不得不遏制他使用暴力。(restrain)
2860. 价格上涨应该会约束消费。(restrain)
2861. 新的法律限制销售手枪。(restrict)
2862. 开车过快难免会出事故。(result)
2863. 选举结果将于午夜公布。(result)
2864. 我们还在处理过去的错误遗留下来的问题。(result)
2865. 他对本年度的工作进行了摘要性的总结并祝愿协会下一年工作顺利。(resume)
2866. 参加笔试之前,请将个人简历寄给我们。(resume)
2867. 你有权继续占有这些产品。(retain)
2868. 你的计算机可以存储很多信息。(retain)
2869. 洪水正在慢慢退却。(retreat)
2870. 目前的经济问题迫使政府撤回对削减税收的承诺。(retreat)

2871. 马修从树上取回他的风筝。(retrieve)
2872. 计算机被用来有效地存储和检索信息。(retrieve)
2873. 他透露出自己曾坐过两次牢。(reveal)
2874. 帘幕揭开展现出这一大奖。(reveal)
2875. 哈姆雷特在设法报杀父之仇。(revenge)
2876. 首先,他们期望筹集到足够的钱来支付自己的活动。(revenue)
2877. 政府的大部分收入来自税款。(revenue)
2878. 我什么都不欠你的,如果有什么的话,你倒欠我的。(reverse)
2879. 英国十便士硬币的背面有一只狮子。(reverse)
2880. 失掉参议院的选票给总统重重一击。(reverse)
2881. 有些家庭里,父亲出去工作,母亲待在家里。另外一些家庭的情况正好相反。(reverse)
2882. 我们作为孩子和监护人的位置倒过来了。(reverse)
2883. 报纸发表了一篇关于她的书的评论文章。(review)
2884. 所有的费用都要被复查。(review)
2885. 我们会回顾一下你的处境,然后再决定如何帮助你。(review)
2886. 布莱德曼将对这些新的儿童书籍进行评论。(review)
2887. 本书的几个章节需要修订。(revise)
2888. 我们已经修正过对人口增长的估计。(revise)
2889. 过去十年里,教育界经历了一次变革。(revolution)
2890. 地球每年绕着太阳转一周。(revolution)
2891. 警方悬赏寻求任何与抢劫有关的线索。(reward)
2892. 当看到自己的书被印刷出来,他觉得自己所有艰辛的工作都得到了回报。(reward)
2893. 我没有节奏感,因此我舞蹈跳得很糟糕。(rhythm)
2894. 这种荒唐的赌博会让他把钱全部输光。(ridiculous)
2895. 她死板的控制着自己的情感生活。(rigid)
2896. 他通过艰苦的训练和严密的纪律组建这支队伍。(rigid)
2897. 每种新药在上市之前都要经过严格的安全检查。(rigorous)
2898. 这种车经过严密的道路表现测试。(rigorous)
2899. 把轮胎按在轮辋上。(rim)
2900. 那些苹果还没熟。(ripe)
2901. 这块土地已经具备了发展工业的条件。(ripe)

2902. 如果你在考虑创办公司，要认真地想想所涉及的各种风险。(risk)
2903. 希娜辞了职，转到一家竞争对手公司工作。(rival)
2904. 林中风声呼啸。(roar)
2905. 他看上去很健壮。(robust)
2906. 一度强健的经济如今已衰败。(robust)
2907. 你能用最低的价钱买到黑白电视机。(rock-bottom)
2908. 这次演出的成功，每个人都有份。(role)
2909. 巴巴拉·卡特兰是一位浪漫的小说作家。(romantic)
2910. 我们认为埃及是一个不可思议的传奇国家。(romantic)
2911. 这里是童子军所有成员的值勤表。(roster)
2912. 这个俱乐部拥有数名签约的优秀球员。(roster)
2913. 卫星在绕地球旋转的同时缓慢的自转。(rotate)
2914. 首先给你的文章写篇草稿。(rough draft)
2915. 他睡得太沉，叫不醒。(rouse)
2916. 指挥员设法激励他们都行动起来。(rouse)
2917. 去剑桥的最佳路线怎么走。(route)
2918. 通过另一条渠道，肯尼迪得到了同一个结论。(route)
2919. 工作没有固定的常规——每一天都是不同的。(routine)
2920. 我的工作如此死板乏味——我讨厌它。(routine)
2921. 孩子们被要求站成一排。(row)
2922. 这场雨把我们的假期毁了。(ruin)
2923. 他们拒绝证实或否认关于计划裁员的流言。(rumour)
2924. 我跑过去开门。(run)
2925. 撒切尔夫人想要第四次参加竞选。(run)
2926. 她在波斯顿开了一段时间餐馆。(run)
2927. 乡村生活往往比城市生活更安静。(rural)
2928. 印度仍然是个乡土味极其浓重的国家。(rural)
2929. 汽车上有大块的锈斑。(rust)
2930. 他们访问了伊斯兰圣地。(sacred)
2931. 你为事业牺牲健康是不值得的。(sacrifice)
2932. 为了保丰收而祭神是很普通的事。(sacrifice)

2933. 人们像祭坛献上一头羔羊作为他们赎罪的祭品。(sacrifice)
2934. 作出牺牲是抚养孩子的一部分。(sacrifice)
2935. 新条例已被制定以保护环境。(safeguard)
2936. 新的法律对消费者的权益有没有提供足够的保障。(safeguard)
2937. 这一设备达到了安全标准。(safety)
2938. 救火队员将孩子们带到了安全地点。(safety)
2939. 他们采集血样,检测肝炎。(sample)
2940. 抽样调查的成年人中百分之十八的人承认曾经有过酗酒的问题。(sample)
2941. 你有机会去尝试乡间生活的愉悦了。(sample)
2942. 按照医生的看法,在凶案发生时他的神智是清醒的。(sane)
2943. 这是一个明智的决定,一个我们全都尊重的决定。(sane)
2944. 检查过公共卫生的安排之后,他们下令整个地方都要消毒。(sanitary)
2945. 她新买了一个放在浴室的体重秤。(scales)
2946. 他们仔细查看他的大脑,寻找受伤的迹象。(scan)
2947. 她粗略的看过这篇论文。(scan)
2948. 他右臂上有个疤。(scar)
2949. 冬天水果总是稀少,而且价格昂贵。(scarce)
2950. 我们才开出去一英里,车就坏了。(scarcely)
2951. 地形几十万年来几乎没有什么变化。(scarcely)
2952. 地板上到处散放着书。(scatter)
2953. 突然一声枪响,人群向四处逃散。(scatter)
2954. 想象一下只有百分之二十的人有工作会是什么样的局面。(scenario)
2955. 最糟糕的方案就是,他必须动手术。(scenario)
2956. 在最后一幕里,哈里告诉萨布莉娜自己爱她。(scene)
2957. 几分钟之内记者就赶到现场。(scene)
2958. 夜晚的空气中弥漫着玫瑰的香味。(scent)
2959. 他如何将每件事情都安排进他那繁忙的日程表呢?(schedule)
2960. 大多数假期航班都准时起飞和降落。(schedule)
2961. 这笔钱将用于教师培训计划。(scheme)
2962. 她策划毒死他。(scheme)
2963. 他的那本关于汉语动词的书是一部学术性很强的著作。(scholarship)

2964. 波拉是靠奖学金到牛津大学求学的。(scholarship)
2965. 母亲今天早上责备我对你没礼貌。(scold)
2966. 对那个问题的全面讨论超出了这本书的范畴。(scope)
2967. 经济拥有进一步发展的广阔空间。(scope)
2968. 开赛两小时二十分钟后，最终比分为三比二。(score)
2969. 他的智商为120分。(score)
2970. 数十名记者聚集在法庭外。(score)
2971. 所有剧组的成员都不必脱离剧本。(script)
2972. 他仔细审阅这份文件。(scrutinise)
2973. 学院开设雕塑课。(sculpture)
2974. 五年中等教育结束后要参加两种考试。(secondary)
2975. 社交技巧不一定被看做没有学术成就重要。(secondary)
2976. 飞机的尾部在一块玉米田里找到了。(section)
2977. 这一疾病在城里的贫民区蔓延。(section)
2978. 家用电脑数量的增加促进了电子部门的发展。(sector)
2979. 我们希望自己孩子的未来无忧无虑。(secure)
2980. 这年头没有牢靠的工作。(secure)
2981. 军队被派去保卫边界。(secure)
2982. 这家公司最近和福特公司签署了一份两千万美元的合同。(secure)
2983. 昨天一个犯人越狱，此后上级命令监狱加强安全保卫。(security)
2984. 不管是谁发行的这些证券，我们都会对其运用同样的原则。(security)
2985. 河流正给大海带来大量沉积物。(sediment)
2986. 你认为总统会竞选连任吗？(seek)
2987. 如果这些症状仍然存在，请征求医生的意见。(seek)
2988. 水没有排走，而是向下渗进地里。(seep)
2989. 各段护墙板被漆上不同的颜色。(segment)
2990. 橙子瓣 (segment)
2991. 他一把抓住我的手，把我从窗户旁拉开。(seize)
2992. 叛乱分子已在暴力政变中夺取了政权。(seize)
2993. 荣誉学位颁发给少数杰出的学生。(select)
2994. 他有希望入选国家队。(select)

2995. 我们做出选择不容易。(selection)
2996. 秋季学期始于八月二十八号。(semester)
2997. 每周我们上一次现代政治理论的研讨课。(seminar)
2998. 来自13个国家的出版商和作家出席了这一讨论会。(seminar)
2999. 她在中学里教公民课，那里的高年级学生已经有选举资格了。(senior)
3000. 她丈夫比她大九岁。(senior)
3001. 年龄较大的学生有一定的特权。(senior)
3002. 普通员工、中级管理人员和高级管理人员各有各的餐厅。(senior)
3003. 我认为那是最明智的做法。(sensible)
3004. 他看上去并不知道未来的困难。(sensible)
3005. 她在整个职业生涯里都对批评意见很敏感。(sensitive)
3006. 如果这些部位哪里容易疼，就告诉我。(sensitive)
3007. 体育馆和桑拿分别在两个不同的大楼里。(separate)
3008. 我妻子和我各有一个独立的账户。(separate)
3009. 灯塔与陆地被一个宽阔的海峡分隔开来。(separate)
3010. 他已经经历了一连串生意上的失利。(sequence)
3011. 按正确的顺序小心地将这些动作完成。(sequence)
3012. 路上已有一系列的事故。(series)
3013. 星期一，各州州长要和布什举行一次工作会议。(session)
3014. 法庭现在开庭。(session)
3015. 我们每星期上五个小时的英语课，包括一次在语言实验室集合。(session)
3016. 他可能收到的最严厉的惩罚是十年监禁。(severe)
3017. 一名乘客受了严重的擦伤和划伤。(severe)
3018. 非洲的一些地方存在严重的食物短缺问题。(severe)
3019. 这些日子你在电视上看到的都是色情和暴力。(sex)
3020. 请在表格上方填上你的姓名、年龄和性别。(sex)
3021. 邻家的房屋在我们的花园里投下阴影。(shadow)
3022. 她父亲的病给她孩子的出生蒙上了一层浓重的阴影。(shadow)
3023. 溪很浅，所以我们都能够涉水而过。(shallow)
3024. 我认为那部电影相当肤浅。(shallow)
3025. 我们的桌子是椭圆形的。(shape)

3026. 他就宣言的形式大致地谈了一些自己的想法。(shape)

3027. 透过窗口，我可以看见外边的街道上有个黑漆漆的人影。(shape)

3028. 他开始把面团做成面包卷。(shape)

3029. 研究成果经常被用于设计社会政策。(shape)

3030. 我们后院有一间工具房。(shed)

3031. 他很担忧东欧向自由市场思维的转变。(shift)

3032. 达维昨天不得不轮班工作12个小时。(shift)

3033. 她把目光从我的身上转向鲍比。(shift)

3034. 他拒绝改变立场。(shift)

3035. 朱厄妮塔冻得直发抖。(shiver)

3036. 电影在快到六点的时候放完了。(shortly)

3037. 为什么电话铃总会在我淋浴时响起来？(shower)

3038. 预报明天山区有强阵雨。(shower)

3039. 那些男孩子吓得直往后退。(shrink)

3040. 如果可能的话，你应该拿窗帘去干洗，这样不大会缩水。(shrink)

3041. 全世界的森林面积正在以令人惊恐的速度缩小。(shrink)

3042. 看等号两边的数字。(sign)

3043. 经济没有好转的迹象。(sign)

3044. 司机打了个往右转的信号。(signal)

3045. 他最重要的政治成就是取消了死刑。(significant)

3046. 日本人相当一部分财富投资在西方。(significant)

3047. 车子又开到了野外，我们驶过一块路标，可是我读不懂。(signpost)

3048. 我的老师给了我一些指导，指出我接着该学什么。(signpost)

3049. 这条路的路标不是很好。(signpost)

3050. 这一演说和今年早些时候美国总统所做的演讲惊人地相似。(similar)

3051. 在研究小孩子和其他动物的幼崽时，我们可以看到两者在行为上的一些类似之处。(similarity)

3052. 设法解释的简明一些，好让孩子们听懂。(simplify)

3053. 他发现不可能假装悲哀。(simulate)

3054. 可以在教室进行模拟面试。(simulate)

3055. 两个孩子同时回答了老师的问题。(simultaneously)

3056. 他们相信自己是因为罪孽而受到惩罚。(sin)

3057. 请把此物连同我的诚挚祝福一并收下。(sincere)

3058. 他本性温和诚实。(sincere)

3059. 镇上购买了维拉大街上的一块地皮建新的图书馆。(site)

3060. 这房子建在中世纪时的一个监狱的旧址上。(site)

3061. 控制中心设在好几英里之外。(situated)

3062. 艰难状况下他应付得很好。(situation)

3063. 现在的局面我一天也无法忍受了。(situation)

3064. 孩子们应该喝牛奶以帮助增强骨骼。(skeleton)

3065. 我的书有了框架——现在我只需要加上细节。(skeleton)

3066. 该书的导论为其内容提供了一个概述。(sketch)

3067. 艺术系学生每人都被要求画一张树的素描。(sketch)

3068. 阅读和写作是两种不同的技巧。(skill)

3069. 全队队员都技艺娴熟，信心十足地进行比赛。(skill)

3070. 慢火炖过肉之后，把表面的脂肪撇去。(skim)

3071. 浏览一下第二部分就行，节约时间。(skim)

3072. 小羊羔们在田里跳来跳去。(skip)

3073. 这本书的这个部分不是十分有趣，所以我将它跳过。(skip)

3074. 她身段苗条，留着一头长长的黑发。(slender)

3075. 你还要片火腿吗？(slice)

3076. 你能为我切一片很薄的蛋糕吗？(slice)

3077. 我们厨房里装了那种可滑动开关的门。(slide)

3078. 他说，政府必须采取措施以阻止国家经济滑坡陷入衰退。(slide)

3079. 我们将有一场幻灯表演。(slide)

3080. 她比她姐姐高一点。(slightly)

3081. 经常运动会使你更加苗条。(slim)

3082. 有人幸存下来的可能性极小。(slim)

3083. 小心！地板很滑。(slippery)

3084. 我们这次新的促销活动需要一条广告语。(slogan)

3085. 地板有点倾斜。(slope)

3086. 屋顶呈30度斜角。(slope)

3087. 我失手把盘子掉在地上，摔得粉碎。(smash)

3088. 拉里用拳头猛击桌子。(smash)

3089. 我午饭吃得很饱，所以晚饭我只要一些点心就可以了。(snack)

3090. 人们经常告诫小孩不要一把抢过东西，因为这是粗鲁的行为。(snatch)

3091. 我当时急于脱离教学岗位，因此毫不犹豫地想办法抓住这工作。(snatch)

3092. 雨被风吹进了卧室，打湿了床。(soak)

3093. 整个夜晚焰火在高空升腾。(soar)

3094. 我去看了该剧作家的所谓大作，非常失望。(so-called)

3095. 这个人号称专家，却不能告诉我们哪里出了问题。(so-called)

3096. 到处是压制和社会不公平现象。(social)

3097. 这是一种扩大他们社交接触圈子的机会。(social)

3098. 你需要特殊的软件去看文档中的信息。(software)

3099. 他的鞋底是软皮底儿。(sole)

3100. 格里菲斯是这次撞车事件里唯一的幸存者。(sole)

3101. 只有这家公司有权推广埃尔顿·约翰的唱片。(sole)

3102. 连牛奶也冻结了。(solid)

3103. 我们很高兴来到陆地上。(solid)

3104. 双方都在努力寻求和平解决的方案。(solution)

3105. 稀淡的糖溶液 (solution)

3106. 价格比我预期的要高一些。(somewhat)

3107. 老练的读者理解了这本书隐含的意义。(sophisticated)

3108. 我想这个问题需要用一种更复杂的方法来解决。(sophisticated)

3109. 他对我父亲的去世表示悲痛。(sorrow)

3110. 他大学中途退学，这使他的父母十分伤心。(sorrow)

3111. 你用的是哪一种洗发水？(sort)

3112. 它们是一种巧克力。(sort)

3113. 他在整理一堆干净的短袜。(sort)

3114. 我对她略有所闻，但不知道她是谁。(sort)

3115. 特德总会给你提出明智的忠告。(sound)

3116. 豆类是很好的蛋白质来源。(source)

3117. 我们已经发现这个麻烦的由来。(source)

3118. 在文章的最后列出所有的文字出处。(source)

3119. 他花了一个上午购买纪念品。(souvenir)

3120. 我有一间宽敞且陈设舒适的起居室。(spacious)

3121. 新政府只用了两年的时间就使国家的经济形势有所改观。(span)

3122. 如果私下和他说这件事情,就不会使他尴尬了。(spare)

3123. 务请抽点时间在这本书上签个名。(spare)

3124. 指挥官对他们的勇敢印象如此之深以至于饶了他们一命。(spare)

3125. 他们把此事原原本本登在《皇室新闻》上,任何细节都未放过。(spare)

3126. 没有多余的椅子。(spare)

3127. 你所需要带的全部东西是一件备用衬衫和一套备用内衣。(spare)

3128. 煤气泄漏时,任何一个小火花都会引起爆炸。(spark)

3129. 我给她讲了一点我自己在他这个年龄时的生活情况,发觉他流露出一点兴趣。(spark)

3130. 蛙鱼奋力回游到河里产卵。(spawn)

3131. 贫困引发了无数次的宗教运动。(spawn)

3132. 我去找了一位专科医生,他发现我血糖过低。(specialist)

3133. 西蒙专门研究合同法。(specialize)

3134. 鲨鱼有250多种。(species)

3135. 瑟曼不愿谈这个生意的具体详情。(specific)

3136. 霍华德先生给了我们明确的指示。(specific)

3137. 电厂雇员必须遵守特定的安全规则。(specific)

3138. 总统没有说明访问秘鲁的日期。(specify)

3139. 一百多位教师将会收到该辞典的样本。(specimen)

3140. 调查表上的问题覆盖面极广。(spectrum)

3141. 在公共事业领域里,妇女常常被排除在权力地位以外。(sphere)

3142. 这道咖喱饭菜需要再加一点调料。(spice)

3143. 千万别让水洒到地板上。(spill)

3144. 教皇是基督教会的精神领袖。(spiritual)

3145. 在高温下木质地板裂开了。(split)

3146. 关于如何处理这一局势,政府意见分歧。(split)

3147. 我真希望别下雨,那会毁了一切的。(spoil)

3148. 我没看过这部电影,所以不要把内容告诉我,以免破坏我的兴致。(spoil)

3149. 她父母用玩具和各种花样来宠她，纵容她。(spoil)

3150. 如果你不把甜食放进冰箱，它就会变质。(spoil)

3151. 她家在布里斯托尔的朋友同意做她的保人。(sponsor)

3152. 在你拿到居留英国的签证之前，你需要有一个能正式资助你的人。(sponsor)

3153. 通常他的领带上有几点油污。(spot)

3154. 看来这是个很好的野餐地。(spot)

3155. 据调查，在60%的家庭中夫妻双方都出去工作。(spouse)

3156. 我们看见一辆大汽车将水喷洒在路面上。(spray)

3157. 现在就像春天一样，傍晚时天色越来越亮了。(spring)

3158. 我觉得沙发弹簧断了——它摸上去很软。(spring)

3159. 几年下来，床垫失去了它的弹性。(spring)

3160. 山泉 (spring)

3161. 把柠檬切成两半，再把汁挤在碗内。(squeeze)

3162. 24小时以后病人的情况开始稳定下来。(stabilize)

3163. 宽广的基底将使得构架更加稳定。(stable)

3164. 他明显不是个很坚定的人。(stable)

3165. 成千上万的足球迷涌进了体育场来看杯赛的决赛。(stadium)

3166. 这所学校的教职员是非常优秀的。(staff)

3167. 在这个阶段走捷径可能要付出巨大代价。(stage)

3168. 我走上舞台开始唱起来。(stage)

3169. 不流动的水池里产生青苔。(stagnant)

3170. 人到中年停滞不前就会像李子脯一样干枯、缩水。(stagnant)

3171. 要是冷水除不掉污迹，就用温水和肥皂试试。(stain)

3172. 委员会在评估地方医院的医疗标准。(standard)

3173. 我们支付给他们标准价格。(standard)

3174. 在机场找行李现在是常事儿。(standard)

3175. 他满腹狐疑地盯着我们。(stare)

3176. 对于该国的经济状况存在着恐惧。(state)

3177. 国家政府已经为这一紧急事件特别拨款。(state)

3178. 请说出你的姓名和地址。(state)

3179. 票价标在票的背后。(state)

3180. 他拒绝给警方供词。(statement)
3181. 她在官方声明中正式宣布辞职。(statement)
3182. 只有在停车时才动用手刹车。(stationary)
3183. 我们成批购买文具和卫生纸这类东西。(stationery)
3184. 统计数据来自英国政府最近进行的一项研究。(statistic)
3185. 统计学是数学的一个分支。(statistic)
3186. 人们说罗马是一座有很多雕像的城市。(statue)
3187. 从传统上讲，医生享有较高的社会地位。(status)
3188. 这些文件在英国没有法律地位。(status)
3189. 拿稳手电筒，这样我才能看清楚。(steady)
3190. 当时在这个城市很难找到稳定的工作。(steady)
3191. 他们建议大幅提高烟卷税。(steep)
3192. 他们在浑然不知如何操舵的情况下出发了。(steer)
3193. 他把我领到桌前，让我在椅子上坐下。(steer)
3194. 他头疼是由于视力问题引起的。(stem)
3195. 他从所受的训练中将学到某些陈规老套。(stereotypes)
3196. 他们到处张贴海报，有的贴在墙上，有的贴在路灯柱子上。(stick)
3197. 战争已大大刺激了武器技术的发展。(stimulate)
3198. 在微火下轻轻搅拌汤汁。(stir)
3199. 鼓起劲来，否则我们怎么也别想把这件事干完。(stir)
3200. 最新经济数字引起人们对通货膨胀的恐惧。(stir)
3201. 我看汤需要搅动一下。(stir)
3202. 她的演说引起了轰动。(stir)
3203. 资料存在硬盘上又用软盘做了备份。(stir)
3204. 人们喜欢在较大的商店购物，因为这样他们就能在同一商店买到所有的东西。(store)
3205. 他在地下室储存了大量葡萄酒。(store)
3206. 她有一头金色的直发。(straight)
3207. 你干脆对她坦诚相告，告诉她你的感觉。(straight)
3208. 我回到家后直接上床睡觉。(straight)
3209. 我们不必马上走——我们还有10分钟的时间喝咖啡。(straight)
3210. 新的网络系统很简单，你不应该有任何问题。(straightforward)

3211. 杰克是个强硬的人，但总是很坦率，也很公正。(straightforward)
3212. 公司必须首先解决战略问题。(strategy)
3213. 这座桥梁需要加固。(strengthen)
3214. 他们一直在加强边界的防御来为战争做准备。(strengthen)
3215. 瑜伽功对于缓解压力很有效。(stress)
3216. 鲍威尔强调纪律的重要性。(stress)
3217. 他着重强调了平衡饮食的重要性。(stress)
3218. 为了考试而学习总使我感到很大的压力。(stress)
3219. 我的 T 恤衫在洗的时候被拉长了。(stretch)
3220. 在剧烈运动前舒展一下身体是个好主意。(stretch)
3221. 那条大路绵延二百多英里，贯穿该国的中心地带。(stretch)
3222. 我的父母在我小的时候对我很严厉。(strict)
3223. 克莱尔从门廊上跳下，大步走过草坪。(stride)
3224. 一个雪球打中了他的后脑勺。(strike)
3225. 警方说他们担心此人可能再次袭击。(strike)
3226. 卡罗尔突然意识到她说海伦的那些话也适合他自己。(strike)
3227. 她和她母亲惊人的相像。(striking)
3228. 杰克脱掉衣服，跳进淋浴间。(strip)
3229. 埃文斯上尉被判有罪，被免去了军衔。(strive)
3230. 我们必须继续争取更高的效率。(strive)
3231. 她平稳地用力游泳。(stroke)
3232. 鞭子每抽一下，马就跑得快一些。(stroke)
3233. 麦克斯用画笔迅速、果断地画了几下。(stroke)
3234. 很多到英国游玩的游客发现英国的阶级架构很难理解。(structure)
3235. 引进了新的管理体系。(structure)
3236. 展览围绕三个主题进行安排。(structure)
3237. 你喝的那是什么东西？(stuff)
3238. 正餐将以自助冷餐的形式进行。(style)
3239. 房间装饰成现代派。(style)
3240. 文章中使用缩写形式是不太好的文风。(style)
3241. 这些鞋以最大程度的舒适为目的而设计。(style)

3242. 他们称自己为"双胞胎煞星"。(style)
3243. 我们能不能谈点别的？(subject)
3244. 念书时我最喜欢的科目是历史和地理。(subject)
3245. 他是英国公民。(subject)
3246. 所有建筑公司都要服从严格控制。(subject)
3247. 汽车的国内税很高。(subject)
3248. 侵略者很快征服了当地部落。(subject)
3249. 公司的账目接受了仔细的审查。(subject)
3250. 作为评论家，她的文章过于主观。(subjective)
3251. 所有的申请都必须于星期一前递交。(submit)
3252. 德里克已同意接受问话。(submit)
3253. 一想到被属下进行评估，一些经理就不舒服。(subordinate)
3254. 女人隶属于男人。(subordinate)
3255. 女性在我们的社会中处于次要的地位。(subordinate)
3256. 这些技术被后世子孙承袭下来。(subsequent)
3257. 美国的农夫正在应付因为减少农业补贴带来的麻烦。(subsidy)
3258. 海洛因是一种违禁品。(substance)
3259. 他的决定只是因为他讨厌外国人，没什么真正的原因。(substantial)
3260. 吃了一顿丰盛的午餐之后他决定休息一下。(substantial)
3261. 那块场地上建有若干大而结实的原木建筑物。(substantial)
3262. 她从祖母那继承了大笔的财产。(substantial)
3263. 教练得给蒂姆找个替补。(substitute)
3264. 维生素片绝对代替不了健康的饮食。(substitute)
3265. 这个食谱说可以用酸奶替代酸的奶油。(substitute)
3266. 这两种方案之间的区别细微而精妙。(subtle)
3267. 十减四等于六。(subtract)
3268. 公司决定搬到郊区，因为那里的房租便宜得多。(suburb)
3269. 他的继任者任职15个月就过世了。(successor)
3270. 冰箱是冰盒的替代者。(successor)
3271. 我们需要充足的时间来解决这个问题。(sufficient)
3272. 这个单词是 usefully，后缀 ly 用不同的颜色标出。(suffix)

汉译英练习

3273. 他欠我一大笔钱。(sum)
3274. 他提出用八万美元购买这个房产。(sum)
3275. 新闻报道结束时，他们常会向你概述一遍主要内容。(summary)
3276. 学生们对这一即决审判满意吗？(summary)
3277. 有没有登上过顶峰？(summit)
3278. 他被任命为总理之日即是他达到事业顶峰之时。(summit)
3279. 西方国家的首脑正云集渥太华以出席本周的峰会。(summit)
3280. 博物馆里珍藏了一批20世纪的艺术极品。(superb)
3281. 当他说男人天生就比女人强的时候，她非常生气。(superior)
3282. 示威者在人数上占优势，而警方在力量上占优势。(superior)
3283. 我们选她做这份工作是因为她是最优秀的应试者。(superior)
3284. 游戏时间内老师们轮流监督孩子们的活动。(supervise)
3285. 我的导师说，他将极力推荐我上这门课程。(supervisor)
3286. 这些报酬对他平常的工资是个补贴。(supplement)
3287. 他正在阅读《星期日报》的增刊。(supplement)
3288. 琪亚靠晚上给别人补习来贴补日常工资。(supplement)
3289. 万一总供水系统出现故障，还有补充供水。(supplementary)
3290. 多数大城镇已有电力供应。(supply)
3291. 北海的石油储存量很大。(supply)
3292. 这不是我们应该讨论的事。(suppose)
3293. 我想他得到这份工作一定会很高兴的。(suppose)
3294. 如果我们误了火车——那该怎么办？(suppose)
3295. 以前中国的皇帝是国家的最高统治者。(supreme)
3296. 大理石的表面光滑而有光泽。(surface)
3297. 关于这一决定是否正确的疑虑开始显露了。(surface)
3298. 他的演出超出所有人的预料。(surpass)
3299. 各公司很可能继续裁减冗员，直至经济明显复苏。(surplus)
3300. 学校里有许多孩子都不住在镇里而是来自周围乡村。(surrounding)
3301. 调查表明，英国的树木都很健康。(survey)
3302. 我们对村里为人父母的人进行了全面的考察。(survey)
3303. 19%的被调查者说他们还没决定。(survey)

3304. 查尔斯比妻子多活了三个月。(survive)
3305. 在袭击过后,她幸存下来。(survive)
3306. 140 位乘客中,只有 12 人幸存。(survive)
3307. 我们都容易受广告的影响。(susceptible)
3308. 警方怀疑他和这次抢劫有关。(suspect)
3309. 他有杀人嫌疑。(suspect)
3310. 屋顶上吊着一盏很大的灯。(suspend)
3311. 两国的对话终止了。(suspend)
3312. 他那天的行为使警方产生了怀疑。(suspicious)
3313. 任何人看到可疑物品请立即与警方联系。(suspicious)
3314. 再次见到她是我的精神支柱。(sustain)
3315. 他们给我的食物几乎不够维持生活。(sustain)
3316. 一群蜜蜂 (swarm)
3317. 成群的游客熙熙攘攘地穿过广场。(swarm)
3318. 树木在微风中轻轻摇动。(sway)
3319. 不要在孩子们面前骂人。(swear)
3320. 你能以你的名誉发誓永远不会告诉任何人吗? (swear)
3321. 请帮我把地板打扫干净。(sweep)
3322. 雷暴席卷中国。(sweep)
3323. 我乘飞机旅行时脚踝就会肿。(swell)
3324. 人群逐渐扩大。(swell)
3325. 我的信得到迅速的答复。(swift)
3326. 弗兰克流利自如地由法语改说英语。(switch)
3327. 请把电视机关掉好吗? (switch)
3328. 今年英语课的教学大纲上安排了两部莎士比亚的戏剧。(symbol)
3329. 鸽子是和平的象征。(symbol)
3330. Fe 是铁的化学符号。(symbol)
3331. 在欧洲,白色象征纯洁。(symbolize)
3332. 房子的设计有一种赏心悦目的对称美。(symmetry)
3333. 琼,你没有表现出很大的同情心。(sympathetic)
3334. 党内有一批人赞成我们的目标。(sympathetic)

3335. 他们举办了多次研究动物保护问题的讨论会。(symposium)
3336. 人口迁移是城乡贫富悬殊的症状。(symptom)
3337. "闭上"是"关上"的近义词。(synonym)
3338. 这件夹克是人造材料做成的。(synthetic)
3339. 系统垮掉了。(system)
3340. 在现行体制下,我们没有任何灵活性。(system)
3341. 他们收集资料的方法条理性不够。(systematic)
3342. 关于电影明星私生活的传闻正是通俗小报所钟爱的消息。(tabloid)
3343. 在这个社会里,人们忌讳在公共场所流露感情。(taboo)
3344. 死亡是人们忌讳的话题。(taboo)
3345. 钓具已放在汽车里了。(tackle)
3346. 计算机可通过程序编制来处理各式各样的错误。(tackle)
3347. 你在行李上系上航空公司的标签了么? (tag)
3348. 我父亲20年来一直让同一个裁缝做他的衣服。(tailor)
3349. 我的确很想吃外卖的印度饭菜。(takeaway)
3350. 市中心有一家中国菜外卖餐馆。(takeaway)
3351. 她有明显的音乐天赋。(talent)
3352. 干这种工作需要有特殊的才能。(talent)
3353. 他是一位振奋人心的泳坛新秀。(talent)
3354. 英格兰队现在的积分是15分。(tally)
3355. 选票的数量与选民的人数不相符。(tally)
3356. 和他制作的其他电影比起来,这是一部枯燥无味的电影。(tame)
3357. 公园里的鸟十分温顺,它们会吃你亲手喂给它们的食物。(tame)
3358. 雕刻是一种可触摸的艺术形式。(tangible)
3359. 如果我们要采取法律行动,就需要实实在在的证据。(tangible)
3360. 我拍拍他的肩。(tap)
3361. 有人没关水龙头。(tap)
3362. 我不喜欢听磁带上自己的声音。(tape)
3363. 将照片用胶带贴在墙上。(tape)
3364. 如果我将谈话录下来,你介意吗? (tape)
3365. 冰箱一侧贴了两张图片。(tape)

3366. 这个地区被军队当做打靶练习区。(target)

3367. 取得英语方面的高学位是外国学生的目标。(target)

3368. 没有配置安全设备的汽车很容易被盗贼盯上。(target)

3369. 生火的活儿分给了我。(task)

3370. 我如何保护自己的投资免于课税？(taxation)

3371. 1337年至1362年之间没有向罗马教皇缴过赋税。(taxation)

3372. 他是2002年世界杯冠军的成员。(team)

3373. 并不是所有的技术用语我都理解。(technical)

3374. 按字面解释，这种做法违反了这一条约。(technical)

3375. 我们使用很多技巧来解决数学问题。(technique)

3376. 处理工业污染有很多工艺。(technique)

3377. 蒸汽机是19世纪最伟大的技术进步。(technique)

3378. 工艺技术的进步已促进农作物产量增长超过了百分之三十。(technology)

3379. 我在交通堵塞中度过了无聊的一个小时。(tedious)

3380. 英国的气候温和——既不酷热，又不严寒。(temperate)

3381. 他有耐心，自律和稳健的习惯。(temperate)

3382. 适度批评能激励人上进。(temperate)

3383. 我们演奏莫扎特这首乐曲的速度比原来演奏的速度要快。(tempo)

3384. 我现在和父母一起住，但只是暂时一起住。(temporary)

3385. 我知道在节食期间不该吃巧克力蛋糕，可我很难抗拒诱惑。(temptation)

3386. 房东若要收回房子得给房客"适当时间的提前通知"。(tenant)

3387. 索菲亚在卧室里照顾儿子。(tend)

3388. 越来越多的人趋向于把金钱看得比生活质量更重。(tendency)

3389. 孩子需要的是亲切而体贴的照顾。(tender)

3390. 梅菲尔德博士已提出辞职。(tender)

3391. 这家公司已经参加了三项新合同的竞标。(tender)

3392. 她试图使紧绷的肌肉放松下来。(tense)

3393. 马里恩因为急于打破令人紧张的沉默而说了一句话。(tense)

3394. 铁丝拉得不够紧，把它们再拉紧点。(tension)

3395. 你可以感受到我们等待考试结果时屋子里的紧张气氛。(tension)

3396. 最近的这次间谍事件使局势变得十分紧张。(tension)

3397. 在英国用来称呼财政部长的术语是"the Chancellor"。(term)

3398. 政府的任期年末届满。(term)

3399. 我们必须讨论一下你的雇佣条款。(term)

3400. 我与邻居的关系一直不错。(term)

3401. 法庭裁决，终止这一合同。(terminate)

3402. 我们的新房子是排屋中的最边上的一栋。(terrace)

3403. 我们的新地毯看上去真棒。(terrific)

3404. 这次会议将在中立国召开。(territory)

3405. 所有的人原先都认为这是一个无人居住的地区。(territory)

3406. 有三种预防，即第一级预防、第二级预防和第三极预防。(tertiary)

3407. 他们估计除中学、大专以及大学教员之外，还需要36万培训人员。(tertiary)

3408. 旁观者没人会出庭作证说他有罪。(testify)

3409. 未关的房门证明他走得很匆忙。(testify)

3410. 一张盘可以存储相当于500页文本的信息。(text)

3411. 他被指控盗窃俱乐部的资金。(theft)

3412. 他报告说他的护照被窃。(theft)

3413. 自然是弗罗斯特的诗歌中反复出现的一个主题。(theme)

3414. 该书的主题思想是爱与责任之间的冲突。(theme)

3415. 男女平等在我们这个社会还只停留在理论上。(theoretical)

3416. 我正在上一门政治理论课。(theory)

3417. 弗洛伊德的学说对心理学有很大的影响。(theory)

3418. 他于1978年成为公民，从而获得了选举权。(thereby)

3419. 他们的主论点是教育水平的提高引起收入的增加。(thesis)

3420. 他撰写了关于当代法国文学的博士论文。(thesis)

3421. 医生仔细思考了片刻，开始写处方。(thoughtful)

3422. 谢谢你打电话问我是否觉得好点，你很体贴人。(thoughtful)

3423. 她扬言要离开家里。(threaten)

3424. 他说这场战争危及全世界的和平。(threaten)

3425. 节俭的概念对我来说是陌生的。(thrift)

3426. 战前那些年里，他的生意兴旺。(thrive)

3427. 低潮时，岩石露了出来。(tide)

3428. 警方正在打击一轮犯罪高潮。(tide)
3429. 保持屋子整洁是非常困难的。(tidy)
3430. 地区建筑用木材大多是从南方引进的。(timber)
3431. 杰克是有总统才干的人。(timber)
3432. 汇率的变动使公司正在下跌的收益适时地得到增长。(timely)
3433. 你拿到今年最新的公车时间表了吗？(timetable)
3434. 今天第一节课老师就会发新的课程表。(timetable)
3435. "你还要一些蛋糕吗？""是的，要，一小块就够了。"(tiny)
3436. 这头长颈鹿被一枝顶端涂有毒药的矛刺死了。(tip)
3437. 不要那样向后倾斜你的椅子，你会摔倒的。(tip)
3438. 他们给了这个服务员五磅的小费。(tip)
3439. 基斯岛是指佛罗里达南端以外的珊瑚岛。(tip)
3440. 她的名字就在我的嘴边说不出来。(tip)
3441. 我们不必给服务员留小费，因为账单里包括了一项服务费。(tip)
3442. 她给了我一个有关种植西红柿的实用窍门。(tip)
3443. 核辐射能侵害活组织中的细胞。(tissue)
3444. 他用一块软布擦拭他的太阳镜。(tissue)
3445. 使用一次性餐巾纸比较卫生。(tissue)
3446. 我喜欢吃烤豆加吐司。(toast)
3447. 面包片冻着时也能烤。(toast)
3448. 在为他送别的聚会上，我们用香槟酒与他干杯。(toast)
3449. 我整个周末一直在辛辛苦苦地写这篇文章。(toil)
3450. 许多老年人特别怕冷。(tolerance)
3451. 过这座桥要付两英镑的通行费。(toll)
3452. 具不可靠消息说平民死亡人数达千人。(toll)
3453. 几个星期以来唯一的话题就是这场婚礼。(topic)
3454. 他把报纸向肩膀后面一抛。(toss)
3455. 他们以抛硬币来决定谁先走。(toss)
3456. 飞机被炸毁，机上人员全部遇难。(total)
3457. 他不是心肠硬，而是果断坚强。(tough)
3458. 许多小商店发现很难和大商店进行激烈的竞争。(tough)

3459. 他是本届锦标赛最佳拳击手。(tournament)

3460. 过量的维生素 D 可能产生毒性。(toxic)

3461. 官员们没能发现任何毒品的痕迹。(trace)

3462. 我看到桑德拉脸上掠过一丝微笑。(trace)

3463. 她已放弃了所有追查失踪女儿的希望。(trace)

3464. 他们追溯自己的祖先是来自于英格兰。(trace)

3465. 那只狐狸没留下任何足迹。(track)

3466. 跟踪他很难。(track)

3467. 两个兄弟都遵循家族传统，做了医生。(tradition)

3468. 改变这一计划是造成这一惨案的主要原因。(tragedy)

3469. 狗经过特殊训练能够追踪狐狸留下的踪迹。(trail)

3470. 尼克探身船外，手向后划水。(trail)

3471. 警察花了好几天时间跟踪那帮家伙。(trail)

3472. 安妮的慷慨是她最受人喜爱的品性之一。(trait)

3473. 一群流浪汉围坐在火炉边取暖。(tramp)

3474. 那天长途跋涉冒雪走回家。(tramp)

3475. 在外币兑换柜台进行的每一笔交易，似乎都要花很长时间。(transaction)

3476. 那家商店关门了，迁到别处去营业了。(transfer)

3477. 将这文档转存到软盘上。(transfer)

3478. 他的转会费为八百万英镑。(transfer)

3479. 应更严格地控制核物质的转移。(transfer)

3480. 人口的增长已经改变了这里的地形地貌。(transform)

3481. 新体系改变了经理人对金钱的看法。(transform)

3482. 里斯本是中转站，每个人都等着前往别的地方。(transit)

3483. 每个地区都有其综合的需求，需要公交系统、供水和排水系统，需要处理固体废物，还需要经济发展。(transit)

3484. 我的书已被翻译成许多种语言。(translate)

3485. 气温是 16 摄氏度，如果转换为华氏，则是 60 度。(translate)

3486. 这一系统通过数字电话线传送信息。(transmit)

3487. 蚊子将疟疾传染给人类。(transmit)

3488. 美国公开赛将体内各国卫星现场直播。(transmit)

3489. 植物在一个透明的塑料盒里,所以孩子们能够看到根的生长。(transparent)
3490. 我希望你的目标一目了然。(transparent)
3491. 一眼即被识破的谎言 (transparent)
3492. 春天来临之前植物应该种在室内,到了春天可以把它们移植到外面去。(transplant)
3493. 医生把一颗猴子的心脏移植到一个两岁的孩子的体内。(transplant)
3494. 缺少肝脏移植的器官捐献者。(transplant)
3495. 过去马匹是唯一的运输方式。(transport)
3496. 提高轨道运输系统对商业至关重要。(transport)
3497. 雕像被运到了伦敦。(transport)
3498. 看了一眼,我就被带回到了童年。(transport)
3499. 这个农夫在他的谷仓里设下了陷阱捉老鼠。(trap)
3500. 这个小男孩逮到了一只老鼠。(trap)
3501. 我们被骗入这样一种境地已经不是第一次了。(trap)
3502. 海盗的故事常包括搜寻被埋葬的珍宝。(treasure)
3503. 马尔萨发表了他的论人口问题的专著。(treatise)
3504. 治疗感冒的最佳方法是休息和多喝流质食物。(treatment)
3505. 对较小的发展中国家应给予特殊待遇。(treatment)
3506. 美国和越南签订了一项和平条约。(treaty)
3507. 一想到她发现真相后会发生的事,我就不寒而栗。(tremble)
3508. 火车经过时,整座屋子都在震颤。(tremble)
3509. 他强忍着怒火,但仍气得声音发抖。(tremble)
3510. 她在那幢房子上花了巨额钱款。(tremendous)
3511. 单身妈妈抚养孩子的趋势不断增强。(trend)
3512. 今年我们将检验一下厨房设计中的最新款。(trend)
3513. 这种新药正在接受临床试验。(trail)
3514. 未经审判就把人关进监牢是不民主的。(trail)
3515. 这个国家这个区域的居民每天都受到艰难生活的考验,精疲力竭。(trail)
3516. 三角形的三角总和为 180 度。(triangle)
3517. 许多过去自治的部落如今是一个更大的国家的一部分。(tribe)
3518. 有一群男孩沿着小径走过来。(tribe)
3519. 在英国,愚人节早上搞恶作剧是传统习俗。(trick)

3520. 诀窍是接球时要屈膝。(trick)
3521. 你似乎有点儿紧张。(trick)
3522. 我不明白你为什么把钱浪费在这类鸡毛蒜皮的小事上。(trifle)
3523. 他瞄准后扣动了扳机。(trigger)
3524. 盗贼碰响了警报器后逃之夭夭。(trigger)
3525. 食物过敏能导致几种精神病。(trigger)
3526. 他细心地修剪了头发。(trim)
3527. 我们有必要把国防预算再消减五亿美元。(trim)
3528. 看那些平整的草地和整洁的花园。(trim)
3529. 她身材匀称。(trim)
3530. 他给自己倒一杯三杯量的威士忌。(triple)
3531. 他们要的钱是我们预料的三倍。(triple)
3532. 这家公司的销售量在三年中增至三倍。(triple)
3533. 为一个似乎微不足道的问题打扰您,我感到抱歉。(trivial)
3534. 使计算机懂得人类语言不是一个简单的问题。(trivial)
3535. 她是个植物学家,花了几年时间在热带地区搞研究。(tropic)
3536. 树皮保护树干和树枝免受极端温度的伤害。(trunk)
3537. 这些用来锻炼躯干的肌肉。(trunk)
3538. 我们将所有的装备都装入了几个铁皮箱子里,然后就乘火车出发了。(trunk)
3539. 电视应该是可靠的信息来源,从中公众可以知道发生的事情。(trustworthy)
3540. 我刚开始上大学的时候,一季度的学费是 350 美元。(tuition)
3541. 我的数学得接受课外辅导。(tuition)
3542. 大海波涛汹涌,我们无法出海。(turbulent)
3543. 只有很少的人来听这么著名的演讲者的演讲,真令人失望。(turnout)
3544. 这个团体的人员更迭极快。(turnover)
3545. 年营业额约为 90 亿英镑。(turnover)
3546. 他们雇了位私人教师帮卡罗斯提高英语。(tutor)
3547. 她是我在德勒姆的导师。(tutor)
3548. 牛津大学一对一的导师个别辅导很有效,但却是一种成本很高的教学方式。(tutorial)
3549. 黄昏时分你们很可能会看到这些动物,它们这时开始夜巡猎食了。(twilight)
3550. 她的祖父用他暮年的大部分时间写一本法国历史。(twilight)

3551. 我和我的兄弟长得太像了，人们经常认为我们是双胞胎。(twin)
3552. 他仰望头顶上方夜空的闪烁繁星。(twinkle)
3553. 马克的双眼洋溢着笑意，闪闪发光。(twinkle)
3554. 这是典型的热带天气。(typical)
3555. 她一向对此都很生气。(typical)
3556. 试验的最终结果不能预知。(ultimate)
3557. 我们的终极目标是国会里女性议员的数量和男性的一样多。(ultimate)
3558. 女性裸体画肯定是对艺术技巧的基本检验。(ultimate)
3559. 一切最终都将取决于下周和董事的讨论。(ultimately)
3560. 评论家们几乎都不喜欢这部电影。(unanimous)
3561. 公司经历了几次重大变化。(undergo)
3562. 他们是在剑桥念本科的时候认识的。(undergraduate)
3563. 出于需要，地铁不断扩展。(underground)
3564. 20世纪30年代，他的父亲在共产党地下组织工作。(underground)
3565. 他作为秘密运动的组织者返回了顺化。(underground)
3566. 接到这一邀请及所代表的来之不易的尊重让我感到很骄傲。(underlie)
3567. 社会问题和贫困问题引发当今大城市的很多犯罪现象。(underlie)
3568. 所有术语下面都划了红线。(underline)
3569. 这一系列胜利将加强他们对超级球队地位的要求。(underline)
3570. 约翰逊博士接受了撰写一本综合性的英语字典的任务。(undertake)
3571. 他保证六个月后还钱。(undertake)
3572. 卡尔打开地图，把它铺在桌子上。(unfold)
3573. 随着故事的展开，我们对马克的童年了解得更多了。(unfold)
3574. 那是一件非常不幸的事故。(unfortunate)
3575. 他还穿着学校的制服。(uniform)
3576. 反应器里各个部分的温度必须保持不变。(uniform)
3577. A级鸡蛋必须大小统一。(uniform)
3578. 对战争的大力支持令全国上下同仇敌忾。(unify)
3579. 他的音乐将传统主题和现代主题融为一体。(unify)
3580. 她具有无与伦比的能力，能和所有动物进行交流。(unique)
3581. 每个人的指纹都是绝无仅有的。(unique)

3582. 卓别林是一位受大众喜爱的喜剧演员。(universal)

3583. 世界毁灭的威胁笼罩着全球。(universal)

3584. 他是一个多才多艺的天才。(universal)

3585. 他们认为地球是宇宙的中心。(universe)

3586. 他们不大可能有亲戚住在附近。(unlikely)

3587. 非官方来源说，骚乱中100多人被击毙。(unofficial)

3588. 本世纪见证了环境受到前所未有的大规模的破坏。(unprecedented)

3589. 我们将全天向您报道这条新闻的最新动态。(update)

3590. 邮寄名单最近一次更新是什么时候？(update)

3591. 我们可以让您升级到商务舱。(upgrade)

3592. 他们想坚持传统的家庭价值观念。(uphold)

3593. 他的判决上诉后维持原判。(uphold)

3594. 我们把一罐油漆打翻在地毯上。(upset)

3595. 我并不想打扰你。(upset)

3596. 他不能吃葡萄——那会使他的胃不舒服。(upset)

3597. 越来越多的人正迁往市区。(urban)

3598. 最要紧的是确保每个人都已经离开了大楼。(urgent)

3599. 抽屉里是一些厨房用品，有勺子、铲子、刀子和搅拌器。(utensil)

3600. 消防队的老楼可以用作剧场。(utilize)

3601. 我们对公众安全极为重视。(utmost)

3602. 孩子们没完没了地要求使她的耐心受了最大限度的考验。(utmost)

3603. 在岛的另一边，景色完全不同。(utterly)

3604. 我们本想七月份在旅馆订一间房，但已经没有空房了。(vacancy)

3605. 我们销售部有几个职位空缺。(vacancy)

3606. 只有几套公寓仍然空着。(vacant)

3607. 今天据称大约有100个全日制工作岗位空缺。(vacant)

3608. 卢克被迫取消全家到阿卡普尔科的度假。(vacation)

3609. 伯恩斯坦夫妇正在欧洲度假。(vacation)

3610. 声波在真空中无法传播。(vacuum)

3611. 法律规范和定义常常是模模糊糊的。(vague)

3612. 她是那种很爱虚荣的人，每到一面镜子前非要照一照之后才会走。(vain)

3613. 我们把桌子和椅子都摆到了花园里,天却下起雨来了,因此我们的努力全白费了。(vain)
3614. 警官必须有令人信服的理由才能让人停车。(valid)
3615. 您的返程机票的有效期为三个月。(valid)
3616. 这是块漂亮的地毯,一定能够保值。(value)
3617. 美元的价值在稳步上升。(value)
3618. 一群运动员给学生们讲大学教育的重要性。(value)
3619. 那些价值超过20万美元的油画在她家被盗。(value)
3620. 雪莉很重视自己的隐私。(value)
3621. 汽车消失不见了。(vanish)
3622. 南美的许多动物已经灭绝。(vanish)
3623. 暖一些的空气比冷空气能容纳更多的水蒸气,因此湿度也就更高。(vapour)
3624. 试验中有太多可变因素,因此很难精确预言实验结果。(variables)
3625. 其实,白面包只是法式面包的变体。(variation)
3626. 这一研究表明,不同的CD播放器的差异很小。(variation)
3627. 女孩们来自各种各样的背景。(variety)
3628. 湖里有20多种鱼。(variety)
3629. 有各种方式来回答你的问题。(various)
3630. 植物的高度从8厘米到20厘米不等。(vary)
3631. 大面积的亚马逊雨林都被毁坏了。(vast)
3632. 政府将不得不借贷大量资金。(vast)
3633. 她是一个严格的素食主义者。(vegetarian)
3634. 森林的地面上植物并不茂盛。(vegetation)
3635. 你的车锁了吗? (vehicle)
3636. 弗莱明胜利地回到舞台,这是最好的手段。(vehicle)
3637. 他觉得那项投机过于冒险了,因此不想参与。(venture)
3638. 如果我有足够的钱,我也许真的会涉足广告行业。(venture)
3639. 乐队将在尽可能多的场地进行演出。(venue)
3640. 她把车子停在路边,沿着路边植草带走到了紧急电话那儿。(verge)
3641. 你能证明你的理论吗? (verify)
3642. 多才多艺的表演者 (versatile)
3643. 尼龙是一种有多种用途的材料。(versatile)

3644. 多娜对那晚发生的事情的描述准确吗？(version)

3645. 大多数人都同意意大利版听起来更好。(version)

3646. 中国队对意大利队 (versus)

3647. 周五美元相对其他主要货币贬值了。(versus)

3648. 大乌龟可以活150年，是脊椎动物中寿命最长的。(vertebrate)

3649. 鸟类、鱼类和哺乳动物都是脊椎动物。(vertebrate)

3650. 一条垂直线把这一页分成两半。(vertical)

3651. 在他的航运事业高峰期，他拥有60艘远洋船只。(vessel)

3652. 他们将一只大炊具装满了蔬菜，然后放到营火上面焖。(vessel)

3653. 心脏病发作是有输送血液到心肌的血管堵塞造成的。(vessel)

3654. 国防部有权否决所有英国武器出口。(veto)

3655. 政府否决了这个提案。(veto)

3656. 我们途经巴黎飞往雅典。(via)

3657. 您可以通过因特网进入我们的主页。(via)

3658. 细菌在温度达65摄氏度时还能生长，而且几近沸点时仍能存活。(viable)

3659. 什么时候潮汐发电机可望成功？(viable)

3660. 国会已经同意向飓风受灾难民提供经济援助。(victim)

3661. 这是走向胜利道路上迈出的第一步。(victory)

3662. 将大力为失业人员找到其他工作。(vigorous)

3663. 34名抗议者由于违反刑法而被捕。(violate)

3664. 盗窃案的受害者常常感到私人生活受到了侵犯。(violate)

3665. 首相已经拒绝与恐怖主义者谈判，除非他们放弃暴力。(violence)

3666. 生活在乡下的话，拥有一辆车实际上很有必要。(virtual)

3667. 我们接受某些宗教原则和传统美德。(virtue)

3668. 这个计划的长处之一是它的实施费用比较低。(virtue)

3669. 据估计超过3000万人感染了这一病毒。(virus)

3670. 不可能从电子邮件本身中毒。(virus)

3671. 我得到了去德国的签证。(visa)

3672. 山脉的轮廓清晰可见。(visible)

3673. 检查一下这株植物，看看有没有明显的得病迹象。(visible)

3674. 泪水模糊了她的视线。(vision)

3675. 总统简要地概括了他对未来的憧憬。(vision)

3676. 艺术家将他们的理念转变成了视觉形象。(visual)

3677. 这些措施对国家安全极其重要。(vital)

3678. 她穿着一条色彩鲜艳的粉红色裙子。(vivid)

3679. 我童年时代的一些片段还是这么栩栩如生,就好像是昨天的记忆。(vivid)

3680. 阅读是扩大词汇量的最佳方法之一。(vocabulary)

3681. 此后,学生开始参加职业培训和实习。(vocational)

3682. 松糕鞋又重新流行了。(vogue)

3683. 花卉地毯变成了时髦货。(vogue)

3684. 他听出了我的声音。(voice)

3685. 非洲代表表达了他们愤怒。(voice)

3686. 火山喷射出大量的灰尘进入大气平流层。(volcano)

3687. 1940 年至 1945 年这一阶段在第九册。(volume)

3688. 这一容器的容积为一万立方米。(volume)

3689. 近年来道路交通量迅猛增长。(volume)

3690. 她给红十字会做了很多志愿工作。(voluntary)

3691. "保健诊所"依靠志愿者管理办公室和接电话。(volunteer)

3692. 过去从英国航行到印度要用六个月。(voyage)

3693. 孤独生活的老人尤其脆弱。(vulnerable)

3694. 俄国漫长的战线非常容易受到德国攻击。(vulnerable)

3695. 他们为提高工资和改善工作条件而罢工。(wage)

3696. 产业界同保守党一起开展了一场全面的反国有化运动。(wage)

3697. 我们在这座港口小镇四处漫步。(wander)

3698. 他觉察到我心不在焉。(wander)

3699. 她神志开始有点恍惚了,有时认不出我是谁。(wander)

3700. 她负责三间不同的病房。(ward)

3701. 她父母死后,她被指定由法院监护。(ward)

3702. 辟邪的戒指 (ward)

3703. 我们来织条地毯吧。(weave)

3704. 我喜欢他笔下精心构筑的情节。(weave)

3705. 它大约 12 磅重。(weight)

3706. 他似乎很快乐，只是他体重增加了很多。(weight)
3707. 我不能干重活，也不能再拿重的东西。(weight)
3708. 他没有疯，但却是有些怪。(weird)
3709. 我们唯一关心的是孩子的福利。(welfare)
3710. 商业决策人认为假期对他们的康乐至关重要。(well-being)
3711. 老系统相当复杂，但是新系统却实在很简单。(whereas)
3712. 这个购物中心设计了一个计划，经常购物的顾客可以通过它获得折扣。(whereby)
3713. 上个月批发价格下跌了。(wholesale)
3714. 我们只批发，不零售。(wholesale)
3715. 这对婴儿和父母都有良好影响。(wholesome)
3716. 当然，这个邪恶的巫婆最后被处死了。(wicked)
3717. 一则广泛范围的调查发现工人的不满情绪日渐高涨。(wide-ranging)
3718. 暴风雨带来大面积的损失。(widespread)
3719. 这次战争拥有广泛的支持。(widespread)
3720. 地毯的宽度足以覆盖楼梯。(width)
3721. 我开始习惯于美国街道的宽阔。(width)
3722. 她说阿拉斯加州是最后一片大荒原。(wilderness)
3723. 这些化学药品会毁灭庄稼和一切野生生物。(wildlife)
3724. 这一合并可能意味着股东会获得22亿美元的意外之财。(windfall)
3725. 人们的常识是男孩子比女孩子成熟得慢一些。(wisdom)
3726. 当地人置疑将如此多的钱花在新修一条路上是否明智。(wisdom)
3727. 她有着具感染力的微笑，而且非常机智敏锐。(wit)
3728. 奥斯卡·王尔德是个著名的说话风趣的人。(wit)
3729. 如果父母乐意，他们有权不让孩子上宗教教育课。(withdraw)
3730. 我想从账户中取出500英镑。(withdraw)
3731. 多番劝说之后，他同意撤回辞呈。(withdraw)
3732. 他们必须把墙壁筑得非常牢固以经受住大风。(withstand)
3733. 一位事故的目击者说，司机看起来好像喝醉了。(witness)
3734. 几个居民声称亲眼看到了袭击行动。(witness)
3735. 托尼·理查森承认自己是个工作狂，他记不起上次休假是什么时候了。(workaholic)
3736. 公司正在裁员。(workforce)

3737. 现在妇女代表大约一半的劳动力。(workforce)

3738. 他们主办了很多研讨会和讲习班。(workshop)

3739. 音乐会吸引了全球十几亿的电视观众。(worldwide)

3740. 他强烈反对年轻人中普遍存在的金钱崇拜。(worship)

3741. 他们经常去拜神。(worship)

3742. 囚犯不允许拜他们自己的神。(worship)

3743. 食品必须加包装以便隔绝空气。(wrap)

3744. 许多西班牙船只曾在北美近海海域失事。(wreck)

3745. 我没有很好地按说明书说的去做，结果把好端端的一台立体音响弄坏了。(wreck)

3746. 沉船所在的海底平坦而多岩石。(wreck)

3747. 横坐标轴标注了对生产的关注。(x-axis)

3748. 这两地的劳动力价格在纵坐标轴上有所表现。(y-axis)

3749. 有时我只是渴望一人独处。(yearn)

3750. 与管理方的会谈没能产生任何结果。(yield)

3751. "我们不会对压力屈服，"总统说道。(yield)

3752. 在过去的50年中，美国的农作物产量以每年1%—2%的速度稳步增长。(yield)

3753. 我们努力为考试中没有取得理想成绩的年轻人找到上学的机会。(youngster)

3754. 我对我的工作投入了极大的热情。(zeal)

3755. 汤姆感到生活中有些乐趣已经消失了。(zest)

3756. 旧金山处在地震带。(zone)

3757. 政府建立了一个经济特区来促进私企的发展。(zone)

答 案

1. They were accused of abandoning their own principles.
2. "Dr" is the written abbreviation of "Doctor".
3. The health center serves all the people, regardless of their ability to pay.
4. They have an abnormal interest in drinking.
5. They managed to wipe out the entire aboriginal population.
6. Plants absorb carbon dioxide.
7. Have you absorbed all the details of the plan?
8. She was absorbed in her thoughts.
9. He was asked to make an abstract of the novel.
10. Human beings are the only creatures capable of abstract thought.
11. Your problem is that you can not abstract the important points from the lectures.
12. His imagination so abstracted him that his name was called twice before he answered.
13. Drug and alcohol abuse contributed to Peter's early death.
14. I never expected that he would abuse the trust I placed in him.
15. People who were abused as children often turn into child-abusers themselves.
16. He possessed no academic qualifications.
17. Her husband is working in the Chinese Academy of Sciences.
18. This thesis deals with the functions of the academy in modern society.
19. The car accelerated to overtake the bus.
20. They use special chemical substances to accelerate the growth of crops.
21. Access to the papers is restricted to senior management.
22. Access is by means of a small door on the right.
23. The new technology was acclaimed as a medical breakthrough.
24. The island was used to accommodate child refugees.
25. Her eyes took a while to accommodate to the darkness.
26. Children under 14 must be accompanied by an adult.

27. The disease is accompanied by sneezing and fever.
28. How were they able to accomplish so much so quickly?
29. The accomplishment of this policy goal took 6 months.
30. Cutting the budget was an impressive accomplishment.
31. I believe you gave a very good account of what happened.
32. I would like to open an account with you.
33. We'll certainly take your feelings into account.
34. How do you account for the dent in the car?
35. Computer software accounts for 70 percent of our range of products.
36. Fat tends to accumulate around the hips and thighs.
37. It is difficult to get accurate figures on population numbers.
38. He was accused of robbery.
39. It'll take time for me to accustom myself to the changes.
40. She eventually achieved her goal of becoming a professor.
41. These oranges are very acid.
42. When she spoke, her tone was acid.
43. Vinegar is an acid.
44. Both defendants refused to acknowledge the authority of the court.
45. We wish to acknowledge to the support of the university.
46. Tom acknowledged her presence by a brief glance.
47. He has a lot of business acquaintances but few real friends.
48. He got the job through his acquaintance with the President.
49. The college acquired a reputation for very high standards.
50. He spent many years on acquiring his skills as a surgeon.
51. Their team was devoted to the acquisition of new sites for further development of their firm.
52. The Art Society is holding an exhibition of recent acquisitions.
53. The fish's sense of smell is very acute.
54. The children are finding it hard to adapt to the new school.
55. Many children buy the books that have been adapted for television programs.
56. He was addicted to chocolate.
57. He took out his pen and wrote down his name and address.
58. She gave an address to the Royal Academy.
59. She addressed the letter and stuck a stamp on it.

60. You will have to address your complaints to the head office.
61. The adequacy of treatment with antibiotics has been tested.
62. Her performance is adequate but lacks originality.
63. The company has yet not provided an adequate explanation for its actions.
64. The eggs of these fish adhere to plant leaves.
65. We adhere to the principle of equal rights and freedom of expression for all.
66. We stayed in adjacent rooms.
67. My parents had trouble adjusting to living in an apartment.
68. The territory had been administered by South Africa.
69. The test was administered fairly and impartially.
70. We are looking for someone with experience in administration.
71. The problem has been ignored by the Nixon Administration.
72. I've always admired her paintings.
73. We stopped half way up the hill to admire the view.
74. Admission to the exhibition will be by invitation only.
75. The court may interpret your silence as an admission of guilt.
76. They would charge 5 yuan admission.
77. He admitted his guilt/ mistake.
78. Only ticket holders will be admitted into the stadium.
79. The party was full of spotty adolescents.
80. He is so adolescent sometimes.
81. California has adopted a tough stance on the issue.
82. Congress finally adopted the law after two-year debate.
83. The couple are unable to have children of their own, but hope to adopt.
84. She adored her sister.
85. People will adore this film.
86. Some children found it hard to talk to adults.
87. He lived most of his adult life in Scotland.
88. The film is rated R for the language and adult themes.
89. He arrived half an hour in advance.
90. Remarkable advances have been made recently in medicine.
91. We have advanced greatly in our knowledge of the universe.
92. One of the many advantages of living in New York is that you can eat out at almost any time of

day.
93. She had some exciting adventures in Egypt.
94. They received a lot of adverse publicity about the changes.
95. We decided to advertise our car in the local newspaper.
96. He has always advertised his willingness to talk to the press.
97. She is a passionate advocate of natural childbirth.
98. He is the advocate of the defence in that case.
99. Extremists were openly advocating violence.
100. From an aesthetic point of view, it's a nice design.
101. The chair may be aesthetic but it's not very comfortable.
102. One of the central questions in aesthetics is whether beauty is in the eye of the beholder, or whether there is something within itself which makes it beautiful.
103. We were all deeply affected by her death.
104. She had little affection for him and certainly didn't love him.
105. He tried to win her affections by bringing her flowers.
106. The suspect affirmed that he had been at home all evening.
107. She gave an affirmative answer to his question.
108. He did not feel very affirmative about what was happening.
109. They both come from relatively affluent families.
110. The government set an agenda for constitutional reform.
111. Attempts to restrict parking in the city center have further aggravated the problem of traffic congestion.
112. The smaller minorities got an aggregate of 1,327 votes.
113. Sheila's earning from all sources aggregated $100,000.
114. He has been granted the legal aid.
115. She looked around in alarm.
116. The alarm went off.
117. He accepted the job, albeit with some hesitation.
118. I never touch alcohol in any form.
119. Most wines contain between 10% and 15% alcohol.
120. It is a country that has had an alien government and an alien language imposed on it by force.
121. On arrival in the United Kingdom you must report to the Aliens Registration Office.
122. All these changes to the newspaper have alienated its traditional readers.

123. The two men alleged that the police forced them to make false confessions.
124. This money should alleviate our financial problem.
125. One million dollars was allocated for disaster relief.
126. While he was at college, his parents gave him such small allowance that he had to earn extra money working in a restaurant.
127. When I go abroad, I hardly ever use all my duty-free allowance.
128. Her faces had not altered much over the years.
129. I had no alternative but to report him to the police.
130. Have you any alternative suggestions?
131. We are currently flying an altitude of 10,000 meters.
132. It was a very amateur performance.
133. John amazed his friends by suddenly getting married.
134. The language in the Minister's statement is highly ambiguous.
135. His ambition is ultimately to run his own business.
136. Foreign aid is badly needed to ameliorate the effects of the flood.
137. The defendant later amended his evidence.
138. You'll have ample opportunities to ask questions after the talk.
139. At school she always would be devising games to amuse her classmates.
140. She drew an analogy between childbirth and the creative process.
141. The cell samples are analyzed by a lab.
142. Further analysis of the data is needed.
143. There were portraits of his ancestor on the walls of the room.
144. He came from an ancient Catholic family.
145. It was announced that the Prime Minister would speak on television that evening.
146. He announced to his wife that he was leaving.
147. You're just saying that to annoy me.
148. The jazz festival has become an annual event.
149. Sales are better than anticipate.
150. I apologize for my late arrival.
151. The new piece of apparatus was used in the experiment.
152. It soon became apparent that we had a major problem.
153. All the organizations involved have sent urgent appeal to the government, asking for extra funding.

154. All prisoners have a right of appeal.
155. The program has a very wide appeal.
156. She is not happy with the decision and plans to appeal.
157. Farmers have appealed to the government for help.
158. The idea of working abroad really appeals to me.
159. The two sisters are remarkably alike in appearance.
160. The fight was soon stopped, thanks to the prompt appearance of the police.
161. The results of client survey are appended to this document.
162. Christine had to go into hospital to have her appendix out.
163. Sudden decrease of appetite is sometimes a sign of illness.
164. Paul has no appetite for had work.
165. The children applauded at the end of the song.
166. These changes will be applauded.
167. I have applied for another job.
168. He wants a job in which he can apply his foreign languages.
169. This chart no longer applies.
170. I'd like to make an appointment to see one of the doctors this morning.
171. He congratulated me on my appointment as editor.
172. I appreciate your concern, but honestly, I'm fine.
173. Her abilities are not fully appreciated by her employer.
174. Most investments are expected to appreciate at a steady rate.
175. Our approach frightened the birds.
176. He decided to adopt a different approach and teach *The Bible* through story-telling.
177. She heard footsteps approaching.
178. I did not feel that this was an appropriate time to mention the subject of money.
179. I don't approve of cosmetic surgery.
180. The conference approved a proposal for a referendum.
181. What is the approximate number of students in each class?
182. This figure approximates to a quarter of the UK's annual consumption.
183. He had an aptitude for journalism.
184. Our decision to go to Italy this summer rather than Spain was quite arbitrary.
185. Many areas of Africa have suffered severe drought this year.
186. The course covers three main subject areas.

187. We were surprised to see a new candidate enter the arena just before the election.
188. I broke the vase during an argument with my husband.
189. We need to provide a convincing argument as to why the system should be changed.
190. The new law has aroused much public concern.
191. The list is arranged alphabetically.
192. Contact your local branch to arrange an appointment.
193. There was a vast array of colors to choose from.
194. an article of furniture
195. Guests are advised not to leave any articles of value in their hotel rooms.
196. There was an interesting article on education in the paper yesterday.
197. The invasion contravened article 51 of the UN Charter.
198. At the age of 80, she was still sharp-witted and articulate.
199. Do you think that women are more able than men to articulate the feelings?
200. I don't like wearing clothes made of artificial fibers.
201. Their cheerfulness seemed rather strained and artificial.
202. The divers have begun to ascend to the surface of the water.
203. Dealing with people is the most important aspect of my work.
204. A large crowd had assembled outside the American embassy.
205. It is nonsense to assert that smoking does not damage people's health.
206. The value of the business was assessed at £1.25 million.
207. The technique is being tried in classrooms to assess what effect it may have.
208. He owns a corporation with $9 billion in assets.
209. I think Rachel would be an asset to the department.
210. Assign each student a partner.
211. Jane's been assigned to the Asian Affairs Bureau.
212. He was killed while on assignment abroad.
213. He was informed of his assignment as vice-consul in Liverpool.
214. You will be employed to assist in the development of new equipment.
215. Jone was one of his business associates.
216. Bloodshed is an associate to war.
217. Peter used to be an associate judge.
218. Sarah was the associate editor of the *Vogue* magazine.
219. At the conference I met many friends from associate organizations.

220. I do not associate him with sports.
221. He did not associate himself with the pro-democracy movement.
222. I don't like these layabouts you're associating with.
223. a small bunch of assorted wild flowers
224. The theory assumes that both labour and capital are mobile.
225. I didn't see your car, so I assumed you'd gone out.
226. Whoever they appoint will assume responsibility for all financial matters.
227. A lot of people make the assumption that poverty only exists in the Third World.
228. His air of assumption made him disliked.
229. The document is genuine, I can assure you.
230. Excellent reviews have assured the film's success.
231. Her political future looks assured.
232. He is generally a self-assured person.
233. You may be assured that everything is all right.
234. It astonishes me that they are getting divorced.
235. Check where Minnesota is in your atlas.
236. The atmospheres of Mars and the Earth are very different.
237. The atmosphere in the room was so stuffy that I could hardly breathe.
238. There's a very friendly atmosphere in our office.
239. A molecule of carbon dioxide (CO_2) has one carbon atom and two oxygen atoms.
240. Attach a recent photograph to your application form.
241. Please fill in and return the attached reply slip.
242. It's easy to become attached to the people you work with.
243. Enemy forces have made an attack on/against the city.
244. Most wild animals won't attack humans unless they are provoked.
245. The government has come under attack from all sides for cutting education spending.
246. She wrote an article attacking the judges and their conduct of the trial.
247. After a year she had attained her ideal weight.
248. He attempted a joke, but it was received in silence.
249. This bomb is the third attempt on the President's life this year.
250. A large number of people attended the funeral.
251. Which school do your children attend?
252. Peter's attitude towards women really scares me.

253. He later became a prominent attorney.
254. These flowers are brightly coloured in order to attract butterflies.
255. The fall in the number of deaths from heart disease is generally attributed to improvements in diet.
256. One should not attribute human motives to animals.
257. What attributes should a good manager possess?
258. Her latest book should appeal to a large audience.
259. The accounts have to be audited by a firm of external auditors.
260. The company has an audit at the end of each financial year.
261. With the birth of his third son, he found it necessary to do something to augment his income.
262. The book gave an authentic account of the awful war.
263. He was the author of two books on China.
264. Mr. Li is a leading authority on Chinese food.
265. The U.S. and Columbian authorities tried to reach an agreement.
266. Could I speak to someone in authority please?
267. Cash machines automate two basic functions of a bank—deposits and withdrawals.
268. An automatic weapon continues to shoot bullets until you take your finger off the trigger.
269. Citizenship is automatic for children born in this country.
270. Life would be impossible if digestion wasn't an automatic process.
271. When there is power shortage, they are counting on the auxiliary power supply.
272. Tickets are available from the box office.
273. One of the world's most beautiful avenues is the Champs Elysees in Paris.
274. We must explore every avenue before admitting defeat.
275. The average age of teachers was thirty-eight years in 1996.
276. We don't want Einstein, just someone of average ability.
277. Prices have risen by an average of 3% over the past year.
278. In Western Europe, a 7-to-8-hour working day is about the average.
279. They were pilots in the early days of aviation.
280. The children are not aware of the danger of taking drugs.
281. He responded well to a very awkward situation.
282. an awkward posture
283. In the background is a tall pine tree.
284. Their marriage will never work. Their backgrounds are too different.

285. Bacteria in drinking water have spread the illness.
286. At the meeting, we all had to wear badges with our names on.
287. The porter helped her into the taxi with her baggage.
288. We all carry a lot of emotional baggage around with us.
289. She had to hold onto the railings to keep her balance.
290. I had to balance the children's needs against my own.
291. Demand and supply could be balanced.
292. The party leader is elected by secret ballot.
293. Staff balloted for strike action yesterday.
294. There should be a ban on talking and eating loudly in cinemas.
295. Smoking is banned in this restaurant.
296. The Beatles are probably the most famous band in the world.
297. Radio signals are transmitted in different bands.
298. Please describe all the information in the bar chart below.
299. What time does the bar close?
300. There weren't any free tables, so I sat on a stool at the bar.
301. a bar of chocolate
302. Don't walk around outside in your bare feet.
303. Their flat has a bare wooden floor.
304. The management and employees eventually made a bargain.
305. The coat was half-price, a real bargain.
306. Trade unions bargain with employers for better conditions of pay and employment.
307. They heard a dog barking outside.
308. The sergeant barked a succession of orders to the new recruits.
309. The land still remained barren.
310. Barren women are rejected by the tribesmen.
311. The mountains form a natural barrier between the two countries.
312. The language barrier makes debate impossible.
313. She just bought a book called *The Basic of Cooking*.
314. The farm lacks even basic equipment.
315. Their claim had no basis in a fact.
316. Bread forms the basis of their daily diet.
317. The general was killed in a battle.

318. The government fought two decisive battles against the National Union of Mineworkers.
319. I could see the beam of his flashlight waving around in the dark.
320. This disaster was more than some of them could bear.
321. It would be unjust for him to bear personally the great expenses involved.
322. I doubt if that chair will bear your weight.
323. Lying in their tent, they could hear the noises of wild beasts moving about in the darkness outside.
324. I knew she was coming that afternoon because she had phoned beforehand to say so.
325. She asked the doctor to speak to her parents on her behalf.
326. The headmaster will not tolerate bad behavior in class.
327. Despite of her behavior off-stage her performances set a new benchmark for singers throughout the world.
328. He bent down and undid the laces.
329. Bend your arms and then stretch them upwards.
330. Most of the effects of science are really quite beneficial to people.
331. I hope that the decision taken today will be to the benefit of the whole nation.
332. You might be entitled to housing benefit.
333. They are working together to benefit the whole community.
334. We do not sell any alcoholic beverages.
335. A new environment can bewilder and frighten a child.
336. Students were evaluated without bias or favoritism.
337. Several factors could have biased the results of the study.
338. Please consult the bibliography for all the books having been referred to.
339. His hands were bound behind the post.
340. My sister's dog bit me.
341. Are the fish biting today?
342. He had some bizarre conversations with his friend.
343. George blames his mother for his lack of confidence.
344. She put the blame on him for the accident.
345. I never know what Jane's thinking—she has such a blank expression.
346. There's a blank space at the bottom of the form for you to sign your name in.
347. Blend the butter and sugar together.
348. This coffee is a rich blend of the best beans, it says on the label.

349. Fortunately we were blessed with fine weather.
350. The priest blessed the people in church, saying "God be with you".
351. Bless you!
352. a large block of ice
353. The museum is just six blocks away.
354. A fallen tree is blocking the road.
355. Their garden was full of wonderful blooms.
356. These flowers will bloom all through the summer.
357. She's been blooming since she came out of hospital.
358. After signing my name I blotted the paper.
359. The wind was blowing harder every minute.
360. On the beach the letter blew away and I had to run after it.
361. The whistle blew for halftime.
362. He was caught trying to steal the blueprint of a top-secret missile system.
363. It is unlikely that their blueprint for economic reform will be put into action.
364. My pencil's blunt.
365. Let me ask a blunt question.
366. He boasted that it was the most expensive film ever made.
367. When the water has boiled let it cool.
368. She didn't know how to boil an egg.
369. It's a bold venture starting a business these days.
370. This sentence is in bold type.
371. The troops bombarded the city, killing and injuring hundreds.
372. After he had stopped speaking, the students bombarded him with questions.
373. He was released on bond.
374. The very act seemed to strengthen her bond with me.
375. My father put all his money into stock market bonds.
376. It takes less than 10 minutes for the two surfaces to bond.
377. He paid me and added a bonus for the new customer I had signed up.
378. We heard a boom in the distance as the boom in the distance as the bomb went off.
379. This year has seen a boom in book sales.
380. The cannons boomed in the night.
381. The leisure industry is booming here.

382. The new resort area has boosted tourism.
383. She was involved in a campaign to boost new fashions.
384. Our company's booth at the exhibition was right next to our main competitor.
385. a telephone booth
386. The train crosses the border between France and Germany.
387. I never bother to iron my shirts.
388. What bothers me is that it won't be legal.
389. Don't bother me with little things like that.
390. You have to stay within your country boundary.
391. He gave a low bow to the audience.
392. They bowed to the Queen before speaking.
393. They bragged that they had never been beaten.
394. Kirby had a sudden brainstorm.
395. Employees get together and brainstorm ideas.
396. The trees were leafless except for the topmost branches.
397. Report to the Branch Manager as soon as you've settled in.
398. Immunology is branch of biological science.
399. What brand of shampoo do you use?
400. The blackbird, like most birds, breeds in the spring.
401. The American Civil Liberties Union filed a brief opposing the decision.
402. Green spent a brief time at Cambridge.
403. The president has been fully briefed on the current situation in Haiti.
404. They brought home heaps of travel brochures.
405. His arms and back were covered in bruises.
406. One or two of the peaches had bruises on them which I had to cut out.
407. In the garden most of the plants are in bud.
408. The trees had already put out their leaves and there were buds everywhere.
409. The budget for photography has been cut.
410. This scheme enables you to budget the cost through fixed monthly payments.
411. The dough will rise until it is double in bulk.
412. The bulk of consumers are based in towns.
413. The office buys paper in bulk to keep down costs.
414. We can bulk out the report with lots of diagrams.

415. I've bumped my head on that shelf again!
416. We bumped along the track in our car holding on to our seats.
417. I bought a bunch of bananas.
418. The cat chased a mouse into its burrow.
419. The worm burrowed its way under the earth.
420. The river was threatening to burst its banks.
421. I knew they were bursting with curiosity but I said nothing.
422. The children burst into the room.
423. I usually eat in the cafeteria.
424. Oil prices are calculated in dollars.
425. It's difficult to calculate what effect all these changes will have on the company.
426. The black response to these laws was a campaign of violence.
427. They are busy campaigning against the building of new motorway near here.
428. Most first-year students live on campus.
429. I phoned the hotel to cancel my reservation.
430. There are three candidates standing in the election.
431. We are prepared to take candidates from any academic discipline.
432. Canteens were set up in the flooded areas.
433. He lifted a canteen to his lips.
434. I'm perfectly capable of looking after myself, thank you!
435. The room had a seating capacity for about 80.
436. The company has the capacity to build 1,500 trucks a year.
437. Australia's capital city is Canberra.
438. She leaves her capital untouched in the bank and lives off the interest.
439. Two of the soldiers were killed and the rest were captured.
440. The city took 24 hours to capture.
441. The American drive to land a man on the moon captured the attention of the whole world.
442. He realized that his acting career was over.
443. Michelangelo carved his figure from a single block of marble.
444. Someone had carved their initials on the tree.
445. I bought some new clothes through a mail-order catalogue.
446. Many plants become extinct before they have ever been catalogued.
447. They hope his election will act as a catalyst for reform.

448. There are five categories of workers.
449. Voters fall into three main categories.
450. This is the biggest event we've ever catered for.
451. Most perfume ads cater to male fantasies.
452. The physician must exercise caution when prescribing anti-depressants.
453. She was cautioned for speeding.
454. The rain ceased and the sky cleared.
455. They celebrated passing their exams with a party.
456. We have a census in this country every ten years.
457. He was present at the opening ceremony of the Olympic Games.
458. It's a certainty that prices will go up soon.
459. You can't say with any certainty where you might be in the future.
460. My examination certificate arrived in the post today.
461. Sign here to certify that this statement is correct.
462. She was certified as a teacher in 1990.
463. Look at the gold chain Sam bought me!
464. the chain of events that led to World War I
465. a chain of restaurants
466. I like the speed and challenge of racing.
467. It was a direct challenge to the Governor's authority.
468. After lunch Carey challenged me to a game of tennis.
469. The heart has four chambers.
470. the world heavyweight boxing champion
471. She swam across St. George's Channel.
472. They are building an irrigation channel.
473. An efficient irrigation system channels water to the crops.
474. Snow and ice have caused chaos on the roads.
475. The economic policy in this country could only be described as chaotic.
476. This chapter discusses power, and how people use it.
477. We hope that they will join us in opening a new chapter of peace and cooperation.
478. A chapter of disasters in his life confined him to bed.
479. People were affected by the character of Paris.
480. Hardy's main character is a young milkmaid whose life ends in tragedy.

481. The creamy richness is characteristic of the cheese from this region.
482. Ambition is a characteristic of all successful businessmen.
483. When you buy a suit, there is no charge for any alterations.
484. Harry will take charge of the department while I'm away.
485. Dick is facing a charge of armed robbery.
486. The restaurant charged us 40 dollars for the drinks.
487. The man they arrested last night has been charged with murder.
488. All the money raised by the concert will go to charity.
489. Several charities sent aid to the flood victims.
490. She was a woman of great charm and she knew how to use it.
491. He is looking at the chart showing last year's sales.
492. The police car was going so fast, it must have been chasing someone.
493. The solicitor's doing everything he can to chase the contract.
494. Let me just check whether the potatoes are cooked.
495. It's wise to check with your doctor before going on a diet.
496. The guide contains a handy checklist of points to look for when buying a car.
497. He is conducting a chemical analysis of the soil.
498. Although I cherish my children, I do allow them their independence.
499. My grandfather cherished his memories of the years he spent in the army as a young man.
500. Chill the champagne in a bucket of ice.
501. Come and sit by the fire, you look chilled to the bone.
502. Chop an onion into pieces.
503. Can you chop some firewood?
504. I'll go shopping when I've done my chores.
505. I find writing reports a real chore.
506. There is a chronic shortage of teachers.
507. The pain was chronic.
508. We arranged the documents in chronological order.
509. Blood circulates around the body.
510. Add his name to the circulation list for this report.
511. The old banknotes are being taken out of circulation.
512. The paper has a circulation of 200,000.
513. I can't imagine a circumstance in which I would be willing to steal.

514. Whether or not you qualify for a loan will depend on your financial circumstances.
515. The judge cited a 1956 Supreme Court ruling in her decision.
516. Garcia was cited for her work with disabled children.
517. Jackson spent the day meeting with local religious and civic leaders.
518. The local art museum is a source of civic pride.
519. They were married in a civil ceremony in May.
520. Many civil cases can be settled out of court.
521. Some people think that nuclear war would mean the end of civilization.
522. How does it feel to be back in civilization after all?
523. The police said that if no one claims the watch, you can keep it.
524. The company claims (that) it is not responsible for the pollution in the river.
525. After her house was burgled, she made a claim on her insurance.
526. Can you give any evidence to support your claim?
527. Could you clarify one or two points for me?
528. The report aims to clarify how these conclusions were reached.
529. Roy scored a classic goal in the 90th minute.
530. He chose a classic navy suit for the ceremony.
531. Jane Austen's *Pride and prejudice* is a classic of English literature.
532. In law, beer is classified as a food product.
533. As a musician, Cage is hard to classify.
534. He just could not distinguish a principal clause from a subordinate clause.
535. A confidentiality clause was added to the contract.
536. Right now he is in a meeting with an important client.
537. I could not bear living in a tropical climate.
538. Small businesses are finding it hard to survive in the present economic climate.
539. The election campaign reaches its climax next week, when the people finally cast their votes.
540. The Olympics climaxed in a spectacular closing ceremony.
541. Cling on or you might fall over.
542. He still clings to (= refuses to give up) his old-fashioned ways.
543. I'm never going to guess the answer if you don't give me a clue.
544. He is the best tennis coach I've ever met.
545. She coaches students in French, usually for exams.
546. The coarse sand was hot and rough under her feet.

547. All reports must be sent in code.
548. Each state in the US has a different criminal and civil code.
549. The Textile Services Association has drawn up a code of practice.
550. He is learning cognitive psychology.
551. They were never a coherent group.
552. The three years of the course are planned as a coherent whole.
553. Historically, sports have been a cohesive force in international relations.
554. His entry to the party coincided with his marriage.
555. The interests of the US and those of the islanders may not coincide.
556. Two writers collaborated on the script for the film.
557. The ancient abbey was in imminent danger of collapse.
558. He lost all his money in the collapse of the stock market.
559. The roof had collapsed long ago.
560. I thought that without me the whole project would collapse.
561. She discussed the idea with some of her colleagues.
562. So when did you start collecting antique glass?
563. This is a collective decision on the part of the management.
564. Their secret to success was manufacturing cheap goods on a colossal scale.
565. A number of factors have combined to create this difficult situation.
566. Good carpet wool needs to combine softness with strength.
567. A lot of Shakespeare's plays are comedies.
568. I looked to my family for comfort when things got difficult at work.
569. I usually dress for comfort rather than style.
570. I tried to comfort him but it was no use.
571. Gathered all-together in this church, we commemorate those who lost their lives in the great war.
572. Your first evaluation will be six months after you commence employment.
573. The speech received much comment in the press.
574. Does anyone have any questions or comments?
575. People were always commenting on my sister's looks.
576. During the war commerce between the two countries halted.
577. The dealer takes a 20% commission on the sales he makes.
578. The Government set up a commission to investigate allegations of police violence.

579. You should at least be ashamed of yourself for the commission of the crime.
580. Women commit fewer crimes than men.
581. He has committed himself to the cause of economic reform.
582. I couldn't go to the meeting because I had other commitments (= other things that had to be done).
583. I don't want children—they're too much of a commitment.
584. He is on the finance committee.
585. Commodity prices fell sharply.
586. Car thefts are commonplace in this part of town.
587. The new arts center will serve the whole community.
588. He is a part of the gay community in San Francisco.
589. The train was packed with sweaty complaining commuters.
590. The dormitory rooms were compact with a desk, bed and closet built in.
591. His dog became his closest companion during the last years of his life.
592. You cannot compare the war in Somalia to the Vietnam War.
593. Comparison with his previous movies shows how Lee has developed as a director.
594. The writer draws comparisons between the two presidents.
595. Stephen's political views often were not compatible with her own.
596. The new software is IBM compatible.
597. He didn't want to visit her but conscience compelled him (to).
598. Her intelligence more than compensates for her lack of experience.
599. He is the only party leader competent enough to govern this country.
600. The two companies are in competition with each other.
601. The document was compiled by the Department of Health.
602. This wine would be a nice complement to grilled dishes.
603. Each new cell will carry its full complement of chromosomes.
604. John and Bob complemented each other extremely well.
605. China was a complex of different societies.
606. I used to have an exaggerated complex about my looks.
607. It was a very complex relationship between two complex people.
608. I had to fill in this really complicated form.
609. She complained that her husband never paid her any compliments any more.
610. I was just complimenting him on his wonderful food.

611. Exercise is one of the key components of a healthy lifestyle.
612. The music was specially composed for the film.
613. There used to be many mysteries in this imperial compound.
614. His problems were compounded by an unsatisfactory relationship with his landlady.
615. His account of the meeting was most comprehensive.
616. This metaphor is beyond his comprehensive ability.
617. The house comprises two bedrooms, a kitchen, and a living room.
618. The committee is comprised of well-known mountaineers.
619. Party unity is threatened when members will not compromise.
620. The government has said that there will be no compromise with terrorists.
621. Swimming was compulsory at my school.
622. Final results had not yet been computed.
623. The path was concealed by long grass.
624. I've looked in every conceivable place for my keys, but I can't find them anywhere.
625. Many people cannot conceive or a dinner without meat or fish.
626. She had difficulty in conceiving.
627. The population is concentrated along the river banks.
628. Doctors are aiming to concentrate more on prevention than cure.
629. It's very simple, once you grasp the concept.
630. One of the concerns that people have is the side effects of treatment.
631. He was moved by her obvious concern.
632. The restaurant is a family concern.
633. The tax changes will concern large corporations rather than small businesses.
634. Issues like food additives do concern me.
635. Make your answer clear and concise.
636. The report concluded that the school should be closed immediately.
637. Did you come to any conclusions at the meeting this morning?
638. The investigation failed to provide any conclusive evidence.
639. It's a depressing gray concrete building with tiny windows.
640. They think she killed her husband but they have no concrete evidence.
641. We've got a general idea of what we want, but nothing concrete at the moment.
642. The exhibition reflected concurrent developments abroad.
643. My opinion are concurrent with yours.

644. I prefer to read in the library. I find it more conducive.
645. The Senator's conduct is being investigated by the Ethics Committee.
646. His conduct of the business was very successful.
647. He was a player who always conducted himself impeccably, both on and off the field.
648. The orchestra is conducted by John Williams.
649. An honorary degree was conferred on him by the university.
650. Franklin leant over and conferred with his attorney.
651. Should I book the conference room for the meeting?
652. She lacks confidence. I've never known anyone so timid and unsure of themselves.
653. She has never experienced life beyond the confines of her own close-knit family.
654. You are asked to confine your use of the telephone to business calls alone.
655. He was confined in a narrow, dark room for two months.
656. The President refused to confirm the rumor.
657. To confirm my diagnosis I need to do some tests.
658. Her remarks confirmed my opinion that she was a very rude young lady.
659. For years the region has been torn apart by armed conflicts.
660. Marx point out the potential conflict is below the surface of society.
661. The new evidence conflicts with previous findings.
662. Students can be expelled for refusing to conform to school rules.
663. All new buildings must conform with the regional development plan.
664. Troops were confronted by an angry mob.
665. We try to help people confront their problems.
666. Customers are confronted with a bewildering amount of choice.
667. You're confusing him! Tell him slowly and one thing at a time.
668. You're confusing me with my sister—it was she who was sick on your sofa.
669. She congratulated me warmly on my exam results.
670. He sent her a note of congratulation on her election victory.
671. an international/medical congress
672. Congress has rejected the recent presidential proposal on firearms.
673. Police are connecting the break-in with other recent thefts in the area.
674. Has the phone been connected yet?
675. Please explain connective tissue to me.
676. The Normans conquered England in 1066.

677. The Zulus conquered all the neighboring tribes.
678. I was conscious that she was ill at ease.
679. The driver was still conscious when the ambulance reached the scene of the accident.
680. This is the fifth consecutive weekend that I've spent working, and I'm a bit fed up with it.
681. Could we reach a consensus on this matter? Let's take a vote.
682. He took the car without the owner's consent.
683. He rarely consents to do interviews.
684. The safety procedures had been ignored, with potentially tragic consequences.
685. The farmers suffered a sever drought and there was a consequent shortage of food in the markets.
686. conservative policies
687. a very conservative attitude to education
688. a very conservative suit
689. The series has aroused considerable interest.
690. The buffet consisted of several different Indian dishes.
691. Happiness does not consist in how many possessions you own.
692. Her work is sometimes good but the problem is not consistent.
693. Scientists were satisfied with this figure, and the constant was left undisturbed until 1975.
694. There was a constant stream of visitors to the house.
695. The number of deaths from road accidents has remained constant over the last five years.
696. He is rather constant to his firm.
697. We must redefine what constitutes a family.
698. The Federation was constituted in 1949.
699. Financial factors should not constrain doctors from prescribing the best treatment for patients.
700. Poor economies abroad may constrain demand for US exports.
701. There are plans to construct a new bridge across the river.
702. Royce has constructed a new theory of management.
703. I need to consult my lawyer.
704. Have you consulted a dictionary?
705. A smaller vehicle will consume less fuel.
706. Alcohol may not be consumed on campus.
707. Consumers will soon be paying higher airfares.
708. There is very little contact between the two tribes.

709. He has a lot of contacts in the media.
710. Please do not hesitate to contact me if you have any queries.
711. The article contains some useful information.
712. Try to contain your anger!
713. Oscar was much admired by his contemporaries at the Academy.
714. The wall hangings are thought to be roughly contemporary with the tiled floors.
715. Her new book is about life in contemporary Britain.
716. The box had fallen over, and some of the contents had spilled out.
717. If the contents of this letter become known to the Foreign Secretary, there would be grave consequences.
718. John seems content to sit in front of the television all night.
719. Simple praise is enough to content him.
720. I strongly oppose that contention.
721. The matter has been settled—it's no longer in contention.
722. Losing three matches in a row has put them out of contention for the championship title.
723. We entered a fishing contest.
724. There is always a contest between the management and the unions.
725. The meaning of "funny" depends on its context.
726. To appreciate what these changes will mean, it is necessary to look at them in context.
727. My computer makes a continuous low buzzing noise.
728. Read the contract carefully before you sign it.
729. Metal contracts as it cools.
730. Doctors contract with hospitals for services.
731. Two-thirds of the adult population there has contracted AIDS.
732. The article flatly contradicts their claims.
733. The witness statements contradict each other and the facts remain unclear.
734. He continued to drink despite of advice to the contrary.
735. Unless there is evidence to the contrary, we ought to believe them.
736. Contrary to popular belief, a desert can be very cold.
737. Two contrary views emerged.
738. The stock lost 60 cents a share, in contrast to last year, when it gained 21 cents.
739. While there are similarities in the two cultures, there are also great contrasts.
740. These results contrast sharply with other medical tests carried out in Australia.

741. City employees cannot contribute to political campaigns.
742. He is one of the several authors contributing to the book.
743. Controversy arose over the use of chemicals on fruit and vegetables.
744. It was announced on Oct.25 that the National Assembly would convene on Nov.4.
745. The government considered only the convenience of the suppliers.
746. A folding bath-tub is a convenience if you can afford it.
747. Alternative medicine can sometimes provide a cure where conventional medicine cannot.
748. I wanted to appear friendly and approachable but I think I gave the converse impression.
749. She enjoyed the chance to converse with someone who spoke her language.
750. They are recent converts to the cause.
751. They converted the spare bedroom into an office.
752. European missionaries converted thousands to Christianity.
753. The stocks can be easily converted to cash.
754. If you see James, do convey my apologies.
755. The officials were eager to convince us of the safety of the nuclear reactors.
756. Leopards cooperate with each other when hunting game.
757. Matching bag and accessories provide a complete ensemble of colour coordinates.
758. The agencies are working together to coordinate policy on food safety.
759. Poor families have to cope with a lot of strain.
760. Who owns the copyright of this book?
761. Remove the cores, and bake the apples for 40 minutes.
762. Debts is at the core of the problem.
763. When I heard the news, I was shaken to the core.
764. The company is moving its corporate headquarters from New York to Houston.
765. She worked for a large corporation.
766. The two halves of the document did not correspond.
767. The description of these events corresponds closely to other accounts written at the time.
768. She stopped corresponding with him after the death of her mother.
769. We're making a few cosmetic changes to the house before we sell it.
770. Are you on the diet for health or cosmetic reasons?
771. I was very much struck by London—the fact that it's so cosmopolitan.
772. Oxford is considered by many cosmopolitan experts to be one of the most agreeable university towns in Europe.

773. The children were dressed in Halloween costumes.
774. Singers performing Mozart's operas often dress in historical costume.
775. Maybe we should see a marriage counselor.
776. There was nobody behind the counter when I went into the bank, and I had to wait to be served.
777. The Prime Minister is to meet his European counterparts to discuss the war against drugs.
778. There are a couple of girls waiting for you.
779. They are a newly married couple.
780. This must be coupled with the creation of an attractive environment.
781. This coupon is worth five pounds.
782. To find out more about our new computers, fill in the coupon and send it to us at the address given below.
783. Meeting Sally changed the whole course of his life.
784. I agreed that this was the only sensible course of action.
785. Andy's doing a one-year journalism course.
786. The ticket includes entry and a four-course meal.
787. Tears coursed down his cheeks.
788. Although she often disagreed with me, she was always courteous.
789. London covers 1,579 square kilometers.
790. The light was so bright that I had to cover my eyes with my hands.
791. This leaflet covers what we've just discussed in more detail.
792. We covered 400 km in three hours.
793. Cambridge dictionaries give very good grammar coverage.
794. What did you think of the BBC's election coverage?
795. I've only got fire coverage for my car.
796. The window cracked when the stone hit it.
797. The whip cracked above the horses' heads.
798. The nurse rocked the cradle.
799. Fossil records indicate that Africa was the cradle of early human evolution.
800. I am teaching the craft to my brother's son.
801. The plane crashed within seconds of taking off.
802. Her mother was killed in a car crash.
803. The software makes it easy to create colorful graphs.
804. Some people believe the universe was created by a big explosion.

805. Several children created a disturbance.
806. The crocodile is a strange-looking creature.
807. I have full credit in your ability to do the job.
808. He quickly acquired credit within the diplomatic community.
809. I don't have enough credits to graduate.
810. Do credit me with a little intelligence!
811. Much of Manchester United's success can be credited to their manager.
812. We crept upstairs so as not to wake the baby.
813. The dog crept under the car to hide.
814. The crime rate continued to increase.
815. My father was a cripple, my mother in poor health.
816. The company is facing a crisis over demands for higher pay.
817. To qualify for a grant, students must satisfy certain criteria.
818. We try to give students constructive criticism.
819. She has read a dozen of articles on literary criticism.
820. This aid money is crucial to the government economic policies.
821. Do you have to be so crude?
822. The package had been badly crushed in the post.
823. I was given a lovely pair of crystal earrings for my 21st birthday.
824. Most of the land there is too poor to cultivate.
825. At this school we aim to cultivate the minds of all the children we teach.
826. If it's culture you are looking for, the city has plenty of museums and art galleries.
827. He is known as a man of great culture.
828. Park your car close to the curb.
829. There will be new curbs on drink-driving from next week.
830. Great efforts have been made to curb drug trafficking.
831. After a year, she was cured of the cancer.
832. There is no known cure for this disease.
833. The best cure for boredom is hard work!
834. Babies are curious about everything around them.
835. A curious thing happened to me yesterday.
836. The little girl's face was framed by golden curls.
837. The bank can supply you with foreign currency.

838. His ideas enjoyed wide currency during the last century.
839. In some schools children study current affairs as a subject.
840. Languages are an essential part of the school curriculum.
841. He missed the ball and cursed violently.
842. She sank back against the cushions.
843. The hovercraft rides on a cushion of air.
844. I have some savings—hopefully they'll act as a cushion while I'm looking for a job.
845. It's the custom for the bride's father to pay for the wedding.
846. He was stopped at customs and questioned.
847. He's got a really cute baby brother.
848. Sometimes the only way to break the cycle of violence in the home is for the wife to leave.
849. The water is cycled through the machine and reused.
850. I usually cycle through the park to get to school.
851. He is watching the cyclic motion of a steam-engine.
852. The earthquake caused extensive structural damage.
853. Take care not to damage the timer mechanism.
854. Don't sit on the grass—it's damp!
855. We dashed along the platform and just managed to catch the train.
856. Waves dashed against the cliffs.
857. The spacecraft has sent back new data about Jupiter's atmosphere.
858. We talked almost until dawn.
859. The deadline for applications is May 27.
860. Cars turn into deadly weapons when they are driven dangerously.
861. She is the new dean of the Faculty of Social Sciences.
862. There was much lively debate about whether women should spend more time in the home.
863. It would have been better to hold the debate during the day.
864. Philosophers debate whether it is right to clone an individual.
865. I debated with myself whether I should tell anyone.
866. They are expected to go on damaging the ozone layer for decades.
867. They claimed that the plastics would not decay if they were buried.
868. I was deceived by uniform—I really thought he was a police officer.
869. They are incapable of expressing themselves in decent English.
870. Can you decipher the writing on this envelope?

871. They declared their support the proposal.
872. There has been a decline in the size of families.
873. There is widely held that educational standards are in decline.
874. Offered the position of chairman, Smith declined, preferring to keep his current job..
875. Car sales have declined by a quarter.
876. Her health has been declining progressively for several moths.
877. They decorated the wedding car with ribbons and flowers.
878. Our share of the market has decreased sharply this year.
879. I'd like to dedicate this song to my wife.
880. From her son's age, I deduced that her husband must be at least 60.
881. The government has suffered a serious defeat.
882. After a long campaign Wellington's army finally defeated Napoleon.
883. I think that there are a lot of defects in our education system.
884. They needed more troops to defend the border against possible attack.
885. The union said they would take action to defend their member's jobs.
886. Who is defending the case?
887. There's a deficiency of really good books on this subject.
888. Deficiencies in the education system have been much in the news.
889. It is difficult to define the duties and responsibilities of this post.
890. I shall now try to define the term "popular culture".
891. The outer boundary of a figure usually defines its size.
892. John had definite ideas about how the new kitchen should look.
893. It is impossible for me to give you a definite answer.
894. Preheat the oven to 425 degrees.
895. 1960s Britain was characterized by a greater degree of freedom than before.
896. Applicants must have a degree in engineering.
897. He wants to delay the meeting a few days, is that ok with you?
898. There has been a delay in the book's publication.
899. Delegates have voted in favor of the motion.
900. A group of four teachers were delegated to represent the school at the union conference.
901. Authority to make financial decisions has been delegated to a special committee.
902. His name was deleted form the list.
903. We made a deliberate decision to live apart for a while.

904. He's deliberating whether or not to accept the new job he's been offering.
905. Molly's health has always been delicate.
906. Delicate plants need to be kept in a greenhouse during the winter.
907. This rose has a very delicate scent.
908. This cake is absolutely delicious.
909. Mail is delivered to our office twice a day.
910. The government refused to give in to the demands of the terrorists.
911. Protesters went on hunger strike to demand that all political prisoners be freed.
912. This is a very difficult piece of music to play. It demands a lot of concentration.
913. Emily is a very demanding child.
914. Her mother could be very demanding at times.
915. You get demerits if you miss a meeting.
916. That building was demolished a few years ago.
917. The study demonstrates the link between poverty and malnutrition.
918. They'll be demonstrating how to handle modern, high performance cars.
919. The English word "family" used to denote all the people in the house, including servants.
920. Crosses on the map denote villages.
921. There will be dense fog in the northern part of the country tomorrow.
922. I have never denied that there is a housing problem.
923. She could deny her son nothing.
924. The train for Edinburgh will depart from Platform 5.
925. At that time, Robert Kennedy was head of the Justice Department.
926. Ellison is now head of the Department of Education.
927. The country depends heavily on its tourist trade.
928. You can depend on Jane—she always keeps her promises.
929. The length of the treatment depends on the severity of the illness.
930. Her paintings depict the lives of ordinary people in the last century.
931. If we continue to deplete the Earth's natural resources, we will cause serious damage to the environment.
932. We put down a deposit on a house last week.
933. You will have to pay one month's rent in advance, plus a deposit of $500.
934. I'd like to make a deposit, please.
935. The female deposits her eggs directly into the water.

936. As the river slows down, it deposits a layer of soil.
937. You are advised to deposit your valuables in the hotel safe.
938. It depresses me that nobody seems to care.
939. Several factors combined to depress the American economy.
940. He claimed that he had been deprived of his freedom.
941. He and his deputy had cooperated very well.
942. Medically, we will derive great benefit from this technique.
943. This word is derived from Latin.
944. The plane started to descend.
945. My mother claims she is descended from Abraham Lincoln.
946. The man described what he had seen.
947. It is often very hot in the desert.
948. After all that hard work you deserve a holiday.
949. Your proposals deserve serious consideration.
950. The new plane is in its final design stage.
951. He has some grand designs for the company.
952. She designed a new logo for the company.
953. I desire nothing other than to be left in peace.
954. He doesn't have much desire for wealth.
955. After six defeats in a row, a sense of despair seems to have settled on the team.
956. He's the despair of his parents because he shows no interest in getting a job.
957. They are living in desperate poverty.
958. Desperate measures are needed to deal with the growing drug problem.
959. Don't do anything desperate!
960. She went to Spain despite the fact that her doctor had told her to rest.
961. Most of the old part of the city was destroyed by bombs during the war.
962. The handle of the saucepan can be detached.
963. He described the process in detail.
964. The report details the progress we have made over the last year.
965. Many forms of cancer can be cured if detected early.
966. Not all such turncoats are detected.
967. The country's economy has been deteriorating for some time.
968. Experts have determined that the signature was forged.

969. The tests will help the doctors determine what treatment to use.
970. These chemicals have a detrimental effect on the environment.
971. The earthquake devastated the whole region.
972. The funds will be used for marketing and product development.
973. New developments are springing up all around the town.
974. The plane had to deviate from its normal flight path.
975. The company makes devices to detect carbon monoxide.
976. Their proposal was only a device to confuse the opposition.
977. He's very good at devising language games that you can play with students in class.
978. They have devoted all their time to helping the stick.
979. The meeting will be devoted to health and safety issues.
980. The doctor has diagnosed it as rheumatism.
981. The teacher drew a diagram showing how the blood flows through heart.
982. A rich variety of dialects still exists throughout the country.
983. The pond is six feet in diameter.
984. It took him a long time to dictate this letter.
985. Landlords can dictate their own conditions when letting their houses.
986. There was a lot of concentration on the voice and good diction.
987. It is important to have a balanced, healthy diet.
988. I will go on a diet next week and hope to lose five pounds before Christmas.
989. Humans differ from other mammals in their ability to speak.
990. It is important to differentiate between fact and opinion.
991. Television is a powerful means of diffusing knowledge.
992. The company has become large and diffuse.
993. Most babies can digest a wide range of food easily.
994. The report contains too much to digest at one reading.
995. Even in the prison camp we tried to retain some human dignity.
996. The President is clearly in a dilemma over how to tackle the crisis.
997. I have no doubt that diligent research will produce results.
998. The lamp gave out a dim light.
999. The dim outline of a large building loomed up out of the mist.
1000. Prospects for an early settlement of the dispute are dim.
1001. We shall need to know the exact dimensions of the room.

1002. We are heading for a catastrophe of enormous dimensions.
1003. You can have a spiritual dimension to your life without being religious.
1004. These drugs diminish blood flow to the brain.
1005. Don't let him diminish your achievements.
1006. He dipped his finger into the jar of syrup.
1007. I am hoping to get my teaching diploma this year.
1008. We are looking for a peaceful, diplomatic solution.
1009. The secretary was poised and diplomatic on the telephone.
1010. The disease disables thousands every year.
1011. The main disadvantages of the project are the cost.
1012. One hundred and twenty people died in this air disaster.
1013. Because of the weather, the parade was a total disaster.
1014. People who discard their little in the streets should have to pay heavy fines.
1015. It is difficult to discern any pattern in these figures.
1016. Martial arts teach respect, discipline, and cooperation.
1017. The book gives parent advice on discipline.
1018. Different cultures have different ways of disciplining their children.
1019. The Security Service is unlikely to disclose any information.
1020. We can discount Liverpool—they have three injured players.
1021. If we have to discount our prices, we aren't going to make a profit.
1022. I bought these shoes at a 40% discount.
1023. You should install locks on all your windows to discourage burglars.
1024. Students soon get discouraged if you criticize them too often.
1025. There is some discrepancy between the two accounts.
1026. The change happens in a series of discrete steps.
1027. Newborn babies can discriminate between a man's and a woman's voice.
1028. Under federal law, it is illegal to discriminate against minorities and women.
1029. The project is under discussion as a possible joint venture between the two space agencies.
1030. Amanda read her exam results with dismay.
1031. He just laughed and dismissed my suggestion as unrealistic.
1032. Bryant was dismissed from his post.
1033. The teacher might dismiss the class early today because of the snow.
1034. Everything was in disorder, but nothing seemed to be stolen.

1035. The family have a history of mental disorder.

1036. There was such disparity in the standards of living between rich and poor.

1037. The supervisor would dispatch a crew to repair the damage.

1038. Coal has been displaced by natural gas as a major source of energy.

1039. Fifty thousand people have been displaced by the war.

1040. They were at the fireworks display last night.

1041. One of the world's oldest cars has gone on display in Brighton today.

1042. Ian did like public displays of affection.

1043. Chinese vases are disposed around the gallery.

1044. The body releases a chemical that disposes you towards sleep.

1045. There has been a border dispute between the two countries.

1046. Few would disputer that travel broadens the mind.

1047. They are disputing with the local government over the proposed new rail road.

1048. The defending army disputed every inch of land.

1049. The judge ordered the jury to disregard the witness's last statement.

1050. One of the organization's aims is to disseminate information about the spread of the disease.

1051. Dissolve the sugar in the water.

1052. Parliament has been dissolved.

1053. The learning needs of the two groups are quite distinct from each other.

1054. The outline of the ship became more distinct.

1055. I got the distinct impression that he was trying to make me angry.

1056. He's colour-blind and can't distinguish between red and green easily.

1057. He distinguished himself in sports at a very young age.

1058. His face was distorted in anger.

1059. His account was badly distorted by the press.

1060. The royal scandal has distracted media attention from the economic crisis.

1061. Some people show signs of distress when they move house.

1062. How can we prevent such poverty, hardship and distress?

1063. I'm sorry if I've distressed you by asking all this.

1064. Clothes and blankets have been distributed among the refugees.

1065. Make sure the weight of the load is evenly distributed.

1066. Which is the richest district of New York?

1067. Sorry to disturb you, but can I use your telephone?

1068. Selma is rather disturbed that she hasn't had her exam results yet.
1069. It is difficult to design a program that will meet the diverse needs of all our users.
1070. People enter the organization from a diverse range of social, economic, and educational backgrounds.
1071. We need to diversify the economy.
1072. Most financiers recommend that investors diversify their assets.
1073. The curriculum will take account of the ethnic diversity of the population.
1074. In Britain, one in three marriages ends in divorce.
1075. They were divorced after only six months of marriage.
1076. Going without sleep for a long time makes me feel dizzy and light-headed.
1077. She received her doctorate in history in 2004.
1078. Several secret documents went missing from his office.
1079. The document could not be used for an independent inquiry.
1080. In the US, manual labour remains a male domain.
1081. This problem is outside the domain of medical.
1082. Unfortunately his domestic life was not very happy.
1083. Domestic flights go from Terminal 1.
1084. The industry is dominated by five multinational companies.
1085. The cathedral dominated the city.
1086. Education issues dominated the election campaign.
1087. The appeal for people to donate blood was very successful.
1088. A sense of doom hung over the entire country.
1089. Mounting debts doomed the factory to closure.
1090. The long-dormant volcano has recently shown signs of life.
1091. The first four sections were printed on a dot-matrix printer using continuous stationery.
1092. You can't park on double yellow lines.
1093. I'll have a double whisky please.
1094. I'd like to book a double room for two nights.
1095. American manufacturing organizations have been downsizing their factories.
1096. Pam often dozed in her chair after lunch.
1097. My dad was eighteen when he got drafted into the army.
1098. Eva is busy drafting her speech for the conference.
1099. He plays a Russian spy in the comedy drama *Sleepers*.

1100. Maggie's life is always full of drama.
1101. I expect to see dramatic improvements.
1102. Landing on the moon was one of the most dramatic scientific adventures of this century.
1103. I once saw a dramatic production of *The lady in White*.
1104. The government have recently taken drastic measures to control public spending.
1105. It is a great city—the only drawback is the weather.
1106. A drawback is made on customs duties on imported goods when they are later exported.
1107. The rubber raft drifted out to sea.
1108. Jenny spent the year drifting around Europe.
1109. an electric drill
1110. a pronunciation drill
1111. The Saudi government has announced plans to drill for water in the desert.
1112. She was drilling the class in the forms of the past tense.
1113. Be careful—your paintbrush is dripping.
1114. A man fell from a bridge and drowned.
1115. Sam drowned his pancakes in syrup.
1116. David has dual British and American nationality.
1117. The rent is due at the end of the month.
1118. The fire was due to a faulty wire in a plug.
1119. I thought the book dull and unoriginal.
1120. The sea had been a dull gray.
1121. These factors affect both intelligent and dull children.
1122. She's been deaf and dumb since birth.
1123. He stared in dumb misery at the wreckage of the car.
1124. Who dumped all these books on my desk?
1125. Let's dump the car and walk the rest of the way.
1126. The thieves were equipped with duplicate keys to the safe.
1127. I lost the original form so they sent me a duplicate.
1128. Can you duplicate this document for me?
1129. Plastic window frames are more durable than wood.
1130. The course is of three years' duration.
1131. The street lights go on at dusk.
1132. Ian felt a sense of duty towards his parents.

1133. The duty on wine has gone up.

1134. Snow White and the Seven Dwarfs/Dwarves

1135. She dwelt in remote parts of Asia for many years.

1136. The report dwells rather too much on violence.

1137. The number of people going to the cinema seems to dwindle steadily.

1138. Markets are dynamic and a company must learn to adapt.

1139. She is clearly a dynamic young woman with big ambitions.

1140. Perhaps I did look a little eccentric at that stage.

1141. In the current economic climate, we must keep costs down.

1142. Inflation is a major problem in many South American economies.

1143. The company announced that it would cut 500 jobs as part of an economy drive.

1144. Only the leaves of the plant are edible.

1145. The news paper edits letters before printing them.

1146. He looks at a film in the editing room and assembles the pieces.

1147. That drink has had quite an effect on me—I feel light-headed.

1148. Training is often much less effective than expected.

1149. The cut in interest rates is effective next Monday.

1150. Service at the restaurant is efficient and friendly.

1151. They're making the most elaborate preparations for the wedding.

1152. The minister said he was resigning but refused to elaborate.

1153. Forbes, 48, a multimillionaire funding his presidential campaign with his own money, has never held elective office.

1154. Create a first-year elective course on social justice.

1155. an elegant person/figure/profile

1156. an elegant idea/plan/solution

1157. Honesty is a vital element of her success.

1158. She does not even know the basic elements of politeness.

1159. They want to elevate the status of teachers.

1160. When her knock elicited no response, she opened the door and peeped in.

1161. Students on a part-time course are not eligible for a loan.

1162. Stephen was regarded as an eligible bachelor.

1163. The credit card eliminates the need for cash or cheques.

1164. Our team was eliminated in the first round.

1165. We embarked at Liverpool for New York.

1166. In 1950s China embarked on a major program of industrialization.

1167. I was really embarrassed when I knocked the cup of tea over my teacher.

1168. George always embodied good sportsmanship on the playing field.

1169. She embraced her son tenderly.

1170. You'd be a fool not to embrace an opportunity as good as that.

1171. This course embraces several different aspects of psychology.

1172. The sun emerged from behind the clouds.

1173. Later it emerged that the judge had employed an illegal immigrant.

1174. He has been eminent in sociology for many years.

1175. The chimney emitted clouds of smoke.

1176. The course places emphasis on practical work.

1177. I'd just like to emphasize how important it is for people to learn foreign languages.

1178. His theory is inconsistent with the empirical evidence.

1179. The company employs 2,000 people worldwide.

1180. Sophisticated statistical analysis was employed to obtain these results.

1181. Young had hoped to emulate the success of Douglas.

1182. The loan enabled Jane to buy the house.

1183. There are plans to enlarge the runway enable jumbo jets to land.

1184. Congress refused to enact this bill.

1185. Please enclose a curriculum vita with your letter of application.

1186. The park that encloses the monument has recently been enlarged.

1187. The houses encompassed about one hundred square meters.

1188. The US proposed the creation of a free trade zone encompassing the entire Western hemisphere.

1189. He did not appear to remember our encounter last summer and just nodded when we were introduced.

1190. She witnessed the hostile encounter between supporters of rival football teams.

1191. When did you first encounter these problems?

1192. The police must deal with criminals without endangering the lives of passers-by.

1193. Engineers are endeavouring to locate the source of the problem.

1194. The expedition was an outstanding example of human endeavour.

1195. It seemed impossible that anyone could endure such pain.

1196. Finally a day came when they could endure no longer.
1197. She's such an energetic little girl!
1198. She is devoting all her energies to the wedding plans.
1199. She was full of energy after her vacation.
1200. Certain vitamins can give you more energy, if you are always feeling tired.
1201. Governments make laws and the police enforce them.
1202. It is unlikely that a record company would enforce its views on an established artist.
1203. If a book doesn't engage my interest in the first few pages, I don't usually carry on reading it.
1204. Why don't you engage a carpenter to make you some kitchen units?
1205. In his spare time, he engages in voluntary work.
1206. The publicity has done little to enhance his reputation.
1207. Should the function of children's television be to entertain or to enlighten?
1208. The team made an enormous effort.
1209. Before the council starts building the new development, they will have to hold a public enquiry.
1210. Education can enrich your life.
1211. The purpose of the colonies was to enrich the colonists and the Spanish realm.
1212. In 1996 he was enrolled in a community college.
1213. His parents enrolled him in a military academy when he was 18.
1214. All the necessary steps had been taken to ensure their safety.
1215. The hospital tries to ensure that people are seen quickly.
1216. For many parents, having children entails certain sacrifices.
1217. Those were the years of private enterprise when lots of small businesses were started.
1218. We hired a magician to entertain the children at the party.
1219. After the incident he lost his enthusiasm for the sport.
1220. They got an entire set of silver cutlery as a wedding present.
1221. Being unemployed entitles you to free medical treatment.
1222. Her last novel, entitled *The Forgotten Past*, is out this week.
1223. The museum work closely together, but are separate legal entities.
1224. Young children often feel happier in the home environment.
1225. Some of these chemicals are very damaging to the environment.
1226. The scheme cost a lot more than we had originally envisaged.

1227. Most people equate wealth with success.
1228. The rooms are equipped with video cameras.
1229. We equip students with the skills they will need once they leave college.
1230. The word has no equivalent in English.
1231. The US Congress is roughly equivalent to the British Parliament.
1232. I had no dollars, but offered him an equivalent amount of sterling.
1233. The fall of the Berlin Wall marked the end of an era.
1234. The government claims to be doing all it can to eradicate corruption.
1235. Although he is now a wealthy man he cannot erase the memories of childhood.
1236. He's very tall and erect for his 78 years.
1237. The war memorial was erected in 1950 in the center of the park.
1238. The cliffs are being constantly eroded by heavy seas.
1239. Repeated exam failures had eroded his confidence.
1240. There must be an error in our calculations.
1241. The doctor has admitted that he was in error.
1242. The decision to expand the company was an error of judgment.
1243. Because of the imposition of martial law there was a violent eruption of anti-government feeling.
1244. The decision to escalate UN involvement has been taken in the hopes of a swift end to the hostilities.
1245. For homework I want you to write an essay on endangered species.
1246. Competition is the essence of all games.
1247. She packed a few essentials.
1248. It is essential to book in advance.
1249. The essential difference between Sam and me was the fact that I took life seriously.
1250. Our goal is to establish a new research center in the North.
1251. Most of the money will be used to establish local industries and mobilize the work-force.
1252. The police must establish the facts of the case before proceeding.
1253. Relatively low esteem is given in this country to vocational education.
1254. The property is part of the deceased's estate.
1255. Her work is highly esteemed by all her colleagues.
1256. According to a government estimate, the number of refugees is at least 18 million.
1257. We are predicting a 10% rise in oil prices—and that is a conservative estimate.

1258. The tree is estimated to be at least 700 years old.
1259. In some religious views, life is seen as an eternal conflict between the forces of good and evil.
1260. Televised news is based on a code of ethics.
1261. The school teaches pupils from different ethnic groups.
1262. Edward can't evade doing his military service forever.
1263. You should be able to evaluate your own work.
1264. We need to evaluate the success of the campaign.
1265. We need to carry out a proper evaluation of the new system.
1266. This year's Olympic Games will be the biggest ever sporting event.
1267. Both sides were happy with the eventual outcome of the talks.
1268. The study produced one interesting piece of evidence.
1269. He refused to give evidence at the trial.
1270. At present we have no evidence of life on other planets.
1271. It was evident to me that he was not telling the truth.
1272. The school has evolved its own style of teaching.
1273. Fish evolved from prehistoric sea creatures.
1274. The exact distance is 1,838 meters.
1275. The blackmailers exacted a total of 100,000 from their victims.
1276. This church is a good example of Gothic architecture.
1277. Her courage is an example to us all.
1278. He was fined for exceeding the speed limit.
1279. His performance exceeded our expectation.
1280. He excels at sports.
1281. You must report here every Tuesday without exception.
1282. Drinking is OK as long as you don't do it to excess.
1283. We might seem to be carrying excess supplies but they would be necessary in the case of an emergency.
1284. Some of the data was specifically excluded from the report.
1285. The press had been deliberately excluded from the event.
1286. At this stage we cannot entirely exclude the possibility of staff cuts.
1287. A month or two later they executed the king.
1288. The directors make the decisions, but the managers have to execute them.
1289. Los Angeles exemplifies American's diversity.

1290. His poor health exempts him from military service.

1291. Pregnant women are exempt from dental charges under the current health system.

1292. If you were to exert your influence they might change their decision.

1293. I find a full day's teaching exhausts me.

1294. They soon exhausted the food resources of the surrounding area.

1295. The exhibits date from the 17th century.

1296. The children's museum has several hands-on exhibits.

1297. Anyone who exhibits extreme anxiety in the face of potential danger is unlikely to become an effective military leader.

1298. Her paintings have been exhibited all over the world.

1299. The computer industry has expanded greatly over the last decade.

1300. Water expands as it freezes.

1301. Legal experts are saying that the man's conviction was unlawful.

1302. I have no expertise in cooking.

1303. My passport is due to expire in three months.

1304. The Government's term office expired in 2004.

1305. The kidnappers have given us explicit instruction not to involve the police.

1306. Be explicit when you talk about money with your family.

1307. A bomb had exploded in the next street.

1308. The population was still exploding.

1309. The country's natural resources have not yet been fully exploited.

1310. The new TV companies are fully exploiting the potential of satellite transmission.

1311. Homeworkers can easily be exploited by employers.

1312. The exploration for new sources of energy is vital for the future of our planet.

1313. Every part of the island has been explored.

1314. The conference explored the possibility of closer trade links.

1315. She is a famous exponent of self-education.

1316. The most famous exponent of this approach to art was probably Charles Mackintosh.

1317. Wheat is one of the country's chief exports.

1318. The company exports tuna to the US.

1319. Italian food has been exported all over the world.

1320. The report revealed that workers had been exposed to high levels of radiation.

1321. Some children are never exposed to classical music.

1322. He lifted his T-shirt to expose a scar across his chest.
1323. The forest extended in all directions as far as the eye could see.
1324. The bank has said that it cannot extend its commitment to the business any further.
1325. We extended the kitchen by six feet.
1326. I should like to extend thanks to you for your kindness.
1327. From the top of the Empire State Building, you can see the full extent of Manhattan.
1328. Exterior to the main house there is a small building that could be used as an office or studio.
1329. The exterior of the house needs painting.
1330. Fishing must stop before the species is exterminated.
1331. Low birth weight may be caused by external factors, such as smoking during pregnancy.
1332. China will not tolerate any external inference in its affairs.
1333. Many tribes became extinct when they came into contact with Western illnesses.
1334. An air hostess made him extinguish his cigar.
1335. We have to extinguish the memory of the defeat.
1336. Recently he's been working an extra two hours a day.
1337. Add one teaspoon of vanilla extract.
1338. I have only seen short extracts from the film.
1339. You will have to have that tooth extracted.
1340. Oils are extracted from the plants.
1341. They aim to extract the maximum political benefit from the Olympic Games.
1342. Most families lacked the money to get their children involved in extracurricular activities.
1343. He told the extraordinary story of his escape.
1344. She considered him extravagant with electricity.
1345. The product does not live up to the extravagant claims of the advertisers.
1346. People are capable of surviving in extreme conditions.
1347. Society does not tolerate the extremes of human behaviour.
1348. These fabrics are specially imported from Italy and France.
1349. These discs are expensive to fabricate.
1350. Jackson was accused of fabricating banknotes.
1351. You look fabulous!
1352. The painting was sold for a fabulous sum.
1353. The unicorn is a fabulous beast.
1354. The facets of a precious stone are the small flat surfaces cut on to it.

1355. Tact was just one facet of his talents as a captain.

1356. Both centers are electronically linked to facilitate communication.

1357. Computers can be used to facilitate language learning.

1358. Gas stoves can be used with greater facility than the old coal-burners.

1359. The hotel has its own pool and leisure facilities.

1360. The rise in crime is mainly due to social and economic factors.

1361. Three is a factor of fifteen.

1362. She had a great faculty for absorbing information.

1363. Finally, he was admitted by the Faculty of Law.

1364. Both faculty and students oppose the measures.

1365. Hopes of a peace settlement are beginning to fade.

1366. The sun had fade the curtains.

1367. There's still a faint hope that they might be alive.

1368. Several fans fainted in the blazing heat.

1369. The public has quite simply lost faith in the government.

1370. We thought it was a genuine antique, but it was only a fake.

1371. It was a relief to be back in familiar surroundings.

1372. This kind of situation was very familiar to John.

1373. I thought he was being a bit familiar with my wife.

1374. These plans of yours are quite fantastic—they can never work.

1375. You look fantastic in that outfit!

1376. The idea of travelling through time fascinates me.

1377. It was fascinating to watch the glass being made.

1378. Long, curly hair is in fashion this summer.

1379. She fashioned hats for them out of newspaper.

1380. Fasten your seatbelt!

1381. Graf made a fatal mistake halfway through the match.

1382. What is your favourite television programme?

1383. How clever of you to buy chocolate chip cookies—they're my favourites.

1384. You always were Dad's favourite.

1385. The electric car is technically feasible.

1386. The construction of this bridge was a brilliant feat of engineering.

1387. Her eyes were her best feature.

1388. An important feature of Van Gogh's painting is their bright colours.
1389. There were a couple of short cartoons before the main feature.
1390. The exhibition feature paintings by contemporary artists.
1391. Violence seems to feature heavily in all of his books.
1392. It is against federal law to discriminate against someone because of religion.
1393. Switzerland is a federal republic.
1394. Park entrance fee have gone up to $15.
1395. The feedback from the customers who have tired the new soap is very positive.
1396. She was voted the best female vocalist for the second year running.
1397. The Nile's regular flooding meant that the surrounding land was very fertile.
1398. Most men remain fertile into old age.
1399. It takes a fertile imagination to direct a film as original as this.
1400. Despite her trouble life she has always had a fervent belief in God.
1401. Most of the people here are fervent supporters of self-determination.
1402. Happy marriages may be more common in fiction than in real life.
1403. We had to keep up the fiction of being a normal couple.
1404. He is the best-known American outside the field of politics.
1405. The two men had been shot during a fierce fighting last weekend.
1406. Write the amount in both words and figures.
1407. He was a central figure in the movement for constitutional reform.
1408. She pulled a blue file from the shelf.
1409. A file of soldiers marched in step.
1410. The contracts are filed alphabetically.
1411. Mr. Green filed a formal complaint against the department.
1412. Does anyone know the final score?
1413. She's not coming with us, and that's final!
1414. We need to raise finance for further research.
1415. She refused to answer questions about her personal finances.
1416. The concerts are financed by the Arts Council.
1417. It was a wonderful film, but not exactly a financial success.
1418. The earth has a finite number of resources which we must protect.
1419. Check that the ladder's firm before you climb up it.
1420. He's just started working for an accountancy firm in Cambridge.

1421. Suddenly there was a flash and a zig-zag of forked lightning.
1422. Bright birds flash through the air.
1423. People used to believe that the earth was flat.
1424. After the excitement of the party, life seems very flat now.
1425. You flatter me. I'm not that important.
1426. The wine has a light, fruity flavour.
1427. This brief description should give you a flavour of what the book is like.
1428. There's a flaw in this cloth, but it's a tiny one.
1429. Did you spot the flaw in his argument?
1430. Along with thousands of others, he fled the country.
1431. Our new computer software is extremely flexible.
1432. We can be flexible about your starting date.
1433. Does this type of wood float?
1434. We floated the canoe out into the middle of the river.
1435. We were followed by a whole flock of sea gulls.
1436. Hundreds of people are flocking to the football match.
1437. While some international bodies have flourished, others have virtually collapsed.
1438. In these waters, bacteria flourish.
1439. Insect populations fluctuate wildly from year to year.
1440. Prices fluctuated between $20 and $40.
1441. Death may result from loss of fluids.
1442. After a month and a half it was still completely fluid at the center.
1443. The focus of recent research has been on environmental issues.
1444. She turned the camera and focused on Martin's face.
1445. Fold the paper along the dotted line.
1446. Fold your arms and sit up straight.
1447. They had obtained a court order forbidding the sale.
1448. It is almost impossible to forecast the future development of a very young child.
1449. What's the weather forecast for the next few days?
1450. Do you foresee any problems with the new system?
1451. He has never forgiven the newspaper for printing this story.
1452. Please look at the enclosed magazine to see the usual format for articles.
1453. The interview was written in a question and answer format.

1454. We now know a lot more about the early stages of planetary formation.
1455. He was an adviser to former President Reagan.
1456. Their farm had been reduced to half its former size.
1457. Our products are handmade from traditional formulas.
1458. We are still searching for a peace formula.
1459. Charles Darwin formulated the theory of natural selection.
1460. We are studying the situation but have not formulated any response yet.
1461. Keep an eye on the noticeboard for forthcoming events.
1462. When no reply was forthcoming, she wrote again.
1463. IBM is usually pretty forthcoming about the markets for its products.
1464. He borrowed it a fortnight ago.
1465. The journal services as a regular forum for the interchange of information and ideas.
1466. Dinosaur fossils can be seen in science museums.
1467. The fossil bones of animals teach us about life in the past.
1468. The castle is founded on solid rock.
1469. Eton College was founded by Henry VI in 1440.
1470. It took the builders three weeks to lay the foundation.
1471. All theories should be built on a foundation of factual knowledge.
1472. The school has served the community since its foundation in 1835.
1473. For a fraction of a second I hesitated.
1474. 1/4 and 0.25 are different ways of presenting the same fraction.
1475. This was only a fragment out of a long conversation with John.
1476. This paper provides a framework for future research.
1477. We have to act within the existing legal framework.
1478. Water freezes at a temperature of 0℃.
1479. Foods like tomatoes lose their texture and taste if they are frozen.
1480. The Government has frozen pensions until the end of next year.
1481. "Freeze or I'll shoot!" screamed the gunman.
1482. The ship carries freight and passengers.
1483. Serious disasters appear to be increasing frequency.
1484. The overall efficiency of the machine is higher because there is less friction.
1485. Family frictions can interfere with a child's schoolwork.
1486. I think the fact that he's working with amateurs really frustrates him.

1487. Their attempts to speak to him were frustrated by the guards.
1488. The current situation is very frustrating for us.
1489. The failed to fulfil their promises to revive the economy.
1490. Now that the children have left home I can go out and fulfil myself.
1491. The nervous system regulates our bodily functions.
1492. The church fulfils a valuable social function.
1493. This room may be hired for wedding and other functions.
1494. Her legs have now ceased to function.
1495. A library is functioning as a temporary hospital to cope with casualties.
1496. A sale is being held to raise funds for the school.
1497. He had a fund of stories about his boyhood.
1498. Read the following introduction to the fundamentals of design and print production.
1499. We have to tackle the fundamental cause of the problem.
1500. Water is fundamental to survival.
1501. I've never been so furious in my whole life.
1502. He wanted to be moved to a nursing home where he could furnish his own room.
1503. The only other piece of furniture was an old-fashioned wardrobe.
1504. He is old and unpopular. Furthermore, he has at best only two years of political life ahead of him.
1505. It was futile to continue the negotiations.
1506. distant stars and galaxies
1507. I'd never before seen such a galaxy of actors and actresses.
1508. The fence was blown down in the gale.
1509. We're forbidden to drink or gamble.
1510. We can't relax our safety standards-we'd be gambling with people's lives.
1511. Several gangs were operating in the area.
1512. Lou has big gaps between her front teeth.
1513. There is a widening gap between the rich and the poor.
1514. Can you take the garbage out when you go?
1515. She wore a long garment in scarlet linen.
1516. I gathered my maps together and tucked them into the folder.
1517. They gathered berries, nuts and fruit for food.
1518. a gay rights demonstration

1519. She felt excited and quite gay.

1520. I spent most of my time gazing out of the window.

1521. John checked the gear on the cycle.

1522. I packed my gear and walked out.

1523. She inherited £20.000 in gold and gems.

1524. There are may be gender differences in attitudes to paid work.

1525. Can we generalize this principle?

1526. The research findings can be generalized to a wider population.

1527. Wind turbines generate electricity for the local community.

1528. The program would generate a lot of new jobs.

1529. Like most of my generation, I had never known a war.

1530. musical genius

1531. Einstein was a genius.

1532. The experts decided that the painting was a genuine Constable.

1533. She looked at me in genuine astonishment.

1534. The germs are easily passed from person to person.

1535. It's just the germ of an idea, but I think we could make something of it.

1536. Covering her face in a gesture of despair, she burst out crying.

1537. The Government has donated £500,000 as a gesture of goodwill.

1538. Have you read any stories of cruel giants and wicked witches?

1539. He was one of the intellectual giants of this century.

1540. the giant pandas

1541. The earrings were a gift from my aunt.

1542. Dee has a gift for making everyone feel at ease.

1543. He was gifted with extraordinary powers of memory.

1544. The cost of the whole operation has been gigantic.

1545. I missed the lecture, can you give me the gist of it?

1546. She glanced around the room to see who was there.

1547. She glared angrily at everyone.

1548. Car lights glared at the end of the street.

1549. The snake glides smoothly towards its prey.

1550. The minister blamed the rise in unemployment on the global economic recession.

1551. We need to take a global view of the situation.

1552. We export our goods all over the globe.

1553. This was yet another glorious victory for the team.

1554. Your roses are glorious!

1555. He stared thoughtfully into the glow of the fire burning in the grate.

1556. The hat seems to be stuck on with glue.

1557. A new piece was glued into place and repainted.

1558. His ultimate goal was to set up his own business.

1559. I scored the first goal.

1560. Many civil servants are sure that they can govern better than the politicians.

1561. She grabbed my arm.

1562. Their grab for real power in this world was doomed to failure.

1563. She has a graceful way of moving.

1564. She finally apologized, but she wasn't very graceful about it.

1565. My brother is in the sixth grade.

1566. He got a grade A in maths.

1567. Pencils are graded according to softness.

1568. Beef is graded on the basis of its fat content.

1569. Computerization has resulted in the gradual disappearance of many manual jobs.

1570. He is a graduate in philosophy.

1571. His father was a Harvard graduate.

1572. Kate graduated from medical school last year.

1573. As an actress she has graduated from small roles to more substantial parts.

1574. How grand the mountains look in the early light!

1575. Finally, the grand moment comes when you make your first solo flight.

1576. A licence to sell alcohol was granted to the club.

1577. His illness is describe in graphic detail.

1578. Photoshop is the program used by most graphic artists.

1579. Make sure you grasp the rope with both hands.

1580. They failed to grasp the full significance of his remarks.

1581. He was grateful that he was still alive.

1582. I couldn't adequately express my gratitude to Francis.

1583. Anything that is dropped falls towards the ground because of the force of gravity.

1584. Carl did not seem to understand the gravity of this situation.

1585. The Consul spoke slowly and with great gravity.
1586. Don't be greedy—leave some cake for us.
1587. The company had become too greedy for profit.
1588. Mr. Tailor got up from behind his desk to greet me.
1589. The grief she felt over Helen's death was almost unbearable.
1590. They grind the grain into flour between two large stones.
1591. *Cats* has made a gross of over $460 million in the United States alone.
1592. The gross earning of his family amounted to just £75 per week.
1593. Brad threw up on the floor at the party. It was really gross.
1594. They offer a two-year guarantee on all their electrical goods.
1595. The bank is holding the airline's assets as guarantees.
1596. The bank will only lend me money if my parents guarantee the loan.
1597. The law guarantee equal rights for men and women.
1598. In movies, talent by no means guarantees success.
1599. He became the legal guardian of his brother's daughter.
1600. The US has represented itself as the guardian of democracy.
1601. This chapter gives you some guidelines to help you in your work.
1602. Don't you have any feeling of guilt about leaving David?
1603. It is up to the prosecution to establish the defendant's guilt.
1604. The teacher said Sam was impossible to control and that the guilt lay with his parents.
1605. He was found guilty of passing on secret papers to a foreign power.
1606. They feel guilty about seeing her so little.
1607. A sudden gust of wind blew the door shut.
1608. A gust of rage swept through him.
1609. He was always at the gym.
1610. We did an hour of gym.
1611. It was probably brought here from its native Mediterranean habitat by the Romans.
1612. James took his habitual morning walk around the garden.
1613. The hail battered on the windows.
1614. Joe slammed on the brakes and the car skidded to a halt.
1615. Women's progress in the workplace is still hampered by male attitudes.
1616. I was going to screw some handles onto the new bathroom cabinet.
1617. Customers are asked not to handle the goods in the shop.

1618. It was difficult situation and he handled it very well.

1619. We said that we wouldn't be relying on handouts from anyone for our future.

1620. The handout explains what that means.

1621. Our hotel room overlooked a pretty little fishing harbour.

1622. They sing in harmony.

1623. Industries and the universities have worked together in harmony.

1624. Plans are now underway to trap some of this power and harness it for our own use.

1625. His family wouldn't survive the harsh winter.

1626. After ten days, the eggs hatch.

1627. If you haul hard you will divert the fish.

1628. This room is said to be haunted.

1629. Our imaginations were still haunted by the war.

1630. The village is a favourite tourist haunt.

1631. Smoking is both a health hazard and a fire hazard.

1632. The cut will soon heal up.

1633. The plaster cast will help to heal the broken bone.

1634. We piled all the newspapers into a heap.

1635. He's getting old and his hearing isn't very good.

1636. They produced less per hectare and employed fewer people per hectare than small farms.

1637. We made a hectic three-day visit to New York.

1638. As the feeling of panic heightened, people started to flee towards the exits.

1639. The earth is divided into the northern and southern hemispheres by the equator and into eastern and western hemispheres by the meridians.

1640. The main part of the brain is divided into the left and right cerebral hemispheres.

1641. The cost of transport is a major expense for an industry. Hence factory location is an important consideration.

1642. a herd of cattle

1643. He believes that science is as much part of our cultural heritage as art or architecture.

1644. She put her hand on the phone, hesitated for a moment, then picked up the receiver.

1645. After some hesitation he agreed to allow me to write the article.

1646. He worked his way up through the corporate hierarchy to become president.

1647. That weekend in Venice was definitely the highlight of our trip.

1648. Your resume should highlight your skills and achievements.

1649. We're going on a four mile hike tomorrow to the lake.

1650. I've been hiking round Scotland for a month.

1651. High interest rates will hinder economic growth.

1652. She made a few hints about her birthday, to make sure that no one would forget it.

1653. I'd like to paint the bedroom in white with a hint of blue.

1654. In the book you may find some useful hints for people traveling to China.

1655. Mum hinted she might pay for my trip to Mexico if I pass all my exams.

1656. How much would it cost to hire a car for a fortnight.

1657. We ought to hire a public relations consultant to help improve our image.

1658. More money is needed for the preservation for historic buildings and monuments.

1659. Hollow blocks are used because they are lighter.

1660. It was very honest of him to give them the money back.

1661. We appreciated the honesty of her reply.

1662. Put your coat on the hook.

1663. A hare hopped straight into the doorway.

1664. The moon rose slowly above the horizon.

1665. The visit to the Far East certainly broadened our horizons.

1666. a horrible murder

1667. Everything was very expensive and the hotel was horrible.

1668. Thanks for your hospitality over the past few weeks.

1669. While I'm studying in London, I'm staying at a student hostel.

1670. The president was given a hostile reception by a crowd of angry farmers.

1671. The hawk hovered in the sky, waiting to swoop down on the rabbit on the ground.

1672. I noticed several reporters hovering around outside the courtroom.

1673. He is hovering between life and death.

1674. Jane threw her arms around him and hugged him tight.

1675. He was hugging a big pile of books.

1676. Paul gave me a big hug and smiled.

1677. a crime against humanity

1678. If only he would show a little humanity for once.

1679. Iacocca rose from humble beginnings to become boss of Ford.

1680. He thanked us again with a bumble smile.

1681. I don't mind hot weather, but I hate this high humidity.

1682. They don't have the same standard of hygiene as we have.
1683. We hope that further research will confirm our hypothesis.
1684. In an ideal world there would be no need for a police force.
1685. Social justice and equality, like many ideals, are difficult to realize.
1686. The ingredients are identical with those of competing products.
1687. The sisters were not identical in appearance and character.
1688. The police took fingerprints and identified the body.
1689. she has always been identified with the radical left.
1690. The identity of the killer is till unknown.
1691. Children need continuity, security, and a sense of identity.
1692. It is least likely that they did fail to keep their ideology to themselves.
1693. A healthy child cannot be idle; he has to be doing something all day long.
1694. The doctor hated wasting time on idle chatter.
1695. Excuse my ignorance, but how does it actually work.
1696. I would have remained in ignorance if Shawn had not mentioned it.
1697. I'm afraid I'm rather ignorant about computers.
1698. Safety regulations are being ignored by company managers in the drive to increase profits.
1699. It is illegal to sell tobacco to someone under 16.
1700. We have an illusion of freedom.
1701. Let me give an example to illustrate the point.
1702. Over a hundred diagrams, tables and pictures illustrate the book.
1703. She peered closely at her image in the mirror.
1704. He paints a very graphic image of working-class communities.
1705. He had no visual image of her, only her name.
1706. Other societies have begun to imitate the wastefulness of the West.
1707. It is a thriving shopping center for the people who live in the immediate area.
1708. They promise immediate action to help the unemployed.
1709. This development has been of immense importance.
1710. Immerse your foot in ice cold water to reduce the swelling.
1711. His father and mother immigrated when he was two.
1712. I believed that war was imminent.
1713. The force of the impact knocked the breath out of her.
1714. The change in leadership will have a huge impact on government policy.

1715. It is still unclear how the new law will impact health care.
1716. His digestion had been impaired by his recent illness.
1717. The music imparts a feeling of excitement to the film.
1718. He told them that he had a terrible piece of news to impart.
1719. Their advance was seriously impeded by the bad weather.
1720. The present conflict might provide fresh impetus for peace talks.
1721. It is best to cut weeds off at he roots with am implement such as a hoe.
1722. They are not the implements of a wise man.
1723. We have decided to implement the committee's recommendations in full.
1724. Three police officers are implicated in the cover-up.
1725. New evidence implicates Mr. Stephen and his wife in the blackmail attempt.
1726. Her words contained an implicit threat.
1727. Planning and reviewing should be implicit in any team meeting.
1728. Free trade implies shared values.
1729. Democracy implies a respect for individual liberties.
1730. The government imposed a ban on the sale of ivory.
1731. Some parents impose their own moral values on their children.
1732. I was hoping to impress my new boss with my diligence.
1733. The weather improved later in the day.
1734. I forgot to bring my notes, so I had to improvise.
1735. Annie improvised a sandpit for the children to play in.
1736. The prime impulse of capitalism is the making of money.
1737. Gerry couldn't resist the impulse to skip work and go down to the beach.
1738. The building's electrical system was completely inadequate.
1739. Awards provide an incentive for young people to improve their skills.
1740. The child's incessant talking started to irritate her.
1741. Why did the incidence of heroin use continue to climb?
1742. Smokers had the highest incidence of colds.
1743. A serious incident along the border increased our fears of war.
1744. They claimed we were inciting people against the government.
1745. My own inclination, if I were in your situation, would be to look for another job.
1746. This was an area of sloping fields and the track mounted a gradual incline.
1747. The telescope is inclined at an angle of 43 degrees.

1748. The accident inclined him to reconsider his career.
1749. It's fully inclusive price.
1750. The rent is 50 pounds a week, inclusive of heating and lighting.
1751. People on a high income should pay more tax.
1752. We've incorporated many environmentally-friendly features into the design of the building.
1753. Our original proposals were not incorporated in the new legislation.
1754. There has been a marked increase in the use of firearms.
1755. The population increased dramatically in the first half of the century.
1756. She's only 12 years old? I find that completely incredible.
1757. The latest missiles are incredible in firing accuracy.
1758. You will receive annual salary increments every September.
1759. The final rewards will more than compensate for any loss you may incur.
1760. An indefinite number of people have already died in the war.
1761. The project has been postponed for an indefinite period due to a lack of funds.
1762. The changing size of an infant's head is considered an index of brain growth.
1763. Sales targets are indicated on the graph.
1764. The study indicates a strong connection between poverty and crime.
1765. All the main economic indicators suggest that trade is improving.
1766. The indigenous medical traditions in the area make extensive use of plants.
1767. In my job, a telephone is indispensable.
1768. Each individual receives two genes, one inherited from each parent.
1769. Each individual leaf on the trees is different.
1770. Children get more individual attention in small classes.
1771. Nothing would induce me to vote for him again.
1772. Patients with eating disorders may use drugs to induce vomiting.
1773. Rosa was an industrious and brilliant student.
1774. He was always rather inept at sports.
1775. Gold is inert to the action of some acids which can dissolve other metals.
1776. Disease was an inevitable consequence of poor living conditions.
1777. The nurse came into the room carrying a newborn infant.
1778. John has started infant school.
1779. The plan was designed to protect infant industries in this country.
1780. People with the virus may feel perfectly well, but they can still infect others.

1781. Lucy's enthusiasm soon infected the rest of the class.
1782. A lot can be inferred from these statistics.
1783. The evidence inferred that the victim knew her killer.
1784. It was a cheap and inferior product.
1785. They felt inferior to the others until the team's international success gave them some pride.
1786. The annual rate of inflation fell.
1787. The Council had considerable influence over many government decisions.
1788. For centuries the country remained untouched by outside influences.
1789. Several factors are likely to influence this decision.
1790. The influx of migrants to the city is estimated at 1,000 per week.
1791. Please inform us of any change of address as soon as possible.
1792. She gave an informative talk on various aspects of child care.
1793. Some countries lack a suitable economic infrastructure.
1794. These plants have devised ingenious ways of snatching nutrients from the air.
1795. Mix all the ingredients together in a large saucepan.
1796. Traveling abroad is an essential ingredient in your business career.
1797. These remote islands are inhabited only by birds and animals.
1798. The inhabitants of the village protested against the new road.
1799. Every business has its own inherent risks.
1800. All her children will inherit equally.
1801. George's inherited his father's bad temper.
1802. An unhappy family life may inhibit children's learning.
1803. His initials are DPH: they stand for David Perry Hallworth.
1804. The initial response has been encouraging .
1805. Intellectuals have initiated a debate on terrorism.
1806. Older people should be injected against flu in winter.
1807. Two people have been critically injured in a road accident.
1808. The driver of the lorry sustained only minor injuries to his legs and arms.
1809. There were several flats overlooking the inner courtyard.
1810. She longed for inner calm.
1811. He firmly believes that she is innocent of the crime.
1812. I was very young and innocent at that time.
1813. He was a financial genius but a political innocent.

1814. The company has successfully innovated new products and services.
1815. Their ability to innovate has allowed them to compete in world markets.
1816. We must encourage innovation if the company is to remain competitive.
1817. Innovations in information technology have completely transformed the way students work.
1818. They received innumerable letters of complaint about the programme.
1819. Increased input of fertilizer increases crop yield.
1820. This is what I have been able to learn in my inquiries.
1821. He looked round in inquiry to make sure that everyone understood.
1822. On further inquiry, however, I discovered that there had been nobody at home that evening.
1823. Most frogs feed on insects.
1824. His hand shook slightly as he inserted the key into the lock.
1825. His manager inserted a new clause into his contract.
1826. The article gives us a real insight into the causes of the present economic crisis.
1827. Nick insisted that he was right.
1828. I got out of the car to inspect the damage.
1829. General Allenby arrived to inspect the troops.
1830. I hope this success will inspire you to greater efforts.
1831. They've installed the new network at last.
1832. I paid one hundred dollars in four monthly installments of twenty-five dollars.
1833. They came across many instances of discrimination.
1834. We hope you will be able to meet our requirements in this instance.
1835. All his instincts told him to stay near the car and wait for help.
1836. Her work experience has been various, including that of director of an environmental research institute.
1837. My colleague is a scientist at the Massachusetts Institute of Technology.
1838. Nearly every state had instituted a student-testing program.
1839. We had no choice but to institute court proceedings against the airline.
1840. These universities accept lower grades than the more prestigious institutions.
1841. Greater effort is needed to instruct children in road safety.
1842. His secretary was instructed to cancel all his engagements.
1843. The lightning had damaged the plane's instruments, and they weren't giving and readings.
1844. Which instrument do you play?
1845. The fireplace was the only thing that remained intact after the tornado.

1846. Try to reduce your intake of fat.

1847. Music should be an integral part of children's education.

1848. Transport planning should be integrated with energy policy.

1849. Bus and subway services have been fully integrated.

1850. He is a man of great integrity.

1851. They have vowed to protect the country's territorial integrity.

1852. He's quite bright but he's not what you would describe as intellectual.

1853. He was born in an intellectual family.

1854. John showed high intelligence from an early age.

1855. According to our intelligence, further attacks were planned.

1856. The article is not really intelligible unless you already know a lot about genetics.

1857. We intend to go to Australia next year if all goes well.

1858. The pain was so intense I could not sleep.

1859. She is a little too intense for me.

1860. After a brief period of intensive training, I was allowed to make my first parachute jump.

1861. She had no intention of spending the rest of her life working as a waitress.

1862. Lucy interacts well with other children in the class.

1863. I'd never interfere with a husband and wife.

1864. It has 104 cubic feet of interior space.

1865. The book is aimed at students at the intermediate level and above.

1866. There is to be an internal inquiry into the whole affair.

1867. The doctor said they found some signs of internal bleeding.

1868. We have no interest in interfering in the internal affairs of other countries.

1869. His refusal to work late was interpreted as a lack of commitment to the company.

1870. They spoke good Spanish, and promised to interpret for me.

1871. Sorry to interrupt but I have an urgent message for you.

1872. The city lies at the intersection of three motorways.

1873. He left the room, returning after a short interval with a message.

1874. He was just establishing his career when the war intervened.

1875. The army will have to intervene to prevent further fighting.

1876. He was very nervous before he had his job interview.

1877. In a television interview last night he denied he had any intention of resigning.

1878. The last interview he gave was recorded the day before he died.

1879. We're interviewing six candidates this afternoon.
1880. Who is the most famous person you've ever interviewed on TV?
1881. She is on intimate terms with important people in the government.
1882. She was asked about the most intimate details of her life.
1883. The watch mechanism is extremely intricate and very difficult to repair.
1884. Flexibility is intrinsic to creative management.
1885. I'm so sorry. Haven't you two been introduced?
1886. When we introduced this system, no one believed it would work.
1887. Your advice has been invaluable to us.
1888. Alexander Bell invented the telephone in 1876.
1889. But I didn't invent the story—everything I told you is true.
1890. Oliver made a fortune by investing in antique furniture.
1891. It was very difficult to leave a home we had invested so much in.
1892. The state police are investigating the incident.
1893. Who should we invite to the party?
1894. The interviewer invited the Senator to comment on recent events.
1895. No invoices had been found for any of the goods.
1896. Have they invoiced us for the stationery yet?
1897. St.Genevieve is often invoked against plagues.
1898. I invoked all Lord Mayor's power to organize a search for you.
1899. Reilly involves himself in every aspect of his company's business.
1900. Running your own business usually involves working long hours.
1901. We are focusing too much on irrelevant details.
1902. The main purposes of the dam were to provide irrigation and produced hydroelectric power.
1903. The town was isolated by the floods.
1904. A nosebleed is an issue of blood from the nose.
1905. The key issue is whether workers should be classified as "employees"
1906. A low grunt issued forth from his throat.
1907. All the workers were issued with protective clothing.
1908. The US State Department issues millions of passports each year.
1909. We went on to the next item on the agenda.
1910. I also saw that news item in the *Sunday Times*.
1911. Travellers who are willing to fix their own itinerary are able to avoid the tourist crowds.

1912. strawberry jam
1913. Sorry we're late. We got stuck in a traffic jam.
1914. I can't unscrew the lid of this jar.
1915. Why are you so jealous of his success?
1916. Do you enjoy your job?
1917. It is my job to make sure that the work is finished on time.
1918. She jogs for twenty minutes every morning before breakfast.
1919. "Who cooked the meal?" "Well it was a joint effort really."
1920. Knee joint
1921. Rain penetrates the joints between the concrete panels.
1922. I was given access to his private papers and journals.
1923. Her book draws on letters diaries, journals and historical sources.
1924. Have you had a good journey?
1925. As she looked through the old photograph albums, she was taken on a nostalgic journey to her childhood.
1926. The company was fined £6 million, following a recent court judgement.
1927. In my judgement, we should accept his offer.
1928. I have known him for years and I trust his judgement.
1929. When driving a car. You should always slow down as you approach a junction.
1930. Either side of the river is dense, impenetrable jungle.
1931. Junior doctors have protested about having to work long hours.
1932. My brother is my junior by three years.
1933. The juniors are performing a play at the end of the semester.
1934. I must get rid of all this junk.
1935. Sometimes I wonder if there's any justice in this world.
1936. We will not rest until her killer is brought to justice.
1937. No one doubts the justice of our cause.
1938. How can we justify spending so much money on arms?
1939. Nothing justifies murdering another human being.
1940. There has been a big increase in juvenile crime in the last few years.
1941. Many people are taking a keen interest in the result of the vote.
1942. There's been a keen competition for the job.
1943. I got a magazine and some cigarettes from a kiosk on the station platform.

1944. The fighter plane's crew all have survival kits in case they are shot down.

1945. She knelt and tried to see under the door.

1946. My granny knitted some gloves for me.

1947. She tried to open the door, but the knob came off in her hands.

1948. Tie a knob in the rope to stop it coming undone.

1949. The boat's top speed is about 20 knots.

1950. You need specialist knowledge to do this job.

1951. Their affair is public knowledge.

1952. She's a knowledgeable woman.

1953. It says "Dry Clean" on the label.

1954. Labels on clothes should be removed for kids with sensitive skin.

1955. The file was labelled "Top Secret".

1956. The newspapers had unjustly labelled him as a troublemaker.

1957. The facility uses animals in laboratory tests for some of its drugs.

1958. Many women do hard manual labour.

1959. Diane went into labour at two o'clock.

1960. Two many teachers are treated with a lack of respect.

1961. Alex's real problem is that he lacks confidence.

1962. You are too lame to be walking like this.

1963. My lame excuse was that I had too much else to do.

1964. I couldn't pick out any landmarks in the dark and got completely lost.

1965. The invention of the silicon chip is a landmark in the history of the computer.

1966. The landscape is dotted with the tents of campers and hikers.

1967. It'll take us several months to landscape the garden.

1968. It is very dangerous to drive fast along narrow country lanes.

1969. I find driving in the fast lane rather stressful so I prefer to stay in the middle lane or the slow lane.

1970. The champion is running in lane five.

1971. The town is at a low latitude.

1972. We give them latitude to generate their own ideas when choosing a career.

1973. In the latter case, buyers pay a 15% commission.

1974. Celebrations are planned for the latter part of November.

1975. Before launching the missile the pilot locks it onto the target.

1976. The government has launched a massive literacy campaign.
1977. A thick layer of dust lay on the furniture.
1978. They were handing out advertising leaflets outside the supermarket.
1979. There's water on the floor—we must have a leak somewhere.
1980. Water was leaking from the pipe.
1981. The news of the pay cuts leaked out quickly.
1982. She took a lease on the house in 1961.
1983. He had persuaded the local council to lease him a house.
1984. He regularly gives lectures on modern French literature.
1985. My father caught me and give me a long lecture about the dangers of drink.
1986. He lectures on European art at Manchester University.
1987. He began to lecture us about making too much noise.
1988. She threatened to take legal action against the hospital.
1989. What the company has done is perfectly legal.
1990. She is writing a thesis on Irish legend and mythology.
1991. Louis Armstrong was a jazz legend.
1992. The legend on the diagram shows how the engine works.
1993. The cave is the home of a legendary giant.
1994. Her handwriting was so tiny it was barely legible.
1995. We must legislate to control these drugs.
1996. Separating the sick from the healthy lessens the risk of infection.
1997. They originally asked for $5 million, but finally settled for a lesser sum.
1998. Employers with a payroll of £45,000 or less will be exempt from the levy.
1999. The government demanded a levy of troops to meet the danger.
2000. If the government wishes to raise tax revenue in order to subsidize the poor, it should levy a tax on films.
2001. The nation levied all able-bodied men for the war.
2002. Taking extra vitamins may reduce your liability to colds.
2003. A child is its parent's liability.
2004. If your liabilities exceed your assets, you may go bankrupt.
2005. My old car's a real liability. I can't use it but I have to pay for somewhere to keep it.
2006. The areas of town near the river are liable to flooding.
2007. You're more liable to injury when you don't get regular exercise.

2008. The law holds parent liable if a child does not attend school.
2009. If only they were as liberal with their cash.
2010. I had quite liberal parents.
2011. The agency has full licence to run operations in any friendly country.
2012. He was arrested for driving without a licence.
2013. Several companies have been licenced to produce these products.
2014. At high speeds the front of the boat would lift out of the water.
2015. Give it one more lift and we'll have it at the top of the stairs.
2016. They took the lift down to the bar.
2017. The clams were delicious. Likewise, the eggplant was excellent.
2018. Only the best linguists can become interpreters at the United Nation.
2019. There are a number of links between the two theories.
2020. Strong family ties still linked them together.
2021. The fuel used by space shuttles is a combination of liquid hydrogen and liquid oxygen.
2022. Water is a liquid.
2023. Mass literacy was only possible after the invention of printing.
2024. The name of the cheese is Dolcelatte, literally meaning "sweet milk".
2025. Dad was literally blazing with anger.
2026. Literature includes novels, shot stories, plays and poetry.
2027. It's important to keep up-to-date with the literature in your field.
2028. There were piles of litter in the streets.
2029. Kate sat on the floor surrounded by a litter of magazines.
2030. The streets were littered with old cans and other rubbish.
2031. We're repaying the loan over a three-year period.
2032. Can you loan me your tennis racket?
2033. I shall meet you in the entrance lobby.
2034. The group is lobbying for a reduction in defence spending.
2035. What kind of leisure facilities are there in the locality?
2036. The business is located right in the center of town.
2037. If you have difficulty locating a particular book, please ask one of the librarians for assistance.
2038. His apartment is in a really good location.
2039. Paul lodged with a family in Bristol when he first started work.
2040. We lodge students during term time.

2041. They went to a shooting lodge in Scotland for the weekend.

2042. What's the logic of your argument?

2043. The detective has to discover the murderer by logical deduction.

2044. The town is at longitude 21° east.

2045. I hesitated before making a long-term commitment of this importance.

2046. As you get closer they loom above you like icebergs.

2047. He loosened his seat-belt.

2048. She won a fortune in a state lottery.

2049. Jack has been a loyal worker in this company for almost 50 years.

2050. The chain might need lubricating.

2051. A few whiskies will lubricate his tongue.

2052. They did not have much luggage.

2053. The bathroom was luxurious, with gold taps and a thick carpet.

2054. The pin was extracted with a magnet.

2055. I want to magnify this picture.

2056. This report tends to magnify the risks involved.

2057. They do not recognize the magnitude of the problem.

2058. She was a tender, watchful maiden.

2059. Britain wants to maintain its position as a world power.

2060. The report found that safety equipment had been very poorly maintained.

2061. Critics maintain that these reforms will lead to a decline in educational standards.

2062. The Prime Minister is here to see you, Your Majesty.

2063. I am changing my major to political science.

2064. There are two major political parties in the US.

2065. The majority of students find it quite hard to live on the amount of money they get.

2066. He became a partner in the family firm on reaching his majority.

2067. Inspection of imported meat is mandatory.

2068. They have made a manifest error of judgement.

2069. They have so far manifested a total indifference to our concerns.

2070. The workmen manipulated some knobs and levers.

2071. You have the constant feeling you are being manipulated.

2072. Consult the computer manual if you have a problem.

2073. It would take too long to do a manual search of all the data.

2074. People in manual occupations have a lower life expectancy.
2075. This firm manufactures cars.
2076. He had manufactured and planted evidence.
2077. Cost will determine the methods of manufacture.
2078. I read his novel in manuscript.
2079. She is sitting on the margin of a swimming pool.
2080. Someone had written a note in the left-hand margin.
2081. You had better allow a margin of 30 pounds in the monthly budget.
2082. a brigade of US marines
2083. What do those marks in the middle of the road mean?
2084. Make sure you don't mark the paintwork while you're moving the furniture around.
2085. Will you mark my test before the end of term?
2086. Company sales improved dramatically following a $2 million marketing campaign.
2087. "My God," Foster marveled, "I've never seen so much money!"
2088. A massive iceberg is floating off the coast of Argentina.
2089. Without a massive increase in investment, the company will collapse.
2090. Could I have six meters of that curtain material?
2091. In some societies, wealth is inherited through the maternal side of a family.
2092. Mature apple trees are typically 20 feet tall.
2093. We are mature enough to disagree on this issue but still respect each other.
2094. She has matured into a fine writer.
2095. The company's main function is to maximize profit.
2096. The career center will help you maximize your opportunities.
2097. He faces a maximum of seven years in prison.
2098. We might have a third child, but that is the absolute maximum.
2099. The maximum temperature in this area is 33 degrees centigrade.
2100. This machine measures your heart rate.
2101. A centimeter is a measure of length.
2102. Stronger measures are needed to combat crime.
2103. These automatic cameras have a special focusing mechanism.
2104. The Army has set up mechanisms to help jobless ex-soldiers get work.
2105. When a person is ill, the body's natural defence mechanisms come into operation.
2106. The scandal was widely reported in the national media.

2107. The former president has agreed to mediate the peace talks.
2108. The injury required urgent medical attention.
2109. What size of shirt does he wear—small, medium or large?
2110. Fry the onions over a medium heat until they are golden.
2111. Sugar melts in water.
2112. You need to develop a positive mental attitude.
2113. It takes a lot of mental effort to understand these ideas.
2114. The center provides help for people suffering from mental illness.
2115. I'd like to examine the merchandise.
2116. I'd have no mercy on them.
2117. The first version certainly has the merit of being clear.
2118. He left a message saying he would probably be a little late.
2119. Some people's metabolism is more efficient than others.
2120. I think we should try again using a different method.
2121. A drop of water from a pond, viewed through a microscope, is full of tiny organisms.
2122. I might go to a concert tonight.
2123. How do birds know when to migrate, and how do they find their way back home?
2124. We had an exceptionally mild winter last year.
2125. Every milestone he passed showed the distance to Stonehenge.
2126. He felt that moving out from his parents' home was a real milestone in his life.
2127. The government has threatened to take military action if the rebels do not withdraw from the area.
2128. The trips are planned with military precision.
2129. Over the millennia the wind and rain destroyed them.
2130. He was mimicking the various people in our office.
2131. This is a continent exceptionally wealthy in minerals.
2132. mineral water
2133. The storm caused only minimal damage.
2134. Every effort is being made to minimize civilian casualties.
2135. We must not minimize the problem of racial discrimination.
2136. She had reduced her consumption of fat and sugar to an absolute minimum.
2137. Her father used to work in the Ministry of Agriculture.
2138. Converted in his early teens, he entered the ministry in 1855.

2139. This film contains material unsuitable for minors.

2140. I am taking history as my minor.

2141. He escaped with only minor injuries.

2142. We have made some minor changes to the program.

2143. There are both pluses and minuses to live in a big city.

2144. They suffered from a trade deficit of minus £4 billion.

2145. At night temperatures sometimes fall to minus 30℃.

2146. The payment will be refunded to you minus a small service.

2147. I'll be back in five minutes.

2148. Check your rearview and side mirrors before you drive away.

2149. The increase in inflation is due to higher prices for food and miscellaneous household items.

2150. You look miserable. What's up?

2151. His mission was to improve staff morale and output.

2152. At the conference you could hear an amazing mixture of languages.

2153. They have insulted us and mocked our religion.

2154. You should have a mock interview before taking part in the test.

2155. They have a relaxed mode of life that suits them well.

2156. To get out of the "auto" mode on the camera, turn the knob to "M".

2157. They showed us a model of the building.

2158. She was a model of honesty and decency.

2159. They used a computer to model the possible effects of global warming.

2160. Jim had always modeled himself on his great hero, Martin Luther King.

2161. We're looking for a house with a moderate-sized garden.

2162. It's a moderate price for a car of its type.

2163. He's very modest about his success of his research in genetics.

2164. They live in a fairly modest house, considering their wealth.

2165. The regulations can only be modified by a special committee.

2166. Make sure the soil is moist before planting the seeds.

2167. Trees have enormous roots that can reach out for moisture far below the surface.

2168. He suspected that his phone calls were being monitored.

2169. The temperature is carefully monitored.

2170. The government is monitoring the situation very closely.

2171. It's monstrous to charge that much for a hotel room.

2172. The splendid National Monument was erected in memory of the country's founders.
2173. I have to question the morality of forcing poor people to pay for their medical treatment.
2174. The rocking motion of the boat made Sylvia feel sick.
2175. A good teacher has to be able to motivate his/her students.
2176. What do you suppose was the killer's motive?
2177. His family motto is "God helps those who help themselves."
2178. For days after the accident, the death toll continued to mount.
2179. He mounted his bicycle and rode away.
2180. The house's windows are double-glazed to muffle the noise of aircraft.
2181. Three multiplied by four is twelve.
2182. Spending on military equipment has multiplied in the last five years.
2183. He was murmuring to himself in a corner.
2184. The next day the muscles in my arm felt sore.
2185. He wished he was more muscular and didn't have such a flat chest.
2186. Unfortunately some poisonous mushrooms look like edible mushrooms.
2187. With a mute bow he indicated to them his gratitude.
2188. The word "debt" contains a mute letter.
2189. Mutual respect is necessary for any partnership to work.
2190. His sudden disappearance was a complete mystery.
2191. Most societies have their own creation myths.
2192. We had a naïve belief that with democracy and freedom would come prosperity.
2193. The children swam naked in the lake.
2194. Switzerland is surrounded by four large neighbors, namely France, Germany, Austria and Italy.
2195. Some of the story was narrated in the film.
2196. Religion matters are very much at a national level.
2197. We refused to sign any treaty that is against our national interests.
2198. You're a very naughty boy! Look what you've done!
2199. That stretch of the river is too shallow to be navigable.
2200. Sailors have special equipment to help them navigate.
2201. The compass is an instrument of navigation.
2202. In the past, navigation depended largely on the position of the stars.
2203. A telephone is an absolute necessity for this job.

2204. The witness's testimony negated what the defendant has claimed.
2205. The decision would negate last year's Supreme Court ruling.
2206. The majority of people, when asked whether or not they are creative, will reply in the negative.
2207. The negatives outweigh the positives on this issue.
2208. He gave a negative answer without any explanation.
2209. My drinking was starting to have a negative effect on my work.
2210. The pregnancy test was negative.
2211. Many of those ideas have been neglected by modern historians.
2212. The government refused to negotiate with terrorists.
2213. Elderly people were carefully negotiating the hotel steps.
2214. I never suffer from nerves when I'm speaking in public.
2215. The dentist was drilling and he hit a nerve. The pain was incredible!
2216. It is important to build up a network of professional contacts.
2217. You are watching CNN, Cable News Network.
2218. I always tried to maintain neutral when they started arguing.
2219. During the World War II, Sweden was neutral.
2220. What you said was true. It was, nevertheless, a little unkind.
2221. Years after the accident I still have nightmare about it.
2222. The first day was a nightmare, but it was far from a total disaster.
2223. The new rich of early commerce and industry aped the nobility.
2224. He followed his principles with nobility.
2225. Hamsters are nocturnal creatures.
2226. The region was extremely beautiful. Nonetheless Gerard could not imagine spending the rest of his life there.
2227. Joyce's style of writing was a striking departure from the literary norm.
2228. Peer evaluation within the teams has become the norm.
2229. It is normal to feel nervous before an exam.
2230. All I want is to lead a normal life.
2231. She will graduate from this Normal University next year.
2232. The book is notable for its striking illustrations.
2233. Alcohol has a noticeable effect on the body.
2234. It was noticeable that no one at the party was under 40.

2235. You will be notified at any changes in the system.
2236. In August we were notified that our article had been rejected.
2237. She had only a vague notion of what she wanted to do.
2238. The traditional notion of marriage goes back thousands of years.
2239. The area was notorious for murders.
2240. Fame and fortune notwithstanding, Donna never forget her hometown.
2241. Will you still be happy after the novelty of the first few weeks is over?
2242. He is still novice as far as film acting is concerned.
2243. This is the first stage of a nuclear reaction which can lead to explosion.
2244. It's such a nuisance that you live so far away.
2245. Numerous attempts have been made to hide the truth.
2246. Do you believe that nature or nurture has the strongest influence on how children develop?
2247. She wants to stay at home and nurture her children, not go out to work.
2248. Nutrition and exercise are essential to fitness and health.
2249. She was an obedient little girl.
2250. I have no objection to anybody coming into my lesson.
2251. He vowed to achieve certain objectives before the end of his presidency.
2252. The world has an objective reality.
2253. It is hard to give an objective opinion about your own children.
2254. Employers are legally obliged to pay the minimum wage.
2255. If there is anything else I can do, I'm always happy to oblige.
2256. I'm much obliged to you.
2257. It's an obscure island in the Pacific.
2258. Official policy has changed, for reasons that remain obscure.
2259. Thick cloud obscured the stars from view.
2260. This accident should not obscure the fact that train travel is extremely safe.
2261. He has been taken to hospital for observation.
2262. I wish to make a few general observations about your work so far.
2263. It was difficult to observe any change in his expression.
2264. The role of scientists is to observe and describe the world, not to try to control it.
2264. I didn't enjoy the party, but the conventions had been observed.
2266. I would only observe that he is well qualified for the post.
2267. Fear of change is the greatest single obstacle to progress.

2268. A small aircraft now obstructed the runway.
2269. A small minority obstructed policies that would help the majority of people.
2270. These obstructions could take some weeks to clear from the canals.
2271. You will need to obtain permission from the principal.
2272. The obvious way of reducing pollution is to use cars less.
2273. Work will occupy your mind and help you forget about him.
2274. A third of accident deaths occur in the home.
2275. It had never occurred to him that he might be falling in love with her.
2276. Flooding under this bridge is a common occurrence.
2277. The study compares the occurrence of heart disease in various countries.
2278. There was something odd about him.
2279. He was wearing odd socks.
2280. A faint, sweet, woody odour hung in the air.
2281. The odour of hypocrisy hung about everything she said.
2282. The President was leaving for a four-day official visit of Mexico.
2283. You will have to get official permission first.
2284. He's an officious little man and widely disliked in the company.
2285. Cuts in prices for milk, butter, and cheese will be offset by direct payment for farmers.
2286. His blonde hair offset a deep tan.
2287. How do parents pass genes on to their offspring?
2288. Please don't omit any details, however trivial they may seem.
2289. The discussions are still ongoing.
2290. A team of three men operate the dam.
2291. Nuns are operating an emergency hospital.
2292. The two women had very different opinions about drugs.
2293. They have a very high opinion of Paula's work.
2294. He is admired even by his political opponents.
2295. He is opposed by other two candidates.
2296. The grocery store was on the opposite side of the street.
2297. I thought the medicine would make him sleep, but it had the opposite effect.
2298. We're in the building opposite the government offices.
2299. The people who live opposite are always making a lot of noise.
2300. Native tribes had been oppressed by the government and police for years.

2301. Strange dreams and nightmares oppressed him.
2302. I do not share his optimism about our chances of success.
2303. Foreign bankers are cautiously optimistic about the country's economic future.
2304. This was not the only option open to him.
2305. Conrad now owns 302,000 shares and options.
2306. The Space Shuttle is now in orbit.
2307. The satellite orbits the Earth every 48 hours.
2308. List your choices in order of preference.
2309. I want to leave my desk in order before I go away.
2310. At 8:00 a.m. we received the order to attack.
2311. The shop phoned to say your order has come in.
2312. Just give me a moment to order my thoughts, and I'll explain the system to you.
2313. The management has ordered a cutback in spending.
2314. I ordered some paste and a mixed salad.
2315. Reproduction is one of the most essential properties of a living organism.
2316. Factories and cities are more complex organisms than self-sufficient villages.
2317. The course was organized by a training company.
2318. He does not need you to organize his life for him.
2319. The Orient is used to refer to the eastern part of the world.
2320. It takes new students a while to orient themselves to college life.
2321. She looked at the street's names, trying to orient himself.
2322. I would prefer to read it in the original.
2323. The land was returned to its original owner.
2324. That is not a very original suggestion.
2325. How did the idea originate?
2326. Who originated the present complaints procedures?
2327. The shop stocks a wide range of garden ornaments, such as statues and fountains.
2328. The building relies on clever design rather than on ornament for its impressive effect.
2329. I can't meet you on Tuesday—I'm otherwise engaged.
2330. Put the milk back in the fridge, otherwise it will go off.
2331. The poor sound quality ruined an otherwise splendid film.
2332. He might have told you he was a qualified engineer, but the truth is quite otherwise.
2333. People who had heard the evidence at the trial were surprised at the outcome.

2334. This drainpipe is an outlet for water when it is raining.
2335. I play racquet ball as an outlet for stress.
2336. A chalk outline of the victim's body was still visible on the sidewalk.
2337. Always write an outline for your essays.
2338. The new president outlined plans to deal with crime, drugs and education.
2339. Output is up 30% on last year.
2340. There has been a huge increase in the output of children's books.
2341. It was clear right from the outset that there were going to be problems.
2342. It's an area of outstanding natural beauty.
2343. The advantages of this plan far outweigh the disadvantages.
2344. The overall cost of the exhibition was £400,000.
2345. They're half an hour overdue. I wish they'd come.
2346. Reform in all these areas is long overdue.
2347. The tiles on the roof overlap.
2348. My vacation overlaps with yours.
2349. The university has a large number of overseas students.
2350. Douglas often travelled overseas when he was in the army.
2351. A team leader was appointed to oversee the project.
2352. An overwhelming majority of people are opposed to this plan.
2353. My boss owes me for the extra work I did last weekend.
2354. I owe an enormous amount to my parents.
2355. He owes his life to the staff at the hospital.
2356. a pacific river
2357. The rebel's pacific gestures have met with little response from the army.
2358. Can you deliver a large package of books?
2359. The bank is offering a special financial package for students.
2360. Those chocolates have been packaged very attractively.
2361. It took me months of painstaking research to write the book.
2362. I picked up a free pamphlet on places to visit in the region.
2363. One of the door panels was badly damaged and had to be replaced.
2364. There will be at least three senior doctors on the panel.
2365. Shoppers fled the street in panic after two bombs exploded in central London.
2366. The Vietnam War has become a powerful anti-war paradigm.

2367. "More haste, less speed" is a paradox.
2368. It's a paradox that in such a rich country there can be so much poverty.
2369. The book is a mixture of all points of view in one paragraph.
2370. There are many parallels between Yeats and the Romantic poets.
2371. Lines AB and CD are parallel.
2372. Social changes in Britain are matched by parallel trends in some other countries.
2373. The railroad tracks paralleled the stream for several miles.
2374. His career parallels that of his father.
2375. The inquiry has to stay within the parameters laid down by Congress.
2376. Well, to paraphrase his words, television has become the opium of the masses.
2377. He made a partial recovery but he was never able to walk properly after the accident.
2378. The reporting in the papers is entirely partial and makes no attempt to be objective.
2379. Everyone in the class is expected to participate actively in these discussions.
2380. Dust particles must have got into the motor, which is why it isn't working properly.
2381. We are hoping to expand our business, particularly in Europe.
2382. Nigeria is our principal trading partner in Africa.
2383. She is a partner in a law firm.
2384. Clare is my tennis partner.
2385. He was guaranteed safe passage out of the country.
2386. The bill was amended several times during its passage through Congress.
2387. My parents could not afford the passage to America.
2388. Biology is their great passion at the moment.
2389. Kathy seems to take a very passive role in the relationship.
2390. Reading was her favourite pastime.
2391. When does the patent expire?
2392. This century there have been over a hundred patented devices to extract energy from the waves.
2393. Many artists were dependent on wealthy patrons.
2394. They provide facilities for disabled patrons.
2395. The book set the pattern for over 40 similar historical romances.
2396. The child showed a normal pattern of development.
2397. There was a pause while Alice changed the tape.
2398. Joe paused to consider his answer.

2399. She paused for a moment.
2400. Mount McKinley is Alaska's highest peak.
2401. Sales this month have reached a new peak.
2402. Sales peaked in August, then fell sharply.
2403. This meat tastes peculiar.
2404. The problem of racism is not peculiar to this country.
2405. Comparing students with their peers outside university, they are more likely to have emotional problems.
2406. There are now stiffer penalties for drunken drivers.
2407. I had to pay the penalty for the wrong decisions I made.
2408. When an X-ray beam penetrates the body, part is absorbed and part passes through.
2409. The company has been successful in penetrating overseas markets this year.
2410. It's hard to penetrate her mind.
2411. They find it hard to live on their state pension.
2412. The park attracts four million visitors per year.
2413. The work was carried out as per your instructions.
2414. Cats are not able to perceive colour.
2415. Even as a young woman she has been perceived as a future chief executive.
2416. I agree with you a hundred percent.
2417. A high percentage of married women have part-time jobs.
2418. Tax is paid as a percentage of total income.
2419. We face the perennial problem of not having enough money.
2420. Roses and geraniums are perennials, flowering year after year.
2421. the performance of his presidential duties
2422. Many people are extremely disappointed with the performance of this government.
2423. After the performance I went round to see her in her dressing room.
2424. The arms race is the greatest single peril now facing the world.
2425. His playing improved in a very short period of time.
2426. I was twelve years old when I started my period.
2427. The periodical is published every month.
2428. Hundreds perished when the ship went down.
2429. The old religion is perishing.
2430. Being exposed to sunlight has caused the rubber to perish.

2431. The blindness that the disease cause will be permanent.
2432. He gave up a permanent job in order to free-lance.
2433. Is it permissible to park my car here?
2434. Smoking is only permitted in the public lounge.
2435. I'll see you after the meeting, if time permits.
2436. You're not allowed to park here unless you have a permit.
2437. This is one reason why we persevered with the diary.
2438. If the pain persists, you must see a doctor.
2439. Childhood experiences have a strong influence on forming personality.
2440. It's partly the architecture which gives the town its personality.
2441. a TV personality
2442. We've advertised for extra security personnel.
2443. She is the head of personnel for a big company.
2444. His father's death gave him a whole new perspective on life.
2445. I finally managed to persuade her to go out for a drink with me.
2446. Your remarks are not pertinent to today's discussion.
2447. After the war a spirit of hopelessness pervaded the country.
2448. The tone of the meeting was pessimistic.
2449. They wanted me to sign a petition against experiments on animals.
2450. She is threatening to file a petition for divorce.
2451. Villagers petitioned the local authority to provide better bus services.
2452. Try the pharmacy on the corner.
2453. Modern pharmacy has solved the problem of sleeplessness.
2454. The first phase of renovations should be finished by January.
2455. There are three phases of this issue that come to my mind presently.
2456. Homelessness is not a new phenomenon.
2457. Language is a social and cultural phenomenon.
2458. Emma studies philosophy at university.
2459. The company explained their management philosophy.
2460. They were kept in appalling physical conditions.
2461. She was in constant physical pain.
2462. the picturesque narrow streets of the old city
2463. A pie chart can help the retailer or business-person see at a glance exactly where the money

goes.
2464. a pinpoint of light at the end of the tunnel
2465. Can you pinpoint it on the map for me?
2466. He was a pioneer of heart transplant operations.
2467. a general hospital which pioneered open heart surgery in this country
2468. He gave me advice on how to avoid the pitfalls of the legal process.
2469. The placement of the buttons and knobs in the car is well thought out.
2470. Records show that jailers made three attempts to find other placements, and then the matter apparently was forgotten.
2471. The town is situated on a plateau high up among the mountains of the north.
2472. She was waiting on Platform 4 for the train to London.
2473. He made a plea for help.
2474. Everyone is horrified about the plight of the starving people.
2475. The plots of his books are basically all the same.
2476. The plot was discovered before it was carried out.
2477. House prices have plummeted in recent months.
2478. The car stopped suddenly and he was plunged forward through the windshield.
2479. The price of oil has plunged to a new low.
2480. The margin of error was plus or minus 3 percentage points.
2481. Most children start school when they are five plus.
2482. This is not an exciting car to drive, but on the plus side it is extremely reliable.
2483. Three plus six equals nine.
2484. There are numerous clubs, plus a casino.
2485. The company has adopted a strict no-smoking policy.
2486. It has always been my policy not to gossip.
2487. It was my duty to polish the silver on Saturdays.
2488. He'd spent the summer polishing his flying skills.
2489. shoe polish
2490. This table needs a good polish.
2491. It's a reasonable movie, but it lacks polish.
2492. A recent poll found that 80% of Californians support the governor.
2493. The result of the poll will not be known until around midnight.
2494. The president's popularity has declined considerably.

2495. Computers become lighter, smaller, and more portable every year.
2496. The other driver must bear a portion of the blame for the accident.
2497. Do you have any children's portions?
2498. The writer portrays life in a working-class community at the turn of the century.
2499. Ann struck a pose and smiled for the camera.
2500. He shed the pose of the sophisticated lawyer and became his real self at last.
2501. We posed for photographs.
2502. Bryce was caught posing as a lawyer.
2503. Officials claim the chemical poses no real threat.
2504. Are you absolutely positive you locked the door?
2505. The response we have had from the public has been very positive.
2506. She has got a really positive attitude to life.
2507. I packed my remaining possessions into the trunk.
2508. The house has been in the family's possession since the 1500s.
2509. He has three postgraduates helping him with his research.
2510. Most of the people in the department hold postgraduate degrees.
2511. The match had to be postponed until next week.
2512. The film is fully of potent images of war.
2513. The company certainly has the potential for growth.
2514. For the first time she realized the potential danger of her situation.
2515. Kim poured some water into a glass.
2516. More than 20% of American families now live below the poverty line.
2517. Candidates should have training and practical experience in basic electronics.
2518. It does not sound like a very practical solution.
2519. Generally practitioners in Berkshire claimed 31.5 night visitor per 1000 population in 1992.
2520. In 1967, Phil was an eagerly practitioner of this dangerous specialty.
2521. Fire precautions were neglected.
2522. Lunch will be preceded by a short speech from the chairman.
2523. In other words, music precedes the idea.
2524. The invasion of Panama set a dangerous precedent.
2525. It was difficult to get precise information.
2526. Although I had precise engineering plans I nevertheless measured and remeasured the place.
2527. It is difficult to predict what the long-term effects of the accident will be.

2528. Immigration is the predominant social issue of the day.
2529. In this painting, the predominant colour is black.
2530. We could eat Chinese, Italian, or Indian—do you have any preference?
2531. In allocating food, preference is given to families with young children.
2532. These words appear to consist of prefix + stem.
2533. All three-digit number in Forden will now be prefixed by 580.
2534. Prejudice against black people is common in many parts of America.
2535. The discussions were preliminary to prepare a policy paper.
2536. A reasonable proficiency in English is a prerequisite for the course.
2537. These pills can be obtained by prescription only.
2538. You presence is requested at the club meeting on Friday.
2539. The presentation of prizes and certificates will take place in the main hall.
2540. The presentation of food can be as important as the taste.
2541. There are two presentations of the cabaret every night.
2542. I think these traditional customs should be preserved.
2543. In August the press are desperate for news.
2544. To judge from the press, the concert was a great success.
2545. the Clarendon Press
2546. They are putting pressure on people to vote yes.
2547. The pressures of work can make you ill.
2548. This little British firm has now gained considerable prestige.
2549. The king wanted to enhance his prestige through war.
2550. From the way he talked, I presumed him to your boss.
2551. Belief in magic still prevail in some rural parts of the country.
2552. Justice prevailed in the end.
2553. She has two children from a previous marriage.
2554. Financial reward is the primary reason most people work.
2555. Counseling was given as primary therapy for depression.
2556. Our primary concern is to provide the refugees with food and healthcare.
2557. Smoking is the prime cause of lung disease.
2558. The hotel is in a prime location overlooking the valley.
2559. Even today the villagers live in a primitive one-crop economy.
2560. She later became a principal with the Royal Ballet.

2561. Another teacher who moved me was an assistant principal named Chow, who doubled as a history teacher.
2562. Teaching is her principle source of income.
2563. It is against my principles to accept gifts from clients.
2564. He prided himself on his moral principles.
2565. Circle any typing errors you made on the printout.
2566. You do not need any prior knowledge of the subject.
2567. His own children have a prior claim to the business.
2568. Buses should have priority over other road uses.
2569. I need some privacy to read the letter properly and understand it.
2570. The new law is designed to protect people's privacy.
2571. One of the privileges of belonging to the club is that you can use its tennis courts.
2572. At school, I received several prizes for chemistry and physics.
2573. Has he ever shown you his prize for collection of antique clocks?
2574. What is the procedure for applying for a visa?
2575. This is standard procedure for getting rid of toxic waste.
2576. The government was determined to proceed with the election.
2577. Contract negotiations are proceeding smoothly.
2578. Coal forms by a slow process of chemical change.
2579. Repetition can help the learning process.
2580. Two million workers are employed processing goods for electronic firms.
2581. All university applications are processed through this system.
2582. Canada produces high-quality wheat.
2583. Sugar became the chief produce of the Caribbean.
2584. Management is always seeking ways to increase worker productivity.
2585. You sing like a real professional.
2586. Sloff was a true professional in the field of insurance.
2587. It is essential to get good professional advice.
2588. This business plan looks very professional.
2589. You need some proficiency in book-keeping for this job.
2590. I only saw her face in profile.
2591. Every week the magazine present the profile of a well-known sports personality.
2592. You don't expect to make much profit within the first couple of setting up a company.

2593. A lot of companies will profit from the fall in interest rates.
2594. The mother's behavior has a profound impact on the developing child.
2595. Because of bad weather, our programme of events has had to be changed slightly.
2596. What's your favorite television programme?
2597. What's programmed for this afternoon?
2598. Little progress has been made on human rights issues.
2599. We made good progress despite the snow.
2600. I asked the nurse how my son was progressing.
2601. Work on the ship progressed quickly.
2602. Smoking is strictly prohibited inside the factory.
2603. Tibai, who had been President since independence, was constitutionally prohibited from serving a further term in office.
2604. The project aims to provide an analysis of children's emotions.
2605. We are doing a project on pollution.
2606. School officials are projecting a rise in student numbers next semester.
2607. She projected the side onto the wall.
2608. All the time people are seeking to prolong life.
2609. The government should be playing a more prominent role in promoting human rights.
2610. He is a promising young actor.
2611. Helen was promoted to senior manager.
2612. Fertilizer promotes leaf growth.
2613. She is in London to promote her new book.
2614. Her situation prompted me to do something about getting a new job.
2615. He is always prompt in answering letters.
2616. You're more prone to illnesses when you're tired and your body is rundown.
2617. The fish moved silently through the water, propelled by short sweeps of its tail.
2618. Their job is to protect private property.
2619. He's got his own property.
2620. One of the properties of copper is that it conducts heat and electricity very well.
2621. an old Testament prophet
2622. He is one of the leading proponents of capital punishment.
2623. The proportion of women graduates has increased in recent years.
2624. Reduce the drawing so that all the elements stay in proportion.

2625. The committee put forward a proposal to reduce the time limit.
2626. Greeks face the prospect of new general elections next month.
2627. Job prospects for graduates do not look good.
2628. A lot of microchip manufacturing companies prospered at that time.
2629. His father was a prosperous farmers and coal merchant.
2630. According to protocol, he was to arrive at the meeting exactly five minutes early.
2631. The companies said they will share technology and develop a standard set of communication protocols.
2632. The appetite, says the proverb, grows with eating.
2633. Children were permitted into the hall for these films, provided they sat at the back.
2634. The agreement includes a provision for each side to check the other side's weapons.
2635. We had enough provisions for two weeks.
2636. We chose the house for its proximity to the school.
2637. You have to use psychology to get people to stop smoking.
2638. He spent his holiday writing reviews for publication.
2639. She was in England for the publication of her new book.
2640. The publication of his results has inspired a new wave of research.
2641. The concert wasn't given much advance publicity, so many tickets remained unsold.
2642. The first edition was published in 1765.
2643. We love reading your letters and we try to publish as many as possible.
2644. He is a very punctual person.
2645. This product should be consumed on the day of purchase.
2646. You can purchase insurance on-line.
2647. Her singing has purity, clarity and strength.
2648. Brian ran across the field with one police officer pursuing him.
2649. She plans to pursue a career in politics.
2650. The company is ruthless in its pursuit of profit.
2651. The robbers fled the scene of the crime, with the police in pursuit.
2652. Eva had excellent academic qualifications, but no work experience.
2653. The certificate qualifies you to work as a dental assistant.
2654. The research involves qualitative analysis of students' performance.
2655. He shows strong leadership qualities.
2656. Much of the land was of poor quality.

2657. Give us a ring if you have any queries about the contract.
2658. Many people are querying whether the tests are accurate.
2659. Both players queried the umpire's decision.
2660. All staff were asked to fill in a questionnaire about their jobs.
2661. We stood in a queue for half an hour.
2662. Some of the people queuing for tickets had been there since dawn.
2663. Jack wants to quit smoking.
2664. He hosts a pop quiz show on television.
2665. I often start the class with a short quiz to revise some vocabulary items.
2666. She quoted one sentences from a newspaper article.
2667. The firm originally quoted £6,000 for the whole job.
2668. She came second in the race.
2669. The law prohibits discrimination on the grounds of color or race.
2670. She has raced against some of the best runners in the country.
2671. We had to race across London to get the train.
2672. The log fire radiated a warm cosy glow.
2673. There are radical differences between the two organizations.
2674. The radius of the throwing circle should be 1.5 meters.
2675. She flew into a rage.
2676. A beggar was dozing on a pile of ragged blankets.
2677. Aircrafts are carrying out raid on enemy ships.
2678. The company has introduced random drug testing of its employees.
2679. The drug is effective against a range of bacteria.
2680. His hometown was situated in the longest range of hills in the Lake District.
2681. His vocal range is amazing.
2682. In the dining room, team photographs were ranged along the wall.
2683. She is now fifth in the world rankings.
2684. Don't go making any rash decisions about your future!
2685. The divorce rate is fantastically high.
2686. The ratio of nursing staff to doctors is 2∶1.
2687. Parents need to be fully informed so they can make a rational decision.
2688. You can eat carrots or raw.
2689. We've gathered a mass of raw data.

2690. Oil is an important raw material which can be processed into many different products, including plastic.
2691. Oil prices reacted sharply to news of the crisis in the Middle East.
2692. You need to be realistic about the amount you can do in a day.
2693. TV is used as an escape from reality.
2694. We reaped by hand.
2695. Don't let others reap the benefits of your research.
2696. He walked towards the rear of the house.
2697. I used to rear chickens.
2698. Our mother was always very reasonable.
2699. The tickets will cost a very reasonable £30.
2700. They apologized and reassured us that the matter would be dealt with immediately.
2701. Afterwards Olivia could not recall what they had talked about.
2702. The Ambassador was recalled from Washington.
2703. Foot steps receded into the distance.
2704. The painful memories gradually receded in his mind.
2705. We've got receipts for each thing we bought.
2706. We have a room kept for the reception of visitors.
2707. We're going to the Dean's reception.
2708. Would you make an appointment at reception?
2709. Radio reception kept fading.
2710. In times of severe recession companies are often forced to make massive jobs cut in order to survive.
2711. Do you know a good recipe for wholemeal bread?
2712. She had been asked to give a piano recital.
2713. Fred launched into a long recital of his adventures.
2714. How much do you reckon it's going to cost?
2715. She reckoned that there was a risk.
2716. She didn't recognize me at first.
2717. British medical qualifications are recognized in Canada.
2718. He was unable to recollect the names too.
2719. Doctors recommend that all children should be immunized against measles.
2720. Can you recommend a good lawyer?

2721. My university tutor wrote me a letter of recommendation to support my job application.
2722. She is likely to make a recommendation in a few days time on whether the company should file a law suit.
2723. Four paintings stolen from the gallery have been recovered.
2724. He is in hospital, recovering from a heart attack.
2725. Emma's only form of recreation seems to be shopping.
2726. Every effort is made to rectify any mistakes before the book is printed.
2727. Fossil fuels cannot be recycled. Once they are gone they are gone forever.
2728. The governor announced a new plan to reduce crime.
2729. Eventually Charlotte was reduced to begging on the street.
2730. Have you got another reel of film?
2731. A vocabulary index is included for easy reference.
2732. There is no direct reference to her own childhood in the novel.
2733. Car makers are constantly refining their designs.
2734. It was a four-week course, aimed at refining our understanding of the managerial role.
2735. She could see her face reflected in the car's windshield.
2736. The drop in consumer spending reflects concern about the economy.
2737. He had time to reflect on his successes and failures.
2738. It is high time that the legal profession reformed itself.
2739. The breeze was refreshing after the stuffy classroom.
2740. It made a refreshing change to talk to someone new.
2741. You can apply for a refund of your travel costs.
2742. I took the radio back, and they refunded my money.
2743. I refuse to take part in anything that's illegal.
2744. The offer is too good to refuse.
2745. Several scientists have attempted to refute Moore's theories.
2746. She refuted any allegations of malpractice.
2747. Teachers are held in low regard in this society.
2748. My husband sends his regards.
2749. The company's problems, in this regard, are certainly not unique.
2750. She stood back and regarded him coldly.
2751. The company is being questioned regarding its employment policy.
2752. The plan for a new railroad went ahead regardless of local opposition.

2753. The regime got rid of most of its opponents.
2754. He came back with a carefully designed regime for himself.
2755. For several years they lived in a remote region of Kenya.
2756. Peter signed the hotel guest register.
2757. Business letters should be written in a formal register.
2758. How many students have registered for English classes?
2759. Her face registered shock and anger.
2760. If the company's total income is over a certain amount, registration for VAT is compulsory.
2761. The company holds regular meetings with employees.
2762. The pipes were placed at regular intervals.
2763. It has long passed his regular bedtime.
2764. Meat and poultry are regulated by the Agriculture Department.
2765. People sweat to regulate their body heat.
2766. There seem to be so many rules and regulations these days.
2767. Who do I see about reimbursement of travelling expenses?
2768. He was given a reimbursement by the gas company for the damage to his house.
2769. Devote most of your time to reinforcing good behavior, with smiles, hugs and compliments.
2770. The dam was reinforced with 20,000 sandbags.
2771. The film reinforces the idea that women should be pretty and dumb.
2772. Sarah rejected her brother's offer of help.
2773. It is obvious why his application was rejected.
2774. Police now believe that the three crimes could be related.
2775. I might be related to him.
2776. A relatively small number of people disagreed.
2777. Gentle exercise can relax stiff shoulder muscles.
2778. A hot bath should help to relax you.
2779. Simon has obtained early release from prison.
2780. Mr. Wilson said that in a news release.
2781. Playing an instrument can be a form of emotional release.
2782. The bears are eventually released into the wild.
2783. He was released from the hospital yesterday.
2784. Her new album will be released at the end of the month.
2785. Relevant documents were presented in court.

2786. Miller was a quiet and reliable man.
2787. Don't worry, my car is reliable.
2788. To our great relief the children all arrived home safely.
2789. Tranquillizers provide only temporary relief from depression.
2790. She could not accept the religious beliefs of her parents.
2791. Our parents were very religious and very patriotic.
2792. Wells finally agreed, but with reluctance.
2793. Many working women rely on relatives to help take care of their children.
2794. Many people now rely on the Internet for news.
2795. He spent the remainder of his police career behind a desk.
2796. Fifteen divided by four gives you a remainder of three.
2797. He prepared the dinner with remarkable speed and efficiency.
2798. The law doesn't provide a remedy for this kind of injustice.
2799. He preferred home-made remedies to even the most modern pharmaceutical products.
2800. The view reminded her of Scotland.
2801. It may happen some time in the remote future.
2802. Reference books may not be removed from the library.
2803. He removed his hat and gloves.
2804. The college removed rules that prevented women from enrolling.
2805. New technology has rendered my old computer obsolete.
2806. We are sincerely grateful to everyone who has rendered assistance to the victims of the earthquake.
2807. He is rendering the book from French into English.
2808. The factory replaced most of its workers with robots.
2809. He hated the school and everything it represented.
2810. This treatment represents a significant advance in the field of cancer research.
2811. She reproached me for my lack of foresight.
2812. She was astonished at the look of reproach on his face.
2813. If you have a burglar alarm fitted, make sure it is done by a reputable company.
2814. She has the reputation of being a good doctor.
2815. The study was done at the request of the Chairman.
2816. Ray made a formal written request to meet with Douglas.
2817. You have to request permission if you want to take any photographs.

2818. What is required is a complete reorganization of the system.
2819. You are required by law to wear a seat belt.
2820. All my attempts to rescue him were in vain.
2821. I am still doing research for my thesis.
2822. It is a good idea to do some research before you buy a house.
2823. You can see the resemblance between Susan and her sister.
2824. He grew up to resemble his father.
2825. The country has foreign currency reserves of $83 billion.
2826. She overcame her natural reserve.
2827. The management reserves the right to refuse admission.
2828. Do you have to reserve tickets in advance?
2829. Rivers and reservoirs overflowed.
2830. History is a reservoir of human experience.
2831. He spent most of his time in Detroit, where his family resided.
2832. Executive power resides in the President.
2833. You have the choice between resignation and dismissal.
2834. Any attack will be resisted with force if necessary.
2835. This special coating is designed to resist rust.
2836. The resolution was passed by a two thirds majority.
2837. The lawyer's advice led to the resolution of this problem.
2838. Carol made a resolution to work hard at school this year.
2839. Recent events strengthened her resolve to find out the truth.
2840. Mary resolved that she would stop smoking.
2841. The Senate resolved to accept the President's proposal.
2842. I think we can solve this problem without resorting to legal action.
2843. In recent years this little town has grown into a fashionable resort.
2844. He got hold of the money legally, without resort to violence.
2845. You have to help me—you're my only resort.
2846. Only limited resources are available to the police.
2847. He proved that he has considerable inner resources.
2848. New teachers have to earn the respect of their students.
2849. I deeply respect David for what he has achieved.
2850. Dave did not respond to any of her emails.

2851. She has responded well to treatment.
2852. Only 62 percent of respondents said they were satisfied.
2853. The law was passed in response to public pressure.
2854. The exhibition has received a positive response from visitors.
2855. The police arrested those responsible for the burglaries.
2856. Each commissioner is responsible for a department.
2857. The government promises to restore the economy to full strength.
2858. The church was carefully restored after the war.
2859. He had to be restrained from using violence.
2860. Price rises should restrain consumer spending.
2861. The new law restricts the sale of hand guns.
2862. Accidents are the inevitable result of driving too fast.
2863. The election results will be announced at midnight.
2864. We are still dealing with problems resulting from errors made in the past.
2865. He gave a resume of the year's work and wished the Society another successful year.
2866. Please send us your personal resume to us before sitting a written test.
2867. You have the right to retain possession of the goods.
2868. A lot of information can be retained in your computer.
2869. The flood waters are slowly retreating.
2870. Current economic problems have forced the government to retreat from its pledge to cut taxes.
2871. Matthew retrieved his kite from the tree.
2872. Computer are used to store and retrieve information efficiently.
2873. He revealed that he had been in prison twice before.
2874. The curtain opened to reveal the grand prize.
2875. Hamlet was seeking revenge for his father's murder.
2876. First, they expect to raise enough revenue to pay for their own activities.
2877. Taxes provide most of the government's revenue.
2878. I owe you nothing. If anything, the reverse is true.
2879. The British ten-pence coin has a lion on the reverse.
2880. Losing the Senate vote was a serious reverse for the President.
2881. In some families the father goes out to work and the mother stays at home. In others, the reverse situation is true.
2882. Our roles as child and guardian had now been reversed.

2883. The newspaper published a review of her book.

2884. All fees are subject to review.

2885. We will review your situation and decide how we can help you.

2886. Bradman will review the best of the new children's books.

2887. A couple of sections of the book will need to be revised.

2888. We have revised our estimates of population growth.

2889. In the last ten years there has been a revolution in education.

2890. The Earth makes one revolution around the sun each year.

2891. The police offered a reward for any information about the robbery.

2892. All his hard work was rewarded when he saw his book in print.

2893. I've got no sense of rhythm, so I'm a terrible dancer.

2894. All his money will go, as a result of this ridiculous gambling.

2895. She maintained rigid control over her emotional life.

2896. He built the team through hard training and rigid discipline.

2897. Every new drug has to pass a series of rigorous safety checks before it is put on sale.

2898. The car is put through rigorous road performance tests.

2899. Fit the tire round the rim of the wheel.

2900. Those apples aren't ripe yet.

2901. The land was ripe for industrial development.

2902. If you're considering staring a business, think carefully about the risks involved.

2903. Sheena left her job and went to work for a rival company.

2904. The wind roared in the forest.

2905. He looks robust and healthy.

2906. The once robust economy now lies in ruins.

2907. You can get black-and-white television sets at rock-bottom prices.

2908. Everyone had a role in the show's success.

2909. Barbara Cartland is a writer of romantic fiction.

2910. We thought that Egypt was an incredibly romantic country.

2911. Here is the duty roster for all the members of the scout troop.

2912. The club has outstanding players on the roster.

2913. The satellite slowly rotates as it circles the earth.

2914. First do a rough draft of your essay.

2915. He was fast asleep and couldn't be roused.

2916. The commander tried to rouse them all into action.
2917. What is the best route to Cambridge?
2918. Kennedy arrived at the same conclusion by a different route.
2919. There's no set routine at work—every day is different.
2920. My job is so routine and boring—I hate it.
2921. The children were asked to stand in a row.
2922. The rain ruined our holiday.
2923. They refused to confirm or deny the rumour of planned job losses.
2924. I ran to the door and opened it.
2925. Mrs. Thatcher wanted to run a fourth time.
2926. For a while, she ran a restaurant in Boston.
2927. Rural life is usually more peaceful than city life.
2928. India is still an overwhelmingly rural country.
2929. There were large patches of rust on the car.
2930. They visited the scared places of Islam.
2931. It's not worth sacrificing your health for your career.
2932. It was common to make sacrifices to the gods to ensure a good harvest.
2933. The people offered a lamb on the alter as a sacrifice for their sins.
2934. Making sacrifices is part of raising children.
2935. New regulations were introduced to safeguard the environment.
2936. Does the new law provide an adequate safeguard for consumers?
2937. The device meets safety standards.
2938. Firefighters led the children to safety.
2939. They took a blood sample to test for hepatitis.
2940. Eighteen percent of the adults sampled admitted having had problems with alcohol abuse.
2941. Here is your chance to sample the delights of country life.
2942. In the doctor's opinion he was sane at the time of the murder.
2943. It was a sane decision and one we all respected.
2944. After examining the sanitary arrangements, they ordered the whole place to be disinfected.
2945. She bought new bathroom scales.
2946. They scanned his brain for signs of damage.
2947. She scanned through the paper.
2948. There was a scar on his right arm.

2949. Fruit was always scarce in winter, and cost a lot.
2950. We had scarcely driven a mile when the car broke down.
2951. The landscape scarcely altered for hundreds of thousands of years.
2952. Books lay scattered all over the floor.
2953. There was a sudden crack of gunfire and the crowd scattered in all directions.
2954. Imagine a scenario where only 20% of people have a job.
2955. The worst-case scenario was that he would have to have an operation.
2956. In the final scene, Harry tells Sabrina he loves her.
2957. Journalists were on the scene within minutes.
2958. The evening air was full of the scent of roses.
2959. How can he fit everything into his busy schedule?
2960. The majority of holiday flights depart and arrive on schedule.
2961. The money will be used for teacher training schemes.
2962. She schemed to kill him with poison.
2963. His book on Chinese verbs is a work of great scholarship.
2964. Paula went up to Oxford on a scholarship.
2965. Mother scolded me this morning for being rude to you.
2966. A full discussion of that issue is beyond the scope of this book.
2967. There is considerable scope for further growth in the economy.
2968. After two hours and twenty minutes of play, the final score was 3:2.
2969. He had an IQ score of 120.
2970. Scores of reporters gathered outside the courthouse.
2971. All members of the cast must not depart from the script.
2972. He scrutinized the document closely.
2973. The college offers classes in sculpture.
2974. Both exams are taken after five years of secondary education.
2975. Social skills shouldn't necessarily be seen as secondary to academic achievement.
2976. The plane's tail section was found in a cornfield.
2977. The disease spread through the poorer sections of the city.
2978. The growth in the number of home computers has boosted the electronics sector.
2979. We want a secure future for out children.
2980. There are no secure jobs these days.
2981. Troops were sent to secure the border.

2982. The company recently secured a $20 million contract with Ford.
2983. The prison was ordered to tighten security after a prisoner escaped yesterday.
2984. We applied the same principles to these securities regardless of who issued them.
2985. Rivers are bringing lots of sediment down to the sea.
2986. Do you think the President will seek re-election?
2987. If the symptoms persist, seek medical advice.
2988. Instead of draining away, water seeps down into the ground.
2989. Different segments of draining away, water seeps down into the ground.
2990. the segments of an orange
2991. He seized my hand and dragged me away from the window.
2992. The rebels have seized power in a violent coup.
2993. Honorary degrees are handed out to a select few.
2994. He had hopes of being selected for the national team.
2995. It was not easy to make our selection.
2996. Fall semester starts the 28th of August.
2997. Every week we have a seminar on modern political theory.
2998. Publishers and writers from 13 countries attended the seminar.
2999. She gave civics lessons at high schools where the seniors were eligible to vote.
3000. Her husband was nine years her senior.
3001. Senior pupils have certain privileges.
3002. There are separate dining rooms for staff, middle management, and senior management.
3003. I think that's the most sensible thing to do.
3004. He did not appear to be sensible of the difficulties that lay ahead.
3005. Throughout her career she remained very sensitive to criticism.
3006. Tell me if any of these spots are sensitive.
3007. The gym and the sauna are in separate buildings.
3008. My wife and I have separated bank accounts.
3009. The lighthouse is separated from the land by a wide channel.
3010. He has a sequence of business failures.
3011. Be careful to perform the actions in the correct sequence.
3012. There has been a whole series of accidents on this road.
3013. On Monday, the governors were to hold a working session with Bush.
3014. The court is now in session.

3015. We have five hours of English a week, including one session in the language laboratory.
3016. The most severe penalty he could get is ten years in jail.
3017. One of the passengers had suffered severe bruising and serious cuts.
3018. In parts of Africa there is a severe food shortage.
3019. All you see on TV is sex and violence these days.
3020. Please put your name, age and sex at the top of the form.
3021. The house next door cast a shadow over our garden.
3022. Her father's illness cast a shadow over the birth of her baby.
3023. The stream was quite shallow so we were able to walk across it.
3024. I though that film was rather shallow.
3025. Our table is oval in shape.
3026. He outlined his ideas about the manifesto's shape.
3027. Through the window, I could see a dark shape in the street outside.
3028. He began to shape the dough into rolls.
3029. Research findings are often used to shape social policy.
3030. We had a tool shed in our back yard.
3031. He is very worried about the shift towards free market thinking in Eastern Europe.
3032. Dave had to work a 12-hour shift yesterday.
3033. She shifted her gaze from me to Bobby.
3034. He refused to shift his ground.
3035. Juanita was shivering with cold.
3036. The movie was over shortly before six.
3037. Why does the phone always ring when I'm in the shower?
3038. Heavy showers are forecast in the hills tomorrow.
3039. The boys shrank away in horror.
3040. You should dry-clean curtains if possible, as they are less likely to shrink.
3041. The world's forests are shrinking at an alarming rate.
3042. Look at the figures on either side of the equals sign.
3043. There is no sign that the economy is on the upturn.
3044. The driver gave a signal that he was going to turn right.
3045. His most significant political achievement was the abolition of the death penalty.
3046. A significant part of Japan's wealth is invested in the West.
3047. Out in the country again we drove past a signpost I couldn't read.

3048. My teacher has given me some signpost towards what I should study next.
3049. The road wasn't very well signposted.
3050. The speech was strikingly similar to one given by the American.
3051. When studying children and other young animals, we can see similarities in their behavior.
3052. Try to simplify your explanation for the children.
3053. He found it impossible to simulate grief.
3054. Interviews can be simulated in the classroom.
3055. Two children answered the teacher's question simultaneously.
3056. They believed they were being punished for their sins.
3057. Please accept it with my sincere good wishes.
3058. He was gentle and sincere by nature.
3059. The town has purchased a site on Villa Avenue for the new library.
3060. The house is built on the site of a medieval prison.
3061. The control center is situated many miles away.
3062. She coped well in a difficult situation.
3063. I cannot put up with the current situation one day longer.
3064. Children should drink milk to help them develop strong skeletons.
3065. My book is in skeleton form— now I just have to add the details.
3066. The introduction to the book provides a sketch of its contents.
3067. The art students were each told to sketch a tree.
3068. Reading and writing are two different skills.
3069. The whole team played with great skill and determination.
3070. After simmering the meat, skim the fat from the surface.
3071. Just skim through the second section to save time.
3072. The lambs were skipping about in the field.
3073. This part of the book isn't very interesting, so I'm going to skip it.
3074. She was slender and had long dark hair.
3075. Would you like another slice of ham?
3076. Could you slice a very thin piece of cake for me?
3077. We've got one of those doors in the kitchen that slides open.
3078. The government must take measures, he said, to halt the country's slide into recession.
3079. We've going to have a slide show.
3080. She's slightly taller than her sister.

3081. Regular exercise will make you slimmer.
3082. There's a slim chance someone may have survived.
3083. Be careful! The floor's very slippery.
3084. We need an advertising slogan for the new campaign.
3085. The floor slopes a bit.
3086. The roof is at a slope of 30°.
3087. I dropped the plane and it smashed.
3088. Larry smashed his fist down on the table.
3089. I had a huge lunch, so I only want a snack for dinner.
3090. Small children are often told not to snatch because it is rude.
3091. I was desperate to find a way out of teaching so when this job came along I snatched at it.
3092. The wind had blown the rain into the bedroom and soaked the bed.
3093. All night long fireworks soared into the sky.
3094. I went to see the playwright's so-called masterpiece and was very disappointed by it.
3095. The so-called experts could not tell us what was wrong.
3096. There's repression and social injustice everywhere.
3097. It is a way to broaden their circle of social contacts.
3098. You need special software to view the information in the file.
3099. The soles of her feet were feathery soft.
3100. Griffiths is the sole survivor of the crash.
3101. The company has the sole rights to market Elton John's records.
3102. Even the milk was frozen solid.
3103. We were glad to be on solid ground.
3104. Both sides are trying to find a peaceful solution.
3105. a weak sugar solution
3106. The price is somewhat higher than I expected.
3107. Sophisticated readers understood the book's hidden meaning.
3108. I think a more sophisticated approach is needed to solve this problem.
3109. He expressed his sorrow at my father's death.
3110. It was a great sorrow to his parents that he dropped out of college.
3111. What sort of shampoo do you use?
3112. They are a sort of chocolate.
3113. He was sorting through a pile of clean socks.

3114. I've sort of heard of him but I don't know who he is.
3115. Ted will always give you sound advice.
3116. Beans are a very good source of protein.
3117. We have found the source of the trouble.
3118. List all your sources at the end of your essay.
3119. She spent the morning buying souvenirs.
3120. I have a spacious, comfortably furnished living room.
3121. Over a span of only two years, the new government has transformed the country's economic prospects.
3122. It will spare him embarrassment if you speak to him about it in private.
3123. Do sign the book when you can spare a minute.
3124. The commander was so impressed by their bravery that he spared their lives.
3125. They had it printed in *the Palace News*, sparing no detail of what was going on.
3126. There were no chairs spare.
3127. All you need to take is a spare shirt and a spare set of underwear.
3128. In a gas leak, any small spark will cause an explosion.
3129. I told her a little about my life at her age, and I saw a spark of interest.
3130. The salmon fight their way back up the river to spawn.
3131. Poverty had spawned numerous religious movements.
3132. I went to a specialist who found I had too little sugar in my blood.
3133. Simon specialized in contract law.
3134. There are more than two hundred and fifty species of shark.
3135. Thurman was reluctant to go into specifics about the deal.
3136. Mr. Howard gave us very specific instructions.
3137. Power plant employees must follow very specific safety guidelines.
3138. The president did not specify a date for his visit to Peru.
3139. Over a hundred teachers will receive specimen copies of the dictionary.
3140. The questionnaire covered an extremely broad spectrum of topics.
3141. Women have often been excluded from positions of power in the public sphere.
3142. This curry needs a bit more spice.
3143. Make sure the water doesn't spill over the floor.
3144. The people is the spiritual leader of the Christian Church.
3145. The wooden floor had cracked and split in the heat.

3146. The government is splitting on how to deal with the situation.
3147. I really hope it doesn't rain; that would spoil everything.
3148. I haven't seen the film, so don't spoil it for me by telling me what happens.
3149. Her parents spoilt and indulged her with toys and treats of every kind.
3150. The dessert will spoil if you don't keep it in the fridge.
3151. She got a family friend in Bristol to agree to be her sponsor.
3152. Before you can get a visa to live in Britain, you need to find someone who will officially sponsor you.
3153. There are usually a few spots of grease on his tie.
3154. This looks like a nice spot for a picnic.
3155. In 60% of the households surveyed both spouse went out to work.
3156. We saw a huge vehicle spraying water on the road.
3157. It really feels like spring now that the evenings are getting lighter.
3158. I think the springs have gone in the sofa—it feels very soft.
3159. Over the years the mattress has lost its spring.
3160. a mountain spring
3161. Cut the lemon in half and squeeze the juice into the bowl.
3162. After 24 hours the patient's condition began to stabilize.
3163. A wide base will make the structure much more stable.
3164. He was clearly not a very stable person.
3165. Thousands of football fans packed into the stadium to watch the cup final.
3166. The school's staff are excellent.
3167. Short cuts at this stage can be costly.
3168. I walked out on the stage and started to sing.
3169. The moss grows in stagnant pools of water.
3170. People who become stagnant at midlife dry out and shrink like prunes.
3171. If cold water doesn't remove a stain, try using lukewarm water and soap.
3172. The committee is assessing the standard of care in local hospitals.
3173. We paid them the standard rate.
3174. Searching luggage at airports is now standard practice.
3175. He stared at us in disbelief.
3176. There are fears for the state of the country's economy.
3177. The state has allocated special funds for the emergency.

3178. Please state your name and address.
3179. The price of the tickets is stated on the back.
3180. He refused to give a statement to the police.
3181. In an official statement, she formally announced her resignation.
3182. Only use the handbrake when your vehicle is stationary.
3183. We buy things like stationery and toilet rolls in bulk.
3184. The statistic comes from a study recently conducted by the British government.
3185. Statistics is a branch of mathematics.
3186. People say Rome is a city with many statues.
3187. Doctor have traditionally enjoyed high social status.
3188. These documents have no legal status in Britain.
3189. Hold the flashlight steady so I can see better.
3190. It wasn't easy to find steady work in the city.
3191. They have proposed a steep increase in the cigarette tax.
3192. They set off with no idea how to steer a boat.
3193. He steered me to a table and sat me down in a chair.
3194. His headache stemmed from vision problems.
3195. His training will have taught him certain stereotypes.
3196. They went round sticking posters on walls and lamp-posts.
3197. The fighting has greatly stimulated weapons technology.
3198. Stir the sauce gently over a low heat.
3199. Stir yourself, or we'll never get this finished!
3200. The latest economic figures have stirred fears of growing inflation.
3201. I think the soup needs a stir.
3202. Her speech created a huge stir.
3203. The data is stored on a hard disk and backed up on a floppy disk.
3204. People like shopping in the larger stores because they can get everything under one roof.
3205. He's got an impressively large store of wine in his cellar.
3206. She's got straight blonde hair.
3207. Just be straight with her and tell her how you feel.
3208. I got home and went straight to bed.
3209. We don't need to go straight off—we've got ten minutes for a coffee.
3210. The new networking system is fairly straightforward—you should not have any problems.

3211. Jack is tough, but always straightforward and fair.
3212. The company must first resolve questions of strategy.
3213. The bridge will need to be strengthened.
3214. They have been strengthening their border defenses in preparation for war.
3215. Yoga is excellent for relieving stress.
3216. Powell laid particular stress on the need for discipline.
3217. She stressed the importance of a balanced diet.
3218. Studying for exams always stresses me out.
3219. My T-shirt is stretched in the wash.
3220. It's a good idea to stretch before you take vigorous exercise.
3221. The road stretched over two hundred miles through the heart of the country.
3222. My parents were very strict with me when I was young.
3223. Clare jumped off the porch and strode across the lawn.
3224. A snowball struck him on the back of the head.
3225. Police say they fear the man could strike again.
3226. It struck Carol that what she'd said about Helen applied to her too.
3227. She bears a striking resemblance to her mother.
3228. Jack stripped off and jumped into the shower.
3229. Captain Evans was found guilty and stripped of his rank.
3230. We must continue to strive for greater efficiency.
3231. She swam with strong steady strokes.
3232. With each stoke of the whip, the horse galloped faster.
3233. Max made a few quick decisive strokes with his brush.
3234. Many visitors to the UK find the British class structure difficult to understand.
3235. A new management structure has been introduced.
3236. The exhibition is structured around three topics.
3237. What's that stuff you're drinking?
3238. The dinner will be served buffet style.
3239. The rooms are furnished in a modern style.
3240. It is not good style to use abbreviations in an essay.
3241. These shoes have been styled for maximum comfort.
3242. They style themselves "the terrible twins".
3243. Can we talk about a different subject please?

3244. My favorite subjects at school were history and geography.
3245. He is a British subject.
3246. All building firms are subject to tight controls.
3247. Cars are subject to a high domestic tax.
3248. The invaders quickly subjected the local tribes.
3249. The company's accounts were subjected to close scrutiny.
3250. As a critic, his writing is far too subjective.
3251. All applications must be submitted by Monday.
3252. Derek has agreed to submit to questioning.
3253. The idea of being evaluated by subordinates makes some managers uneasy.
3254. Women were subordinate to men.
3255. Women had a subordinate status in our society.
3256. These skills were passed on to subsequent generation.
3257. US farmers are having trouble coping with the reductions in agricultural subsidies.
3258. Heroin is an illegal substance.
3259. His decision was based on nothing more substantial than his dislike of foreigners.
3260. After a substantial lunch, he decided to have a rest.
3261. On the site were a number of substantial timber buildings.
3262. She inherited a substantial fortune from her grandmother.
3263. The coach has to find a substitute for Tim.
3264. Vitamin pills are no substitute for a healthy diet.
3265. The recipe says you can substitute yoghurt for the sour cream.
3266. There is a subtle difference between these two plans.
3267. Four subtracted from ten equals six.
3268. The company decided to relocate to the suburbs because the rent was much cheaper.
3269. His successor died after only 15 months in office.
3270. The refrigerator was the successor to the ice box.
3271. We need sufficient time to deal with the problem.
3272. The word is "usefully", with the suffix -ly in a different colour.
3273. He owes me a large sum of money.
3274. He offered to purchase the estate for the sum of 80,000.
3275. At the end of the news, they often give you a summary of the main headlines.
3276. Were students satisfied with this summary justice?

3277. Did anyone reach the summit?
3278. The summit of his career came when he was made managing director.
3279. Western leaders are gathering for this week's Ottawa summit.
3280. The museum has a superb collection of twentieth century art.
3281. It makes her very angry when he says that men are intrinsically superior to women.
3282. The demonstrators were superior in numbers, but the police were superior in strength.
3283. We chose her for the job because she was the superior candidate.
3284. The teachers take it in turn to supervise the children at playtime.
3285. My supervisor said he would strongly recommend me for the course.
3286. The payments are a supplement to his usual salary.
3287. He is reading *the Sunday* supplements.
3288. Kia supplements her regular salary by tutoring in the evenings.
3289. There is a supplementary water supply in case the main supply fails.
3290. Most large towns are supplied with electricity.
3291. There are very large supplies of oil in the North Sea.
3292. This isn't what we're supposed to be discussing.
3293. I suppose he must be delighted about getting the job.
3294. Suppose we miss the train—what will we do then?
3295. The former Emperor of China was the supreme ruler of his country.
3296. Marble has a smooth, shiny surface.
3297. Doubts are beginning to surface about whether the right decision has been made.
3298. His performance surpassed all expectations.
3299. Companies are likely to continue laying off surplus staff well into the recovery.
3300. A lot of the children at the school do not live in the town, but come in from the surrounding countryside.
3301. The survey showed that Britain's trees are in good health.
3302. We conducted a survey of parents in the village.
3303. Nineteen percent of those surveyed say they haven't decided yet.
3304. Charles survived his wife by three months.
3305. She survived the attack.
3306. Only 12 of the 140 passengers survived.
3307. We are all susceptible to advertising.
3308. Police suspected that he had some connection with the robbery.

3309. He's suspected of murder.
3310. A large light was suspended from the ceiling.
3311. Talks between the two countries have now been suspended.
3312. His behavior that day made the police suspicious.
3313. Anyone who saw anything suspicious is asked to contact the police immediately.
3314. The thought of seeing her again was all that sustained me.
3315. They gave me barely enough food to sustain me.
3316. a swarm of bees
3317. Swarms of tourists jostled through the square.
3318. The trees were swaying gently in the breeze.
3319. Don't swear in front of the children.
3320. Do you swear on your honour never to tell anyone?
3321. Sweep the floor clean for me please.
3322. Thunderstorms swept the country.
3323. My ankles tend to swell when I travel by air.
3324. The crowd swelled.
3325. My letter received a swift reply.
3326. Frank switched easily and fluently from French to English.
3327. Can you switch the television off?
3328. Two Shakespeare plays are on this year's English syllabus.
3329. The dove is a symbol of peace.
3330. Fe is the chemical symbol for iron.
3331. In Europe, the colour white symbolizes purity.
3332. The design of the house had a pleasing symmetry.
3333. You're not being very sympathetic, Joan.
3334. There is a group in the party sympathetic towards our aims.
3335. They have held many symposia on animal-welfare issues.
3336. Migration is a symptom of rural poverty and of urban over-privilege.
3337. "Shut" is a synonym of "closed".
3338. The jacket is made of synthetic materials.
3339. The system has crashed.
3340. Under the present system, we do not have any flexibility.
3341. The way they've collected their data is not very systematic.

3342. Information on the personal life of a film star is just the sort of story the tabloids love.
3343. In this society there is a taboo against any sort of public display of affection.
3344. Death is a taboo subject.
3345. The tackle was already in the car.
3346. The computer can be programmed to tackle a whole variety of tasks.
3347. Have you tied the airline tags on the luggage?
3348. My father used the same tailor for his suits for twenty years.
3349. I really fancy an Indian takeaway.
3350. There is a Chinese takeaway in the town center.
3351. She had an obvious talent for music.
3352. This sort of work calls for special talents.
3353. He's an exciting new swimming talent.
3354. England's tally at the moment is 15 points.
3355. The number of ballot papers did not tally with the number of voters.
3356. It was a tame film in comparison to some that he's made.
3357. The birds in the park are quite tame and will take food from your hand.
3358. Sculpture is a tangible art form.
3359. We need tangible evidence if we're going to take legal action.
3360. I tapped him on the shoulder.
3361. Someone left the tap running.
3362. I hate hearing my voice on tape.
3363. Stick a photo to the wall with tape.
3364. Would you mind if I taped this conversation?
3365. There were two pictures taped to the side of the fridge.
3366. The area is used by the army for target practice.
3367. Higher degrees in English are a target for foreign students.
3368. Cars without security devices are an easy target for the thief.
3369. I was given the task of building a fire.
3370. How do I protect my investments from taxation?
3371. Yet after 1337 no further papal taxation was levied until 1362.
3372. He was a member of the team who won the 2002 World Cup.
3373. I did not understand all the technical terms.
3374. This is a technical violation of the treaty.

3375. We use many techniques of problem-solving.
3376. There are various techniques for dealing with industrial pollution.
3377. The steam engine was the greatest technological advance of the 19th century.
3378. Advances in technology have improved crop yields by over 30%.
3379. I spent a tedious hour in a traffic jam.
3380. Britain's climate is temperate—it is neither tropical nor arctic.
3381. He was patient, self-controlled, and temperate in his habits.
3382. Temperate criticism can encourage people to make improvements.
3383. We play the music of Mozart at a faster tempo than it was originally performed at.
3384. I am living with my parents, but it is only temporary.
3385. I know I shouldn't eat chocolate cake when I'm dieting, but I find it hard to resist temptation.
3386. The landlord must give the tenant "reasonable notice" of his intention to call.
3387. Sofia was in the bedroom tending to her son.
3388. There is a growing tendency to regard money more highly than quality of life.
3389. What a child needs is tender, loving care.
3390. Dr. Mayfield has tendered his resignation.
3391. The company has tendered for three new contracts.
3392. She tried to relax her tense muscles.
3393. Marion spoke, eager to break the tense silence.
3394. There is not enough tension in the wires—pull them tighter.
3395. You could feel the tension in the room as we waited for our exam results.
3396. This latest spy affair has created a lot of tension.
3397. The term used to describe the Treasury Minister in Great Britain is "the Chancellor".
3398. The Government's term of office expires at the end of the year.
3399. We will have to discuss your terms of employment.
3400. I've always been on good terms with my neighbours.
3401. The court ruled that the contact must be terminated.
3402. Our new house is an end-of-terrace.
3403. Our new carpet looks terrific.
3404. This meeting is to be held on neutral territory.
3405. Everyone had assumed that it was uninhabited territory.
3406. There are three main types of prevention, known as primary, secondary and tertiary.
3407. They made an estimate that about 360,000 trainers would be needed in addition to school,

college and tertiary education staff.

3408. None of the onlookers would appear in court to testify against him.

3409. The open door testified that he had left in a hurry.

3410. One disk can store the equivalent of 500 pages of text.

3411. He was charged with the theft of club funds.

3412. He reported the theft of his passport.

3413. Nature is a recurrent theme in Frost's poetry.

3414. The book's theme is the conflict between love and duty.

3415. Equality between men and women in our society is still only theoretical.

3416. I am taking a course on political theory.

3417. Freudian theory has a great influence on psychology.

3418. He became a citizen in 1978, thereby gaining the right to vote.

3419. Their main thesis was that the rise in earnings was due to improvements in education.

3420. He wrote his doctoral thesis on contemporary French literature.

3421. The doctor looked thoughtful for a moment and started to write a prescription.

3422. Thank you for phoning to see if I was feeling better— it was very thoughtful of you.

3423. She threatened that she would leave home.

3424. He said that the war threatened the peace of the whole world.

3425. The concept of thrift is foreign to me.

3426. His business thrived in the years before the war.

3427. The rocks were exposed at low tide.

3428. The police are fighting against a rising tide of crime.

3429. It is very difficult to keep a house tidy.

3430. Most of the region's building timber is imported from the south.

3431. Jack is a man of presidential timber.

3432. The change in the exchange rate provided a timely boost to the company's falling profits.

3433. Have you got the new bus timetable for this year?

3434. Teachers will be giving out copies of the new timetable in the first class today.

3435. "Would you like some more cake?" "Yes, please, just a tiny piece."

3436. The giraffe was killed with a spear that had been tipped with poison.

3437. Don't tip your chair back like that; you'll fall.

3438. They tipped the waiter £5.

3439. The Keys are coral islands off the southern tip of Florida.

3440. Her name is on the tip of my tongue.
3441. We don't need to leave a tip for the waiter, because there's service charge included in the bill.
3442. She gave me a practical tip about growing tomatoes.
3443. Nuclear radiation can attack the cells in living tissue.
3444. He used a piece of tissue to clean his sunglasses.
3445. It's more hygienic to use disposable paper tissues.
3446. I like baked beans on toast.
3447. You can toast sliced bread while it's still frozen.
3448. We toasted him with champagne at his leaving party.
3449. I've been toiling away at this essay all weekend.
3450. Many old people have a very limited tolerance to cold.
3451. There's a two-pound toll to cross the bridge.
3452. Independent sources say that the civilian death toll runs into thousands.
3453. The wedding has been the only topic of conversation for weeks.
3454. He tossed the paper away over his shoulder.
3455. They tossed a coin to decide who would go first.
3456. The aircraft was blown up with total loss of life.
3457. He's not hard-hearted but resolute and tough.
3458. Many small shops are finding it difficult to cope with tough competition from large stores.
3459. He was the best boxer in the tournament.
3460. Excessive vitamin D can be toxic.
3461. Officers were unable to find any trace of drugs.
3462. I saw the faintest trace of a smile cross Sandra's face.
3463. She had given up all hope of tracing her missing daughter.
3464. They have traced their ancestry to Scotland.
3465. The fox didn't leave any tracks.
3466. It's difficult to track him.
3467. Both brothers followed the family tradition and became doctors.
3468. The change of flight plans was the principal cause of the tragedy.
3469. The dogs are specially trained to follow the trail left by the fox.
3470. Nick was leaning out of the boat trailing his hand through the water.
3471. Police trailed the gang for several days.

3472. Anne's generosity is one of her most pleasing traits.
3473. A group of tramps huddled around the fire for warmth.
3474. It was a long tramp home through the snow.
3475. Each transaction at the foreign exchange counter seems to take forever.
3476. The shop closed and the business was transferred somewhere else.
3477. Transfer the files onto floppy disk.
3478. He was transferred for a fee of £8 million.
3479. There ought to be tighter control of the transfer of nuclear materials.
3480. Increased population has transformed the landscape.
3481. The new system transformed the way managers thought about their money.
3482. Lisbon was a city in transit—everyone was waiting to go somewhere else.
3483. Each region has integrated needs—for public transit, for water and sewer systems, for solid waste treatment, for economic development.
3484. My books have been translated into many languages.
3485. The temperature is sixteen degrees Centigrade or, if we translate into Fahrenheit, sixty degrees.
3486. The system transmits information over digital phone lines.
3487. Malaria is transmitted to humans by mosquitoes.
3488. The US Open will be transmitted live via satellite.
3489. The plants are in a transparent plastic box, so the children can see the roots growing.
3490. I wanted your goals to be transparent.
3491. a transparent lie
3492. The plants should be grown indoors until spring, when they can be transplanted outside.
3493. Doctors transplanted a monkey's heart into a two-year old child.
3494. There is a shortage of donors for liver transplants.
3495. Horses were the only means of transport.
3496. Improved rail transport is essential for business.
3497. The statue was transported to London.
3498. One look and I was transported back to childhood.
3499. The farmer sets traps to catch rats in his barns.
3500. The little boy trapped a mouse.
3501. This wasn't the first time we had been trapped into a situation like this.
3502. Stories about pirates often include a search for buried treasure.

3503. Malthus published his treatise on population.
3504. The best treatment for a cold is to rest and drink lots of fluids.
3505. There should be special treatment for the smaller developing nations.
3506. A peace treaty was signed between the US and Vietnam.
3507. I tremble to think what will happen when she finds out.
3508. The whole house trembled as the train went by.
3509. His voice trembled with controlled anger.
3510. She's spent a tremendous amount of money on that house.
3511. The growing trend is for single mothers to bring up children by themselves.
3512. Today we shall be examining the latest trends in kitchen design.
3513. The new drug is undergoing clinical trials.
3514. Putting people in jail without trial is not democratic.
3515. People in this part of the country are exhausted by the daily trials of living.
3516. The angles of a triangle total 180°.
3517. Many tribes which in the past governed themselves are nowadays part of a larger country.
3518. There was a tribe of boys coming up the path.
3519. In Britain it's traditional to play tricks on people on the morning of April Fool's Day.
3520. The trick is to bend your knees as you catch the ball.
3521. You seem a trifle nervous.
3522. I don't know why you waste your money on such trifles.
3523. He took aim and squeezed the trigger.
3524. The burglars fled after triggering the alarm.
3525. Certain forms of mental illness can be triggered by food allergies.
3526. He trimmed his hair carefully.
3527. We need to trim the defense budget by a further $500 millions.
3528. Look at those trim lawns and neat flower beds.
3529. She has a trim figure.
3530. He poured himself a triple whisky.
3531. The money they were asking for was triple the amount we expected.
3532. In three years the company had tripled its sales.
3533. I'm sorry to bother you with what must seem a trivial problem.
3534. Getting computers to understand human language is not a trivial problem.
3535. She's a botanist and spent several years researching in the tropics.

3536. Bark protects the trunks and branches of trees from extremes of temperature.
3537. These exercises are designed to develop the muscles in your trunk.
3538. We packed all our equipment into a couple of tin trunks and started out by train.
3539. Television should be a trustworthy source of information from which the public can find out what's going on.
3540. When I started college, tuition was $350 a quarter.
3541. I had to have extra tuition in maths.
3542. The sea was too turbulent for us to be able to take the boat out.
3543. There was a disappointingly poor turnout to hear such a well-known speaker.
3544. The group has an extremely high turnover of members.
3545. Annual turnover is about £9,000 million.
3546. They hired a private tutor to help Carlos with his English.
3547. She was my tutor at Durham.
3548. Oxford's one-to-one tutorials are an effective but also costly way of teaching.
3549. You'll most likely see these animals at twilight, when they begin the night's hunt.
3550. Her grandfather had spent most of his twilight years working on a history of France.
3551. My brother and I look so alike that people often think we are twins.
3552. He stared up at the stars twinkling in the sky above him.
3553. Mark's eyes twinkled with laughter.
3554. It was typical tropical weather.
3555. It was typical of her to get angry about it.
3556. The ultimate outcome of the experiment cannot be predicted.
3557. Our ultimate objective is to have as many female members of Parliament as there are male.
3558. The female nude is surely the ultimate test of artistic skill.
3559. Everything will ultimately depend on what is said at the meeting with the directors next week.
3560. The critics have been almost unanimous in their dislike of this film.
3561. The company underwent several major changes.
3562. They met when they were undergraduates at Cambridge.
3563. But out of necessity, the underground continued to flourish.
3564. His father worked in the Communist underground in the 1930s.
3565. He returned to Shunhua as an organizer for an underground movement.
3566. I am proud of the invitation and the hard-won respect that underlies it.
3567. Social problems and poverty underlie much of the crime in today's big cities.

3568. All the technical words have been underlined in red.
3569. This series of victories will underline their claim to be a top class team.
3570. Dr. Johnson undertook the task of writing a comprehensive English dictionary.
3571. He undertook to pay the money back in six months.
3572. Carl unfolded the map and spread it on the table.
3573. As the tale unfolds, we learn more about Mark's childhood.
3574. It was a very unfortunate accident.
3575. He was still wearing his school uniform.
3576. The temperature must be uniform in every area of the reactor.
3577. Grade A eggs must be of uniform size.
3578. Strong support for the war has unified the nation.
3579. His music unifies traditional and modern themes.
3580. She has a unique ability of communicating with animals of all kinds.
3581. Each person's fingerprints are unique.
3582. Charlie Chaplin is a comic actor of universal appeal.
3583. The threat of universal extinction hangs over all the world.
3584. He was a universal genius.
3585. They thought the earth was the center of the universe.
3586. They are unlikely to have relatives living nearby.
3587. Unofficial sources say that over 100 people were short dead in the rioting.
3588. This century has witnessed environmental destruction on an unprecedented scale.
3589. We'll update you on this news story throughout the day.
3590. When was the last update performed on the mailing list?
3591. We can upgrade you to business class.
3592. They want to uphold traditional family values.
3593. His conviction was upheld on appeal.
3594. I've upset a tin of paint on the carpet.
3595. I didn't mean to upset you.
3596. He can't eat grapes—they upset his stomach.
3597. More and more people are moving to urban areas.
3598. The most urgent thing is to make sure everyone is out of the building.
3599. In the drawer was a selection of kitchen utensils spoons, spatulas, knives and whisks.
3600. The old fire station could be utilized as a theater.

3601. We attach the utmost importance to public safety.
3602. The children's endless demands tried her patience to the utmost.
3603. On the other side of the island, the view was utterly different.
3604. We wanted to book a hotel room in July but there were no vacancies.
3605. We have several vacancies to fill in the Sales Department.
3606. Only a few apartments were still vacant.
3607. Today there are thought to be about 100 full-time posts vacant.
3608. Luke was forced to cancel the family vacation to Acapulco.
3609. The Bernsteins are vacationing in Europe.
3610. Sound waves cannot travel through a vacuum.
3611. Legal norms and definitions often remain vague.
3612. She's one of those vain people who can't pass a mirror without looking into it.
3613. We put tables and chairs out in the garden but it started to rain and all our efforts were in vain.
3614. Police officers must have a valid reason for stopping motorists.
3615. Your return ticket is valid for three months.
3616. It is a beautiful carpet—it should hold its value.
3617. The dollar has been steadily increasing in value.
3618. A group of athletes spoke to the students about the value of a college education.
3619. Paintings valued at over $200,000 were stolen from her home.
3620. Shelly valued her privacy.
3621. The car had vanished from sight.
3622. Many species in South America have vanished completely.
3623. Warmer air is able to hold more water vapour than cold air and so has a higher humidity.
3624. There are too many variables in the experiment to predict the result accurately.
3625. White bread is really just a variation of French bread.
3626. The study concluded that the variation between the different CD players was very small.
3627. The girls come from a variety of different background.
3628. The lake has more than 20 varieties of fish.
3629. There are various ways to answer your question.
3630. The heights of the plants vary from 8cm to 20cm.
3631. Vast areas of the Amazon rainforest have been destroyed.
3632. The government will have to borrow vast amounts of money.
3633. She was a strict vegetarian.

3634. The forest floor is not rich in vegetation.
3635. Have you locked your vehicle?
3636. This is the perfect vehicle for Fleming to make his triumphant return to the stage.
3637. He thought the venture far too risky and didn't want to become involved.
3638. I might actually venture into advertising if I had enough money.
3639. The band will play as many venues as possible.
3640. She left her car by the side of the road and walked along the grass verge to the emergency phone.
3641. Are you able to verify your theory?
3642. a very versatile performer
3643. Nylon is a versatile material.
3644. Could Donnas' version of what happened that night be correct?
3645. Most people would agree that the Italian version sounds better.
3646. China versus Italy
3647. The US dollar fell versus other key currencies on Friday.
3648. Giant tortoises can live for up to 150 years and are the longest living vertebrate animals.
3649. Birds, fish and mammals are all vertebrates.
3650. A vertical line divides the page into two halves.
3651. At the height of his shipping career, he owned about 60 oceangoing vessels.
3652. They filled a large cooking vessel with vegetables and let it simmer over the campfire.
3653. A heart attack is caused by the blood vessels that supply the blood to the heart muscle getting blocked.
3654. The Ministry of Defence has the power of veto over all British arms exports.
3655. The government vetoed this proposal.
3656. We flew to Athens via Paris.
3657. You can access our homepage via the Internet.
3658. Bacteria can grow at up to 65 ℃ and stay viable right up to just below the boiling point of water.
3659. When are tidal electricity generators likely to become viable?
3660. Congress has agreed to provide financial aid to the hurricane victims.
3661. This was the first step on the road to victory.
3662. Vigorous efforts will be made to find alternative employment for those made redundant.
3663. Thirty-four protesters were arrested for violating criminal law.

3664. Victims of burglaries often feel personally violated.
3665. The prime minister has refused to talk to the terrorists unless they renounce violence.
3666. Car ownership is a virtual necessity when you live in the country.
3667. We accept certain principles of religion and traditional virtue.
3668. One virtue of the plan is that it is cheaper to implement.
3669. It is estimated that over thirty million people are now infected with the virtue.
3670. You cannot get a virus from an email message alone.
3671. I obtained a visa to visit Germany.
3672. The outline of the mountains was clearly visible.
3673. Check the plant for any visible signs of disease.
3674. Tears blurred her vision.
3675. The President outlined his vision for the future.
3676. Artists translate their ideas into visual images.
3677. These measures are vital to national security.
3678. She was wearing a vivid pink skirt.
3679. Parts of my childhood are so vivid to me that they could be memories of yesterday.
3680. Reading is one of the best ways of improving your vocabulary.
3681. After that students go off to vocational and on-the-job training.
3682. Platform shoes are back in vogue.
3683. Flowery carpets became the vogue.
3684. He recognized me by my voice.
3685. The African delegates voiced their anger.
3686. Volcanoes discharge massive quantities of dust into the stratosphere.
3687. The period from 1940-1945 is in Volume 9.
3688. The volume of the container measures 10,000 cubic meters.
3689. The volume of traffic on the roads has increased dramatically in recent years.
3690. She does a lot of voluntary work for the Red Cross.
3691. The Health Clinic is relying on volunteers to run the office and answer the telephones.
3692. The voyage from English to India used to take six months.
3693. Elderly people, living alone, are especially vulnerable.
3694. The long Russian frontier was highly vulnerable to a German attack.
3695. They stopped work to press for better wages and conditions.
3696. Together with the Conservative Party, industry waged a full-scale anti-nationalization

campaign.

3697. We wandered round the little harbour town.
3698. He noticed my attention wandering.
3699. Her mind is beginning to wander and she doesn't always know who I am.
3700. She's in charge of three different wards.
3701. She was made a ward of the court when her parents died.
3702. a ring to ward off evil spirits
3703. Let's weave a rug.
3704. What I like is how he weaves elaborate plots.
3705. It was about 12 pounds in weight.
3706. He seemed happy, except that he had gained a lot of weight.
3707. I'm not allowed to do heavy work, nor can I carry heavy weights any more.
3708. He wasn't mad but he was certainly weird.
3709. Our only concern is the children's welfare.
3710. Business executives believe that holidays are vital to their well-being.
3711. The old system was fairly complicated whereas the new system is really very simple.
3712. The mall created a frequent-shopper plan whereby customers earn discounts.
3713. Wholesale prices fell last month.
3714. We only sell wholesale, not to the public.
3715. This has had a wholesome effect on babies and parents.
3716. Of course, in the end, the wicked witch did get killed.
3717. A wide-ranging survey found growing dissatisfaction among workers.
3718. The storm caused widespread damage.
3719. There was widespread support for the war.
3720. The carpet is the full width of the stairs.
3721. I was beginning to get used to the width of American streets.
3722. She said Alaska was the last great wilderness.
3723. These chemicals would destroy crops and all wildlife.
3724. The merger could mean a $2.2 billion windfall for shareholders.
3725. The conventional wisdom is that boys mature more slowly than girls.
3726. Local people are questioning the wisdom of spending so much money on a new road.
3727. She has an infectious smile and a sharp wit.
3728. Oscar Wilde was a famous wit.

3729. Parents have the right to withdraw their children from religious education lessons if they wish.
3730. I would like to withdraw £500 from my current account.
3731. After much persuasion he agreed to withdraw his resignation.
3732. They have to make the walls strong enough to withstand high winds.
3733. One witness to the accident said the driver appeared to be drunk.
3734. Several residents claim to have witnessed the attack.
3735. A self-confessed workaholic, Tony Richardson can't remember when he last had a holiday.
3736. The company is cutting its workforce.
3737. Women now represent almost 50% of the workforce.
3738. They held a number of workshops and seminars.
3739. The concert attracted a worldwide television audience of over a billion people.
3740. He deplores the money worship common among young people.
3741. They regularly attended worship.
3742. The prisoners were not allowed to worship their own god.
3743. The food must be wrapped so that all air is excluded.
3744. Many Spanish vessels were wrecked off the North American coast.
3745. I wrecked a good stereo by not following the instructions properly.
3746. The seabed where the wreck lies is level and rocky.
3747. Concern for production is illustrated on the x-axis.
3748. The wage rates for labour in the two localities are shown on the y-axis.
3749. Sometimes I just yearn to be alone.
3750. The talks with management failed to yield any results.
3751. "We will not yield to pressure," said the president.
3752. Over the past 50 years crop yields have risen steadily in US by 1%-2% a year.
3753. We try to find college places for youngsters who haven't done as well as they'd hoped with their exams.
3754. I show great zeal for my work.
3755. Tom fell that some of the zest had gone out of his life.
3756. San Francisco is in an earthquake zone.
3757. The government has set up a special economic zone to promote private enterprise.